So D

WOMEN, HOUSING AND COMMUNITY

Women, Housing and Community

Edited by
WILLEM VAN VLIET —

Avebury

Aldershot · Brookfield USA · Hong Kong · Singapore · Sydney

Published by

Avebury

363.59
W872

Gower Publishing Company Limited
Gower House
Croft Road
Aldershot
Hants GU11 3HR
England

Gower Publishing Company
Old Post Road
Brookfield
Vermont 05036
USA

ISBN 0 566 05653 4

Contents

v

Acknowledgments

Permission to reprint material is gratefully acknowledged as follows: chapters 1, 2, 3, 4, 5, 6, and 8 (Sociological Focus); chapters 7, 14 and 15 (Ekistics); chapters 9, 10, and 16 (Women and Environments); chapter 11 (Town Planning Review, Liverpool University Press); chapter 12 (Social Service Review, University of Chicago Press); chapter 13 (City Limits); chapters 17 and 18 (Development Forum); chapter 19 (United Nations Bulletin, International Year of Shelter for the Homeless).

This volume would not have come about without technical production assistance made available and orchestrated by, respectively, Raymond G. Studer, Dean, and Jolene Quigley, Director of Administrative Services, of the College of Environmental Design at the University of Colorado at Boulder. Bob Stuit did an outstanding job in typesetting and preparing differently sized publications for uniformly formatted camera-ready material. My thanks also to Lorraine Self and Lori Dewender for reliable clerical help, to Yvo de Boer (UNCHS), Lynn Lickteig, and David Paulson for supplying valuable photographs, and to John Hickman for drawing the figures for Chapters 7 and 15.

Foreword

This collection of articles was organized to help focus attention on the housing and community needs of women in different countries across the world. Owing to various economic, political, and cultural factors, an increasing number of women worldwide are homeless or without adequate shelter. In a recent survey of 47 U.S. cities, the Partnership for the Homeless (1987:13,31) found that families with children, many headed by women, constitute the largest and fastest growing segment of the homeless population in the U.S.A. Many experience severe and multiple problems associated with homelessness (Bachrach, 1987). Numerous others live in comfortable suburban dwellings, but in social isolation and with greatly restricted access to jobs, shops, day care, medical services and other community support functions (e.g., Egar et al, 1985). In the U.S.A., mothers wanting to rent find that one out of every four rental units excludes families with children (Marans and Colten 1985). Other women encounter discriminatory practices when attempting to buy property or land.

During the past decade, a plethora of studies has documented how the organization of space and the built environment in Western countries reflects and reinforces a limited and typically subordinate role reportoire of women that is incongruent with the broader array of needs and aspirations that has emerged in the more recent period (e.g., Fava, 1980; Saegert, 1980; Wekerle, 1980; Keller, 1981; Popenoe, 1981; Zelinsky et al., 1982; Michelson, 1985; Van Vliet--, 1985).

The articles in this collection highlight various aspects of these "mismatched" environments. Thus Wekerle and Saegert are primarily concerned with urban environments, while Egar et al., Fava, and Franck address questions that are more related to suburban environments, characterized by low population densities, predominantly residential land use, and detached single-family dwellings. The significance of housing type is examined more closely by Booth and Choldin in an empirical study of a sample of Chicago mothers and by Imamura who reports on the situation of Japanese housewives.

Much of the early literature on women and their housing and community requirements consisted of documented observations of environments that did not serve the needs of women and families well. These studies laid the groundwork for a more active advocacy on behalf of women and their participation in planning, design and economic development. Examples of such involvement are given by Taylor, Penrose, and Winckler. Although the outcomes of these processes may often not be satisfactory, they contrast with the tragic circumstances of women who are without a secure home or, indeed, without any shelter at all. Women who live under constant fear of sexual harassment by landlords (Fuentes and Miller), women in emergency shelters (Duvall), and women spending their days and nights in the streets without even a home address (Stoner) are also bitter ironical illustrations of the limited scope of feminist critiques that have juxtaposed the private home and the public community as a dichotomy of female and male spheres. Notwithstanding the ostensible validity of this analytical distinction, a more complex reality is evident in the articles in this collection, and it is important to avoid a simple male-female distinction which reifies a convenient polar dualism of role patterns and, thereby, hinders a fuller articulation of the issues (Van Vliet-- 1985).

While most of the articles that follow concern themselves with women's housing and community context in Western countries, this orientation is more a reflection of research on the topic than of existing situations across the world. Evidence of similar incongruities is now available for the Third World. Much anthropological research in less developed countries has traditionally been conducted by males who have relied on male informants. Typically, their distance and segregation from women's affairs provided a restricted data base. In resultant accounts, women generally appeared, if at all, as a "muted group." Studies have also shown that planners often hold erroneous assumptions regarding the daily activities of women in the Third World, and that they are frequently ignorant or misinformed about women's roles in the planning, implementation, and management of housing programs, community projects, and urban services. As a result, planned environments frequently reflect a view of women that exaggerates their domestic roles (Rogers, 1979; Rakowski, 1984). New urban environments have also been found to contribute to social isolation by depriving women of traditional opportunitites for social interaction previously available in their environment, as described for Tunesia by Waltz (1985). A gender-based bias is evident as well in recent evaluation research of low-income housing. Of 126 such studies, only 13 were found to provide information--and then only in passing--on the problems and performance of women (Carlson and Shagat, 1985). There is, however, a growing body of research from which two findings stand out: First, women fulfill roles essential to the proper functioning of home and community, and, second, development plans often overlook (adverse) consequences for women, thereby also hampering their effectiveness.

Examples of women's significant functions are not hard to find. Jellinek's (1977) biographic sketch of a street food trader in Jakarta, Indonesia, may be somewhat atypical, but women's importance as street food sellers, for the individual household as well as the broader community, has been clearly shown for Indonesia, the Phillippines, Senegal, and even a traditional Islamic country such as Bangladesh (Tinker and Cohen, 1985). El Messiri (1985) reports how the wife of Ahmed, a squatter in Cairo, helped build the family's first room and was instrumental in financing subsequent improvements. Wikan (1985), who has conducted painstaking field research among Cairene squatters, describes how women were solely responsible for the management of land purchase transactions, saving for the installments, paying registration fees, obtaining building permits, and so on (some would even hide the deed from their husbands who tried to steal and sell it). Poor women in Cairo also administer collective savings clubs (gam'iyyat) to support long-term projects. Wright (1981) relates how the success of men in Doshman Zairi, Iran, hinged on effective management of economic issues and social relations by their wives. Likewise, Callaway (1981) notes the significant ecnomic, religious, and political positions historically held by Yoruba women in Nigeria, and Ridd (1981) describes women's control of the household budget and organization, the children, and hospitality among "coloureds" in urban South Africa.

A growing number of recommendations for housing and community development in less developed countries acknowledging the importance of women is being formulated. They concern the design of built environments sensitive to women's needs, the support of women's roles in planning, housing, service delivery, food systems, and the protection of natural resources on which the functions of women and the community at large depend (e.g., Waltz, 1985; Women and Environments, 1986; Schmink, 1985; Tinker and Cohen, 1985; Carlson and Bhagat, 1985; United Nations Centre for Human Settlements, 1985; Moser and Peaker, 1987). Also needed are more effective efforts to legitimize roles for women empowering them to help direct processes of housing and community development, particularly where those are innovative in character.

The articles in this book, all recently published and written by respected researchers and experienced practitioners, provide timely coverage of the housing and community context of women in the U.S.A., Canada, Great Britain, Australia, The Netherlands, Japan, and various Third World countries, including Tunisia and Kenya. Obviously, there exist additional issues that could not be engaged in this limited volume and they are found in many more countries than could be included here. However, the questions raised in the articles that follow are sufficiently broad to excite curiousity about those other issues and nations as well.

REFERENCES

Callaway, H. (1981) "Spatial domains and women's mobility in Yorubaland, Nigeria," Ch. 9 in S. Ardener (ed). **Women and Space.** London: Croom Helm.
    Carlson, E. and S. Bhagat (1985) "Housing and economic development." **Ekistics** 52, 310:6-14.

Egar, R., W. Sarkissian, D. Brady, and L. Hartman (1985) "Coping with the suburban nightmare: Developing community support in Australia." **Sociological Focus** 18,2:119-25.

El Messiri, S. (1985) "The squatters' perspective of housing: an Egyptian view," ch. 16 in W. van Vliet--, E. Huttman, and S. F. Fava (eds.) **Housing Needs and Policy Approaches.** Durham, NC: Duke Univ. Press.

Fava, S. (1985) "Gender and residential preferences in the suburban era: A new look?" **Sociological Focus** 18,2:109-17.

Jellinek, L. (1977) "The life of a Jakarta street trader," ch. 19 in J. Abu-Lughod and R. Hay, Jr. (eds.) **Third World Urbanization.** Chicago: Maaroufa Press.

Keller, S. (ed) (1981) **Building for Women.** Lexington, MA: DC: Heath.

Marans, R. W. and M. E. Colten (1985) U.S. rental housing policies affecting families with children: hard times for youth. In W. van Vliet--, E. Huttman, and S. Fava, (eds.), **Housing needs and policy approaches: trends in thirteen countries.** Durham, NC: Duke University Press.

Moser, C. and Peake, L. (1987) **Women, Human Settlements, and Housing.** London: Tavistock.

Michelson, W. (1985) **From Sun to Sun: Daily Obligations and Community Structure in the Lives of Employed Women and Their Families.** Roman and Allanheld.

Partnership for the Homeless. (1987) **National Growth in Homelessness: Winter 1987.** New York: Author.

Popenoe, D. (1981) "Women in the suburban environment: a U.S.-Sweden comparison," Ch. 7 in G. R. Wekerle, R. Peterson, and D. Morley (eds.) **New Space for Women.** Boulder, CO: Westview Press.

Rakowski, C. A. (1987) Production and Reproduction -- a Planned, Industrial City: The Working-and Lower-Class Households of Ciudad Guayana, Venezuela. Working Paper 61. WIDS, MSU.

Ridd, R. (1981) "Where women must dominate: response to oppression in a South African urban community," Ch. 10 in S. Ardener (ed.) **Women and Space.** London: Croom Helm.

Rogers, B. (1979) **The Domestication of Women: Discriminating in Developing Socie ties.** New York: St. Martin's Press.

Saegert, S. (1985) "The androgenous city: From critique to practice." **Sociological Focus** 18,2:161-176.

Schmink, M. (1985) "The 'working group' approach to women and urban services." **Ekistics** 52,310:76-83.

Tinker, I. and M. Cohen (1985) "Street foods as a source of income for women." **Ekistics** 52,310:83-39.

United Nations Centre for Human Settlements (1985) **Women and Human Settlements.** Nairobi: UNCHS.

Van Vliet--, W. (1985) "Communities and built environments supporting women's changing roles." **Sociological Focus** 18(April):73-77.

Waltz, S. E. (1985) "Women's housing needs in the Arab cultural context of Tunisia." **Ekistics** 52,310:28-34.

Wekerle, G. R. (1980) "Women in the urban environment." pp. S188-215 in **Signs** 5,3, Special Supplement on Women and the American City.

Wikan, U. (1985) "Living conditions among Cairo's poor -- a view from below." **The Middle East J.** 39(Winter):7-26.

Women and Environments (1986) "Women nurture the world." Presented at the Women, Environment and Development workshops, Nairobi, 1985. **Women and Environments** 8(Fall)3:19-21.

Wright, S. (1981) "Place and face: of women in Doshman Zairi, Iran," Ch. 7 in S. Ardener (ed.) **Women and Space.** London: Croom Helm.

Zelinsky, W., J. Monk and S. Hanson (1982) "Women and geography: A review and

INTRODUCTION

1 Communities and built environments supporting women's changing roles

WILLEM VAN VLIET —

During the past two decades, new roles for women increasingly have supplemented household work, childcare, and related traditional tasks of housewives and mothers. Most significant is perhaps the continuing increase in female labor force participation, resulting in different and often additional responsibilities for women. Furthermore, demographic developments such as the rise in female-headed households (Yezer, 1980: Davis and Van den Oever, 1982), their concentration in inner-city areas (Cook and Rudd, 1984), and the historic movement of families away from established urban centers (Moen, 1981; Miller, 1983) have relevant societal and environmental implications. Changes in women's role repertoire, concomitant with these trends, are legion and have been well documented. Carefully executed time-budget studies have shown, for example, the "double load" of employed mothers and effects of paid jobs outside the home on women's discretionary activities (Robinson, 1977; Stone, 1978). Other research has examined antecedent conditions, both at the macro level (e.g., the labor market structure; Miller and Garrison, 1982) and the micro level (e.g., husbands' value orientations; Araji, 1977). Furthermore, the implications of women's new roles for women themselves (Huber and Spitze, 1981), their marital relations (Varga, 1972), their children (Hoffman, 1974), and familial decision making (Walker, 1973) have been extensively studied.

By and large, the vast literature that has emerged in the general area of women's changing roles has been oblivious to the significance of the physical environment. The issues are typically couched in social, cultural, and economic terms; the physical environment is a taken-for-granted background. There is no doubt, however, that women's newly emerging roles require a compatible physical stage; the location of a day-care center, for example, may facilitate or hinder the attempts of mothers with young children to combine employment and familial roles (Martensson, 1977; Fox, 1983). As a result of a growing recognition of the potential significance of the physical environment in women's lives, a new field of studies has developed (Peterson et al., 1978; Wekerle, 1980; Richter, 1982; Zelinsky et al., 1982).

1

The authors in this issue extend and build upon this recent work. A common characteristic of their papers is that they are concerned beyond the direct relations between women vis-a-vis their environment with contextual factors within which ensuing questions are embedded. One such factor is the neighborhood. Traditionally, sociologists have studied neighborhoods as territorial frameworks for social integration. Few of these studies have focused specifically on women; if they did, their concern, too, was typically with social interactions (e.g., Williams, 1958). Neighborhoods are, of course, also an important locus for the provision of jobs, services, and facilities — resources required by women with multiple roles. Wekerle's (1985) assessment of the situation of elderly women, single parents, and employed mothers points to the need for such a broadened focus in urban research and planning.

The desired neighborhood is typically socially and functionally integrated, features a mix of public services, contains rental housing, and provides access to efficient, low-cost public transportation. This scenario presupposes relatively high population densities to form the critical population mass required to support these resources in close proximity to women's homes. To attain these densities, apartment housing is generally introduced. In spite of the documented dominant preference in North America for single-family dwellings (Fischer, 1984: 62-63; Professional Builder, 1984: 65-81), research indicates that most employed women prefer living in an apartment near their place of employment to living in a house located at a greater commuting distance (e.g., Michelson, 1977: 251-57). However, findings reported by Booth and Choldin (1985) suggest that these residential choices may involve a trade-off between conditions of housing versus employment. Also, recent data reported by Fava (1985) raise questions as to whether, in the U.S. in any case, "women's place is (still) in the city," as proposed not long ago by observers who saw the city as the antithesis of the restrictive suburban environment (e.g., Wekerle, 1979). Comparing the residential preferences of men and women in a nationally representative sample, Fava (1985) did not find women more attracted to large cities than men. Women tend to choose medium-size cities and small towns as places to live; only 5.5 percent would want their children to grow up in a large city, versus 37.1 percent who prefer a medium-size city or a small place in the suburbs. Fava interprets these findings in the light of changes occuring at present in cities as well as suburbs, particularly in regard to transportation patterns, job location, and safety. The general tenor of these developments is a diminished attraction of cities and enhanced opportunities in increasingly self-sufficient suburbs which provide a widening array of education, medical, cultural, and commercial services, expanding job markets, and an extensive assortment of retail goods.

These trends notwithstanding, many suburbs still remain impoverished, low-density residential environments. Egar et al. (1985) describe a federally funded neighborhood-development program in one such traditional suburb of Adelaide, Australia. This program stressed action initiatives by local women and has resulted in significant community improvements. These and similar efforts at neighborhood self-help by women certainly merit attention. However, O'Donnell and Stueve (1985) bring into focus some less positive aspects of communities whose mortar consists of economically unrewarded activities performed chiefly by women. Their comparison of childrearing-related volunteering by a sample of working and middle-class mothers and their husbands shows how such volunteer work may become a source of tension for women, stemming largely from continuing community demands that have become incongruous with newly emerging, preferred lifestyles. The authors point to alternative temporal, spatial, and organizational arrangements which would support community involvement by women *and* men, and argue

2

that, above all, recognition of the legitimacy of such involvement, regardless of gender, is essential.

The theme of gender integration is echoed and amplified by Franck (1985) who examines how ideas about gender and family in American society have helped shape the built environment which, in turn, has reinforced the differential assignment of functions considered appropriate for men and women. Saegert (1985) further elaborates the notion of the "androgenous city," in which values historically associated with women's pursuits and stereotypically masculine concerns would have equal priority in planning. Drawing on her work in two contrasting localities — one rapidly growing, the other characterized by decline and disinvestment — Saegert formulates various recommendations for planning communities which support a full range of functions without biasing access on the basis of gender.

MASCULINE ENVIRONMENTS, FEMINIST ALTERNATIVES, AND BEYOND

The papers in this issue throw into bold relief blatant mismatches which have emerged between the needs of certain groups of women and the community environment. These incongruences derive from the social, economic, and environmental organization of western communities which reflects assumptions pertaining to a stereotypical household consisting of a male working from 9 to 5, a nonemployed housewife, and one or more children. In fact, only 16 percent of the U.S. population fits this category and there are numerous other household types.

The concern with the environmental needs of women is paralleled by a concern for the needs of other "non-modal" groups (Michelson, 1985). There is, however, an important difference. The environmental requirements of, for example, children, the elderly, and handicapped people are intrinsic to their lifecycle stage and behavioral potential. In contrast, the significance of the built environment for women is not *inherently* related to gender. Suburban locations may make it difficult for mothers to find and hold a job (Popenoe, 1980) to be sure (and this *is* an environmental constraint), but it is social norms that postulate that the father should be the breadwinner, that the mother's responsibilities should consist primarily of childcare and household maintenance, and that suburbia should be the family's living environment in the first place. Likewise, a single-family home may bring with it more household tasks than does an apartment (Michelson, 1977), but it is social norms that govern the familial division of labor and residential choice. Similarly, the provision of low-cost housing specifically for female-headed households, if anything but an interim solution, signifies a failure to perceive the real roots of the problems and merely exacerbates existing incongruities. First at issue and logically prior are unfair earning differences between men and women, and discriminatory practices faced by women in the rental sector and in dealings with mortgage lending institutions. Also after elimination of these and related flagrant disparities, many women will still need assistance to access the housing market. However, they will do so then on an equal basis along with men; aid programs will not stigmatize them and will not reinforce prevailing socioeconomic inequities by superimposing analogous inequities in the built environment. These observations emphasize that efforts to make environments more congruent with women's needs are inextricably linked to conceptions of women's roles in society and to decision-making processes bearing on the provision of opportunities for such roles to materialize.

By implication, one also has to be somewhat skeptical about allegedly "feminist" guidelines for environmental planning and design as offering a panacea for the extant

3

problems. It is hard to conceive of a theoretical framework from which to derive such uniquely feminist guidelines. In addition to this lack of conceptual justification for and clarity of exclusively feminist planning, there are sobering empirical realities. For example, a recent nationwide survey failed to show relevant differences between the role choices and value orientations of male and female planners (Howe, 1980; Howe and Kaufman, 1981). It would seem more profitable to explore how women's environmental needs coincide with those of other population groups and, further, to enhance inputs in the institutional contexts of environmental decision-making where women's interests are currently not well represented (Taub and O'Kane, 1981; Merritt, 1980; Epstein and Coser, 1981). In all of the above, it is fundamental to avoid the simple male-female distinction which reifies a convenient dichotomy of role patterns and, thereby, narrowly restricts the focus to a small segment of a much richer spectrum of lifestyles, crossing boundaries archaically delimited by gender.

These comments and those of the authors of the articles of this special issue of *Sociological Focus*, do not detract from the real impact which the built environment may have on women's lives; rather they point out that the development and implementation of policies intended to bring about "environmental justice" should articulate the issues in a much broader context which incorporates consideration of political, economic, and cultural factors operating concurrently with and antecedently to the planning of the built environment.

REFERENCES

Araji, S. K.
1977   "Husbands' and wives' attitude-behavior congruence on family roles." Journal of Marriage and the Family 39,2:309-20.
Booth, A., and Harvey Choldin
1985   "Housing type and the residential experience of middle-class mothers." Sociological Focus 18,2:97-107.
Cook, C. C., and N. M. Rudd
1984   "Factors influencing the residential location of female householders." Urban Affairs Quarterly 20,1:78-96.
Davis, K., and P. van den Oever
1982   "Demographic foundations of new sex roles." Population and Development Review 8,3:495-511.
Egar, R., W. Sarkissian, D. Brady, and L. Hartman
1985   "Coping with the suburban nightmare: Developing community supports in Australia." Sociological Focus 18,2: 119-25.
Epstein, C. F., and R. L. Coser (eds.)
1981   Access to Power: Cross-National Studies of Women and Elites. London: Allen and Unwin.
Fava, S.
1985   "Gender and residential preferences in the suburban era: A new look?" Sociological Focus 18,2:109-17.
Fischer, C.
1984   The Urban Experience. Second Edition. New York: Harcourt, Brace and Jovanovich.

Fox, M. B.
1983   "Working women and travel: The access of women to work and community facilities." Journal of the American Planning Association (Spring), pp. 156-70.
Franck, K.
1985   "The social construction of the physical environment: The case of gender." Sociological Focus 18,2:143-60.
Hoffman, L. W.
1974   "Effects of maternal employment on the child: A review of research." Developmental Psychology 10,2:204-28.
Howe, E.
1980   "Role choices of urban planners." Journal of the American Planning Association (October), pp. 398-408.
Howe, E., and J. Kaufman
1981   "The values of contemporary American planners." Journal of the American Planning Association (July), pp. 266-78.
Huber, J., and G. Spitze
1981   "Wives' employment, household behaviors, and sex-role attitudes." Social Forces 66:150-69.
Martensson, S.
1977   "Childhood interaction and temporal organization." Economic Geography 53:99-125.
Merritt, S.
1980   "The recruitment of women to suburban city councils — Higgins vs Chevalier." Pp. 86-115 in D. W. Stewart (ed.), Women in Local Politics. Metuchen: Scarecrow Press.

Michelson, W.
1977 Environmental Choice, Human Behavior and Residential Satisfaction. New York: Oxford University Press.
1985 From Sun to Sun: Daily Obligations and Community Structure in the Lives of Employed Women and Their Families. Roman and Allanheld.
Miller, J., and H. H. Garrison
1982 "Sex roles: The division of labor at home and in the work place." Annual Review of Sociology 8:237-62.
Miller, R.
1983 "The Hoover in the garden: Middle-class women and suburbanization, 1850-1920." Environment and Planning D: Society and Space 1:73-87.
Moen, E.
1981 "Women in energy boom towns." Psychology of Women 6,1:99-113.
O'Donnell, L., and A. Stueve
1985 "Community demands and supports for childrearing related volunteer work." Sociological Focus 18,2:127-42.

Peterson, R., G. R. Wekerle, and D. Morley
1978 "Women and environments: An overview of an emerging field." Environment and Behavior 10:511-34.
Popenoe, D.
1980 "Women in the suburban environment: A U.S.-Sweden comparison." Pp. 165-75 in G. R. Wekerle, R. Peterson, and D. Morley (eds.), New Space for Women. Boulder: Westview.
Professional Builder
1985 "What 1985 buyers want in housing." (December), pp. 65-81.
Richter, L.
1982 "The ephemeral female: Women in urban histories." International Journal of Women's Studies 5,4:312-29.
Robinson, J. P.
1977 Changes in Americans' Use of Time: 1965-1975. Cleveland State University: Communication Research Center.

Saegert, S.
1985 "The androgenous city: From critique to practice." Sociological Focus 18,2:161-76.
Stamp, J.
1980 "Toward supportive neighborhoods: Women's role in changing the segregated city." Pp. 189-201 in G. R. Wekerle, R. Peterson, and D. Morley (eds.), New Space for Women. Boulder: Westview.
Taub, N., and G. E. O'Kane
1981 "Women, the family, and housing: Legal trends." Pp. 175-95 in S. Keller (ed.), Building for Women. Lexington, MA: Lexington.
Varga, K.
1972 "Marital cohesion as reflected in time-budgets." Pp. 357-75 in A. Szalai et al. The Use of Time: Daily Activities of Urban and Suburban Populations in Twelve Countries. The Hague: Mouton.
Walker, K.
1973 "Household work time: Its implications for family decision making." Journal of Home Economics 65,7:7-11.
Wekerle, G. R.
1979 A Woman's Place is in the City. Cambridge, MA: Lincoln Institute of Land Policy.
1980 "Women in the urban environment." Pp. S188-215 in Signs 5,3, Special Supplement on Women and the American City.
1985 "From refuge to service center: Neighborhoods that support women." Sociological Focus 18,2:79-95.
Williams, J. H.
1958 "Close friendship relations of housewives residing in an urban community." Social Forces 36:358-62.
Yezer, A.
1978 How Well Are We Housed? Female Headed Households. Washington, D.C.: U.S. Department of Housing and Urban Development, Office of Policy Development and Research.
Zelinsky, W., J. Monk, and S. Hanson
1982 "Women and geography: A review and prospectus." Progress in Human Geography 6,3:317-67.

Reprinted with permission from **Sociological Focus,** vol. 18, no. 2, pp. 73-78, 1985.

PART I
URBAN ENVIRONMENTS

2 From refuge to service center: Neighborhoods that support women*

GERDA R. WEKERLE

The sociological literature on the neighborhood has tended to overemphasize its function as a locale for social interaction while paying scant attention to the neighborhood's function in the delivery of essential urban services to residents at various stages of the life cycle. From the extensive work on the neighborhood as a focus for social integration have emerged two dominant images — the neighborhood as refuge and the non-place network. The paper focuses on recent research on women's needs in the urban environment which criticizes both these images from a theoretical and empirical base and points to a new image — the neighborhood as service center — as the appropriate focus for research and urban policy.

NEIGHBORHOOD AS REFUGE

One of the key questions in neighborhood research since the turn of the century has been whether the neighborhood is losing functions with the increasing scale of cities. In his review of the literature from 1915 to 1978, Olson (1982) finds that research on the broad range of neighborhood functions has been sparse: four out of the five major themes in studies of the neighborhood have focused on the neighborhood as a social unit. Sociological studies have tended to focus on the neighborhood as a form of social organization where primary ties are developed and maintained. Starting with the Chicago School's preoccupation with social disorganization and the effects of mass society (Wirth, 1938), the neighborhood was considered a key element in stemming the social breakdown and moral disorder which they assumed was the logical consequence of rapid urbanization. Cooley (1909) was influential in stressing the importance of the neighborhood as a source of primary relationships. Robert Park also advocated the creation of local communities to establish opportunities for the attachment of urban residents to primary groups (Olson, 1982; Banerjee and Baer, 1984). This focus has dominated sociological studies of the neighborhood to the present.

The neighborhood unit concept, articulated by Clarence Perry (1939) expressed in physical terms the interests of a diverse group including housing reformers, settlement house workers, and urban planners in creating a sense of community by dividing the city

*I am very grateful for the suggestions and encouragement of Slade Lander, among others, whose comments raised new questions and helped focus the argument more clearly.

7

up into small physical and social units (Bauer, 1952:27; Mumford, 1968:61; Banerjee and Baer, 1984). The neighborhood unit concept and the many planned communities based on it incorporated several key features (Perry, 1939): small size (usually the population required for one elementary school); clear physical boundaries; open spaces; sites for schools and local shops; an internal street system which protected homes from heavy traffic. It was hoped that turning the neighborhood inward, giving it an identity, and providing shared facilities would promote face-to-face contact and strengthen bonds among residents (Banerjee and Baer, 1984:21). The neighborhood unit concept was viewed as a way to create a refuge to support normal family life and protect it from the hostile, competitive world outside. Basic to the neighborhood unit was a uniformity of dwelling units planned for families with children. Restrictive covenants guaranteed social homogeneity and protected the investment of the homeowner. Banishing commercial and industrial uses to arterial roads and other parts of the city created a spatial segregation of home and work which continues today.

Banerjee and Baer (1984:26) document the diffusion of the neighborhood unit concept throughout the world, its adoption and translation into standards by such professional organizations as the American Public Health Association, the American Society of Planning Officials, and the Urban Land Institutes, and its lasting impact on the form of new suburban developments. As automobile ownership spread, elements basic to Perry's initial plan — the small local shops and community facilities, accessibility by foot and mass transit — were eliminated from later applications. Increasingly, planners came to view the rightness of the natural separation of residential, commercial, and industrial uses.

Their continued faith in the importance of promoting community spirit and neighborly relations in local areas was bolstered by the sociological studies documenting the persistence of local communities in large cities. These are the classic studies of ethnic and working-class communities which documented the rich community life and strong identification with a local area in inner city neighborhoods previously viewed as disorganized (Whyte, 1955; Young and Willmott, 1957; Gans, 1962; Liebow, 1967). Studies of the many early planned suburban communities (Merton, 1948; Festinger, et al., 1950; Whyte, 1957) focused on the design and physical layout of the neighborhood, its effect on social life, and the development of a familistic lifestyle organized around childrearing, homeownership, and a high level of interaction with neighbors.

Early criticisms of this research pointed out that housing design and physical planning determined social relations only under very specific conditions of social homogeneity, isolation, and limited options (Isaacs, 1945; Dewey, 1950). The kind of lifestyle and family uniformity which intensified the formation of social networks was often also created by exclusionary zoning and segregation. Even the celebrated "urban villages" were often the result of constraint rather than choice, inhabited by people with limited resources and few linkages to the wider society. After reviewing the large body of literature illustrating the persistence of community ties, Fischer (1976:119) concluded that neighborhoods with active social groups were exceptions rather than the rule since they tended to result from outside threats, be ethnic or occupational enclaves, or were populated by people with little physical mobility, e.g., carless housewives. Many suburban communities never had the kind of intense neighborhood patterns and community spirit documented in the early studies. Instead of a community orientation, the emphasis was on family privacy and a home-centered way of life, yet the neighborhood itself was still viewed as an escape from the problems of urban living (Fischer, 1976; Knox, 1982:45).

8

When researchers found that the neighborhood had declined in importance as a social unit (or was actually less important than initially thought), one of the conclusions drawn was that the neighborhood was only of minimal and residual importance to urban residents. The network view of the neighborhood (Wellman and Leighton, 1979) foresaw that people would be released from neighborhood ties due to improvements in personal mobility, the development of technology, and the spatial separation of home, workplace and recreational opportunities. It was anticipated that social ties based on work or lifestyle interests would tend to replace primary relations based on either neighborhood or kin. A popular typology in neighborhood research categorized urban residents as either locals or cosmopolitans (Foley, 1952; Merton, 1961; Michelson, 1967:87) Locals tended to be the ethnic minorities, rural migrants, and working-class people who brought to the city a culture from another time and place. The truly "urban" seemed to be the cosmopolitans who were not tied to a local area but developed networks of social ties and supports throughout the urban region by taking full advantage of the mobility and access provided by the private automobile and the new communications technology.

In the planning field, Webber's (1963) influential article, "Order in Diversity: Community Without Propinquity," expressed a common view in the growth-oriented sixties: that neighborhood-based inequalities in services and facilities could be overcome by increasing the personal mobility of the vast majority of urban dwellers to the point where they could use services in the whole urban system. These ideas provided a partial justification for the centralization of shopping and urban services in regional centers and the emphasis on expressways at the expense of the pedestrian or transit user.

In hindsight, the potential for physical mobility was overemphasized and the role of space and distance as a constraint was underestimated. In the seventies, there has been a new emphasis in studying indepth specific user groups in urban environments; on time-geographic studies of activity patterns; on analyzing the distributional effects of the location of housing, services, and jobs. From these studies, it is apparent that not only have the poor and ethnic minorities not faded away, but, in addition, there is a new locally-oriented population defined largely by gender.

THE NEIGHBORHOOD AS SERVICE CENTER

An emergent theme seems to be that the neighborhood of the eighties plays a critical role in modern urban life (Hunter, 1979; Olson, 1982; Connerly, 1982). But instead of focusing on one aspect of neighborhood life, current research emphasizes that neighborhoods have a range of specialized functions, the importance of which varies over time in a given neighborhood and also varies with the characteristics and needs of specific households (Suttles, 1972; Hunter, 1975, 1979; Connerly, 1982). Hunter (1979) identifies four key functions of neighborhoods: socialization/sociability, political, economic, and administrative. Data collected both by Hunter (1975) and Connerly (1982) show that these functions are independent of one another in residents' actual use of a particular neighborhood. Thus, as Hunter (1975) found in a Rochester neighborhood, residents may socialize and identify with the local community, but their use of local facilities may decline. Similarly, there may be a relatively low level of social interaction and political organization, but a high use of local facilities. The circumstances will vary with the makeup of each particular community.

Current research goes beyond the internal workings of the neighborhood to examine the links between the local social/spatial structure, individuals' daily lives and the institutions of the larger society. One place where these links are being made is in the developing literature on women's needs in the urban environment. From the small body of recent empirical work on women's environmental needs emerges a picture of an increasingly locally-oriented population, defined largely by gender, for whom distance is not elastic: the elderly, single parents, and working women. For them, the neighborhood serves a critical function as a place for the delivery of essential services.

Recent research on women's lives in the urban environment (Popenoe, 1977; Wekerle, Peterson, Morley, 1980; Wekerle, 1981; Mackenzie and Rose, 1983; Michelson, 1983; Hayden, 1984) has been critical of the dominant refuge image of the neighborhood on the grounds that it contributes to women's inequality by reinforcing the separation of the private sphere of the home and family from the public sphere of urban life. The neighborhood has been able to function as a community in the past because women at home created relationships with neighbors, provided mutual aid, and acted as community volunteers. Yet these activities also served to reinforce the image that the home and neighborhood were the proper place for women. By making connections between the location of home, work, and services on the one hand, and women's inequality in both the home and workplace on the other hand, this new research suggests that a key function of the neighborhood is to provide essential services to households, thereby dissolving some of the traditional separation between home and work, public and private spheres that have been the defining characteristic of the modern metropolis.

Much of the current research begins from the perspective of women as users of the urban environment: studies of suburbia which focus on women's lives and the opportunities and constraints of the suburban environment (Popenoe, 1977; Rothblatt et al., 1979); research on residential choice and satisfaction which compare responses from men, women, and children living in the same household (Michelson, 1973, 1976; Saegert and Winkel, 1980); historical and architectural research which establish the links among the development of suburban environments based on single-family homeownership, domesticity, and the development of corporate capitalism (Hayden, 1981, 1984; Wright, 1981; Mackenzie and Rose, 1983); time-geography studies which document the relationship between space-time constraints and gender roles (Palm and Pred, 1974; Rosenbloom, 1978; Hanson and Hanson, 1981; Michelson, 1983); and detailed studies of the housing and neighborhood needs of women, especially single parents and the elderly (Ahrentzen, forthcoming; Anderson-Khlief, 1981; Berheide et al., 1981; Gutowski, 1981; Hitchcock, 1981; Klodawsky et al., 1983; McClain and Doyle, 1984; Lawton and Hoover, 1981a). In the last decade, growth in the numbers of elderly women, women heads of households, and mothers outside the home has increased the importance of these studies' viewpoint, of their conclusions, and of continuing similar research.

THE NEIGHBORHOOD NEEDS OF ELDERLY WOMEN

Although policymakers and planners working with the elderly have long accepted the view that the neighborhood environment is a key mediator of personal independence and satisfaction (Regnier, 1981: 181), it is only recently that research has begun to examine the precise nature of the relationship between the supportiveness of the neighborhood setting and the use patterns of residents.

Between 1970 and 1980, there was a 23 percent increase in the U.S. population 65 and older, compared with only an 11 percent increase for the total U.S. population (Rudzitis,

10

1982:2). By 1982, 11.6 percent of the population was older than 65 years of age; 67 percent of them were women (U.S. Department of Commerce, 1984:34,35). By the year 2000, a 40 percent increase over current numbers is expected in the elderly population (Rudzitis, 1982:2).

In 1982, slightly more than one-third of women over 65 were living alone (U.S. Department of Commerce, 1984) and the median yearly income of all elderly living alone was $5,607 — well below the poverty level. Three-quarters of the older population lives in owner-occupied housing on a reduced income (Struyk and Soldo, 1980:30). The housing of the elderly tends to be undermaintained and is often of lower quality than the housing of the nonelderly (Struyk and Soldo, 1980:5). In neighborhoods with a high concentration of elderly residents, a key policy question is not just how to maintain the quality of the housing stock, but also how to prevent deterioration of the neighborhood often associated with poorly maintained housing and lower property values.

Nearly 50 percent of the U.S. elderly live in central cities (Struyk and Soldo, 1980: 156). As cities grow, the elderly age in place and become disproportionately represented in the older core areas of major metropolitan areas which effectively become "gray ghettos" (Struyk and Soldo, 1980; Rudzitis, 1982). They tend to be long-term neighborhood residents, with one study finding that the median occupancy of older homeowners was 22.25 years compared with 6 years for nonelderly homeowners (Struyk and Soldo, 1980:7). When moves do occur, they are generally within the same neighborhood (Struyk and Soldo, 1980:7; Gunn et al., 1983:44).

Given the residential inertia of elderly residents, their attachment to the local community through homeownership, and the anticipated growth in the elderly population, it is important to examine their interaction with the local neighborhood environment. With age, the immediate neighborhood seems to gain in importance. Struyk and Soldo (1980: 166) estimate that older persons spend 80-90 percent of their time in the immediate home environment consisting of the dwelling, local store, and church. Yet neighborhoods with a high concentration of elderly residents are frequently also decaying areas with a declining level of services and higher crime rate (Struyk and Soldo, 1980:5).

In a recent survey, Lawton and Hoover (1981a:21) found that elderly households were highly dissatisfied with three aspects of the local environment: public transportation, lack of shopping, and poor access to medical resources. Similarly, Struyk and Soldo's (1980:54) analysis of the elderly's responses to the 1974 and 1976 U.S. Housing Surveys found that lack of adequate public transportation was viewed as the greatest service inadequacy. (This was also a complaint of the nonelderly who are seen as less dependent on public transportation.) The elderly were also more dissatisfied with the lack of shopping than the nonelderly. The dependency of low-income, elderly residents on their neighborhood is illustrated by a case study of an inner-city Los Angeles neighborhood which found residents dependent on a range of services within a five-block area: a drug store, small grocery store, supermarket, variety store, restaurant, and bank (Regnier, 1981:182). A national probability sample of residents living in U.S. elderly housing projects found that distance from a given service was the single most important predictor of its use (Newcomer, 1976). This author suggests that on-site locations are needed for laundromats and senior centers; a one-block radius is needed for public transportation and a three-block radius for outdoor areas. Convenience goods such as grocery stores, supermarkets, banks, post office, department stores, cleaners, barber/beauty shops are all recommended to have maximum distances of from three to six blocks.

Few suburban neighborhoods have this range of services within walking distance, yet a major trend is the growth of the elderly population in the suburbs (Rudzitis, 1982).

11

Lawton and Hoover (1981b:6) note that in the mid-1970s more older whites lived in suburban areas than in central cities and that the older population in the suburbs increased at three times the rate of the total suburban population. Several studies (Gutowski, 1981; Paaswell and Recker, 1974; Social Planning Council of Metropolitan Toronto, 1980; Wekerle and Mackenzie, forthcoming) suggest that the service needs of the suburban elderly may be even more acute than the needs of those living in center-city neighborhoods because suburban neighborhoods were designed almost exclusively for family households and assumed high personal mobility through car ownership. What is often missing are those services which allow the elderly to live independently in their own home in a familiar neighborhood: meals on wheels, chore and home repair services; a broader range of housing options including smaller rental units, specialized senior housing, and extended care; and accessible public transportation.

One response to the locale dependence of the elderly has been the creation of flexible, on-site services attached to seniors' housing. At one Philadelphia project, researchers documented the positive effects on the health and well-being of the elderly of living in service-enriched housing which included meals, household maintenance, shopping, recreation, medical services, and transportation (Brody and Liebowitz, 1981:251). Currently, there is also widespread interest in rezoning single-family neighborhoods, especially in the suburbs, so that they will accommodate a broader range of housing options. One alternative is to permit homeowners to convert single-family houses to accommodate an additional rental unit. This is seen as one solution to the housing and service needs of the elderly, as the homeowner can simultaneously gain income, improve her own housing, and minimize isolation (Ontario Ministry of Municipal Affairs and Housing, 1983; Hare, 1981).

Accessible public transportation stands out as a key element which is both lacking in many neighborhood environments and is seen as contributing to a better quality of life for the elderly. Statistics related to auto ownership and drivership show that the elderly are much less mobile than the nonelderly (Wachs, 1979:16). Car ownership varies significantly with income and elderly women with low incomes are least likely to have access to an automobile (Wachs, 1979:18-19). Most severely disadvantaged are the elderly who live in the suburbs where conventional bus service is of the lowest quality and even specialized transit services organized for the elderly are lacking (Wachs, 1979:248). Wachs (1979:249) concludes that the travel needs of this group will be difficult to meet through any combination of conventional transit or paratransit services. Although more of these elderly suburban residents will continue to drive, problems of physical incapacity and low incomes will eliminate this option for many. Wachs (1979:248-54) suggests the need for an examination of various options to increase the mobility of the elderly from subsidized taxi services, to car pooling, to the manufacture of small low-cost community automobiles.

THE NEIGHBORHOOD NEEDS OF SINGLE PARENTS

A growing segment of the urban population in U.S. cities is families headed by women. Seventy-three percent of all female household heads live in urban areas and women head 15 percent of all U.S. families (U.S. Department of Commerce, 1980b). With a median income less than half that of all families in the United States, families maintained by women are more likely to have incomes below the poverty level (U.S. Department of Commerce, 1980a, 1980c), thus limiting both the kind of housing and neighborhoods available to them.

Very little research has been conducted on the neighborhood environments of women heads of families, their activities, and level of satisfaction. For the most part, recent studies have limited themselves to an examination of single-parent housing and residential location decisions and it is here that we find some references to the functions that neighborhoods serve for single parents.

While single parents are not a homogeneous group, varying in age, social class, and lifestyle, a picture emerges of a group whose housing conditions share some striking similarities to those of elderly women. Female heads of households are more likely to rent rather than own (42 percent of all women household heads compared with 25 percent of all familes) (U.S. Department of Commerce, 1980a) and to live in dwellings in greater need of repair, with fewer amenities (U.S. Department of Housing and Urban Development, 1978; Ahrentzen, forthcoming). A major problem is finding affordable rental housing which will accommodate children (Anderson-Khlief, 1980; Weiss, 1980) and the typical pattern for both middle-class and working-class, newly-divorced mothers is to move into inadequate apartments in undesirable neighborhoods (Anderson-Khlief, 1980). While divorced women in professional and business families tend to stay in the family home, like the elderly female homeowner they become house poor, spending too much of their income on housing and stinting on repairs (Anderson-Khlief, 1980; Rothblatt et al., 1979:122).

Various studies show that divorced mothers try to remain in a familiar territory even if this means accepting housing of a lower quality (Anderson-Khlief, 1980; Ahrentzen, forthcoming). Working-class women often choose to move back to their former neighborhood where parents and relatives can provide assistance with housing, childcare, and jobs. Among middle-class women, part of the motivation to stay in the marital residence is the desire to remain among friends and maintain a sense of community security (Anderson-Khlief, 1980).

Despite the preference for a familiar neighborhood environment, on average, women heads of families move more frequently than the general population. Many of them make a series of moves in rapid succession, initially to reduce housing costs, subsequently to balance often conflicting needs for adequate and affordable housing, maintaining children's friends and school settings, finding childcare, getting within reasonable commuting distance of jobs (U.S. Department of Housing and Urban Development, 1980:3-4; Weiss, 1980). After interviewing 200 single parents, Weiss (1980) comments that: "They are likely to be imperfectly aware of the importance to them of a supportive neighboring community," and the frequent moves reflect the trial-and-error involved in attempting to create a better fit between the family's new circumstances, its housing, and the neighborhood environment.

Carol Brown (1978) focuses directly on the critical role played by the neighborhood environment in the life of the single parent:

> For a divorced mother, the resources previously obtained from a husband must now be obtained from outside the family — from formal organizations, from community services from friends and relatives. . . . Social location is partly also physical location — the kind of housing, the kind of neighborhood, the access to services and to institutions, the proximity of friends and family can make a divorced mother's life easier or harder. The resources she needs come from people — landlords, employers, bureaucrats, businessmen — and these are located in specific places. Specific locations are more, or less, hostile to divorced mothers.

Often the very same residential environment which was chosen because it was "good for family life" — the suburban, low-density, single-family neighborhood — is less supportive of the needs of the single parent (Anderson-Khlief, 1980; Brown, 1978; Rothblatt et al., 1979; Weiss, 1980). In their study of women living in suburban San Jose, California, Rothblatt et al. (1979) found that suburbia is less satisfactory for divorced women than for married women. At the neighborhood level, they found a lack of casual neighborly contacts, fewer people to rely on, and less involvement in informal groups. They concluded that single parents do not really belong to the neighborhood in a social sense and are isolated in a couples world (Rothblatt et al., 1979:124).

Yet single parents, with only one adult present in the home, may be even more dependent on neighbors for socializing and assistance than are traditional nuclear families. Essential services, such as childcare and after-school care, are often missing in suburban neighborhoods and single parents seem to be less satisfied than married women with community services (Rothblatt et al., 1979:121). Many single parents can no longer afford an automobile, and there is little time to chauffeur children (Weiss, 1980). Accessible public transportation becomes essential to gain access to a range of work opportunities. Jobs close to home and in the neighborhood become important as long commutes leave single parents with less time for children (Brown, 1978).

Carol Brown argues that the neighborhood as a community of personal ties becomes more important to single parents as friends and family are needed for assistance, socializing, childcare, information and referrals. Yet her picture of the types of neighborhoods that provide the necessary interpersonal support to single parents bears little resemblance to the neighborhood designed to provide a refuge to the family from the public sphere of urban life. These are neighborhoods which meet a range of functions: social support, collective services, and accessibility. They include stable, working-class areas; public housing; heterogeneous, older neighborhoods with a mix of classes, housing, and family organization; suburban planned unit developments; and condominium developments (Brown, 1978; Rothblatt, 1979). Collective services are essential in replacing some of the functions traditionally met within the family. These might include household maintenance, shared outdoor space, childcare, and shopping. Several authors agree that facilities within walking distance, accessible public transit, the location of home, work, and community services to minimize travel times, become extremely important to the single parent (Brown, 1978; Rothblatt, 1978; Weiss, 1980). Essential to a supportive neighborhood is that it accept the single parent and her children, that it is safe, and that it have other families.

This profile of the good neighborhood for single parents is supported by the findings of Rothblatt et al.'s (1979) study of single parents living in San Jose, California. They also point to the desirability of older, inlying, single-family neighborhoods, with good accessibility, employment opportunities, and supportive social networks. Yet subsequent research has not gone any further to test this on a larger sample or in different locations and much further work is needed.

A different focus has been research examining the characteristics of housing planned specifically for single parents (France, 1985; Klodawsky and Spector, forthcoming; Leavitt, 1982, 1984, 1985). These include short-term (3-6 months), second-stage housing for battered women and their children; permanent, nonprofit, cooperative housing projects; and philanthropic projects targeted at single parents and their children. Common to many of them are good locations, accessible public transportation, play areas for children, and available childcare. Projects like Nina West Homes of London, England, Warren Village of Denver (Hayden, 1984) and Hubertusveriniging of Amsterdam (France, 1985) incorporate social services such as family counseling, job counseling, and help in finding housing. In these projects, there is an attempt to provide an integrated set of housing, childcare, and support services, as a bridge between marital dissolution and independent family living. In the planning stages in many North American cities are housing projects for single parents which combine some level of on-site services with a supportive community (Leavitt, 1984; 1985). These are important demonstration projects as they call attention to the critical link between housing and services, between community support and the neighborhood environment.

THE NEIGHBORHOOD NEEDS OF MOTHERS IN THE LABOR FORCE

As married women with children continue to enter the paid labor force in unprecedented numbers there is a reexamination of how well the neighborhood environment supports this change. In 1982, while 52 percent of all married women in the U.S. were in the labor force, almost two-thirds (63 percent) of mothers with children under the age of 17 were in the labor force. Among the group of mothers who traditionally have had the lowest labor force participation rates — mothers with children younger than six years of age — 49 percent were in the workforce (U.S. Department of Commerce, 1984). These statistics reveal an ever-increasing population of women with severe constraints on their time as they juggle on a daily basis the triple roles of wage earner, parent, and homemaker. The implications for the neighborhood are two-fold: fewer women are home during the day to do the neighboring, volunteer work, chauffeuring, and management of household consumption; and secondarily, families may choose types of housing and neighborhoods which support their new needs.

Two-earner households have been the focus of several studies of residential location. Roistacher and Young (1981) suggest that these households will choose less space in more central locations to minimize journeys to work of both husband and wife and to gain better access to public transportation and services. Duker (1970) and Berheide et al. (1981) support these findings. Some authors (Gale, 1979; Ginzberg, 1978) argue that the demand for housing in gentrified neighborhoods is due to the increase in two-earner households attracted by proximity to a diversity of employment opportunities, mix of public and private services, and a range of cultural, recreational, and social services. While the case studies included in Laska and Spain (1980) would seem to bear this out, the studies also reveal that gentrified neighborhoods attract primarily two-earner households without children since frequently these neighborhoods do not have the quality schools, security, and children's play space that middle-class households with children seek.

Berheide et al. (1981) find that two-earner families with children try to balance the needs of the adults and children. Like traditional nuclear families, they look for neighborhoods with good schools, but they also look for neighborhoods which offer childcare, parks, and convenient shopping. While working mothers often prefer multi-unit rental housing in more central locations, the research of Saegert and Winkel (1980) find that they frequently defer the satisfaction of their own needs and choose instead to live in single-family, suburban houses which are viewed as better environments for the children and preferred by the husbands. In this study and in Michelson's (1973), married women moving to suburban locations are often less satisfied than husbands after the move, they have fewer employment opportunities, and spend more time in household tasks. Van Vliet (1981) suggests that the segregation of land uses found in the typical suburban environment limits outside employment because of the constraints of time and distance.

When families moved from the suburbs to the city, Michelson (1973) finds that women use the city for a wider range of functions than men do: work, shopping, cultural activities, childcare, and neighborhood participation. In a survey of 825 women living in San Jose, California, Rothblatt et al. (1979) report that mothers most satisfied with their communities lived either in older city neighborhoods or newer, planned, high-density suburbs.

15

Basically, we found that women want the more efficient environment. They want fewer demands on their time and they want better supportive services such as the socializing facilities condominiums usually provide, the childcare services that are usually nearer the city, the lack of yard work and the reduced commuter time (Rothblatt et al., 1979:274).

Popenoe's (1977) comparative study concludes that mothers living in an American suburb are less likely to be employed than a comparable group in a Swedish suburb, due to the lack of facilities essential to working women: local jobs, childcare close to home, access to good public transportation.

Local jobs seem to be important to working mothers. In a study of mothers in a Boston-area community, O'Donnell and Stueve (1981) report that 60 percent of mothers compared with 17 percent of fathers worked within the boundaries of the community. Women's jobs were often chosen because of their proximity to home and work and served to reinforce their local involvement. Many of these women worked part-time in order to accommodate both work and home roles. Similarly, Harman (1981) reports a greater mobility of employed men, while women in her sample tended to work locally. Cichocki's (1980) sample of women living in a suburban community of Toronto worked either close to home or downtown within easy access of public transit. Madden and White (1978) report that women are twice as likely as men to work at home or walk to work. Hitchcock's study (1981) of four Toronto neighborhoods found that a high proportion of women in the two city neighborhoods worked either at home or in their own neighborhood: 49 percent in the high-status city neighborhood and 27 percent in the moderate-status neighborhood. Almost half worked less than twenty hours a week, a result, he feels, of the availability of neighborhood jobs.

Considerable research has focused on the effects of gender role constraints on women's mobility especially as this relates to travel patterns (Rosenbloom, 1978; Fox, 1983; Michelson, 1983). The studies conclude that working women are heavily "transit dependent" compared with working men, i.e., they have less access to a private automobile, are more likely to be passengers rather than drivers, and use public transportation more than men. The explanation lies in the division of labor within the family and women's more limited access to the resources of the family. Because of married women's dual worker role, time constraints force them to trade off travel time in order to meet family responsibilities. Compared with men's work trips, for instance, women make shorter distance trips, spend less time per trip, and use public transportation more (Fox, 1983). The combination of work outside the home, family responsibilities, and dependence on public transportation creates considerable stress and puts a heavy premium on saving time by trying to meet basic needs in the neighborhood.

There are indications that women's nonwork trips are largely pedestrian and neighborhood-centered (Paaswell and Paaswell, 1978). A few studies have begun to examine the relative convenience of city and suburban neighborhoods in their access to shopping and other services (Hitchcock, 1981; Bowlby, 1984; Hanson and Hanson, 1981; Coupland, 1982). Hitchcock (1981) found substantial differences in women's access to shopping and work between city and suburban neighborhoods. Despite the commonly-held view that suburban shopping malls provide more convenience and economies of scale for the consumer, he found greater convenience and the most choice for residents shopping in city neighborhoods served by commercial strips. Similarly, Bowlby (1984) found that in England, while supermarkets and shopping malls may decrease time spent in shopping, consumption and costs are higher than when women shop locally.

O'Donnell and Stueve (1981) point out the seeming paradox that employed mothers may be more dependent on the local environment just when work attachments take them out of the neighborhood and home.

> Rather than decreasing in importance . . . the local community may actually be emerging as more consequential to women during their child rearing years, as more mothers add employment to their family and community responsibilities. As the primary locus of both jobs and childcare, the community itself shapes and constrains women's choices and their abilities to sustain what are still highly valued commitments.

CONCLUSIONS

Recent empirical work on women's needs in the urban environment indicates a convergence of needs centered around the local neighborhood. Elements of the supportive neighborhood environmen. 'or elderly women, single parents, and mothers in the labor force include a wide range of housing options, collective services, and accessible public transportation. This represents a basic shift away from the view of the good neighborhood as predominantly a refuge and haven from the public world, to a focus on its linkages with the larger society of production and its ability to deliver a broad range of services. In answer to the question of whether the neighborhood is losing functions with the increasing scale of cities and advances in technology, my review of the literature on the neighborhood needs of three groups of women indicates that their dependence on the local environment may be increasing rather than decreasing. What these studies seem to indicate is that the neighborhood as a social unit where residents have close ties with friends and kin is of vital importance to both elderly women and single parents. However, this cannot be interpreted solely as a preference for community-based ties over dispersed social networks, as it may just as well be a realistic assessment of the fact that friends and relatives are often the only source of assistance for women with limited resources. When women also have low mobility and heavy time pressures, time and distance become significant constraints on their participation in the public sphere. The neighborhood becomes important as a location which mediates between home and the public sphere — a place where essential services can be co-located to maximize access and minimize time and distance constraints for the household. For women in the labor force, a neighborhood environment which includes services such as childcare, shopping, jobs, and good access to public transportation becomes pivotal in allowing them to link family responsibilities and work roles without incurring considerable stress. For elderly women, a neighborhood environment incorporating these elements often allows them to live independently in their own homes instead of moving to institutional settings.

The dominance of the paradigm of the neighborhood as community has tended to limit the questions asked and the range of research done. It has also limited planning and policy responses since planners often rely on sociological research to provide intelligence about changing social needs at the neighborhood level. Sociologists studying the neighborhood have tended to focus primarily on its function as a form of social organization examining in-depth the social-interactional patterns in particular communities and their cultural symbolic functions. Although recent surveys have acknowledged that neighborhoods are often organized around the delivery of services and still serve important economic functions (Hunter, 1979), these aspects of neighborhood life have not been subject to intense scrutiny.

In a recent article, Herbert Gans (1984) critiques the dominant paradigms in urban sociology and suggests the need for the development of an alternative paradigm which begins from the perspective of users and traces their relationships with the suppliers and producers of services. This approach is similar to some of the recent work in the left-liberal tradition of social geography (e.g., Harvey, 1973) which has concerned itself with questions of equity in the distribution of services and the effects of public decisions about facilities location on various groups in society. For the most part, however, these studies do not start with the individual, relying instead on mapping the distribution of services in urban areas with a particular population composition.

Time-geographic studies (Hagerstrand, 1974; Michelson, 1983) are more promising as they combine the focus on the individual with attention to what is possible to do in a given community. Using this perspective, the neighborhood as an environment is seen as providing both opportunities and constraints for activities. Land use densities, the spacing of activities, the time it takes to overcome distance are all seen as part of the environment to which individuals respond. Time-geographic studies informed by a socialist-feminist theoretical framework seek to explain women's spatial inequality in terms of the structure of social relations. By focusing on the spatial expressions of the shifting relationships between production and reproduction, home and work (McDowell, 1983), this paradigm has the potential of linking research on the family, home, neighborhood, and wider urban context. This would satisfy Gans' requirement that a new paradigm for urban sociology must ask "macro-sociological questions for micro-sociological aims: to obtain a client's customer's, taxpayer's view of the world, instead of a professional's, entrepreneur's, or planner's view."

While we now know something about the stress created for women by the segregation of land uses in suburban environments, we have little insight into the kinds of neighborhood environments that would be ameliorative. We need detailed studies of women living in different kinds of neighborhood environments. We need evaluations of existing housing created by and for women: women's cooperatives, single-parent housing, economic development projects (Hayden, 1984; Wekerle, 1980, 1981, 1982; France, 1985) which combine housing, services, and jobs to assess the relative importance attached to community, services, and housing. We need more research on the neighborhood needs of the elderly: the mix of local services required and long term effects on well being and independent living; the effects of housing conversion on individuals and the community; the impacts of levels of service of transportation systems and the consequences of implementing a range of alternatives. Creating housing purpose-built for single-parent households is a new trend. We need data on the housing that already exists for this group, who it serves, and how well. To answer the question of whether single-parent families are best served by the market place or by tailor-made housing arrangements in selected neighborhoods (McClain and Doyle, 1984), we need to study single-parent families living in different types of neighborhoods with a mix of services and housing. With the continued outward migration of family households to the periphery, we need to know more about how these families (many of them with working mothers) are combining family and work responsibilities at a time when municipalities are not able to deliver many new community services. As many service industries switch to a part-time work force, we need to study the implications for the local neighborhood of people working irregular hours and having more time to spend in the neighborhood. We need to evaluate the impact on the neighborhood environment of an increase in the numbers of women working in electronic cottage industries.

These are only a few of the many questions that arise when we think of the neighborhood as a basic service center for a range of family types. They are sociological questions about the organization of family life, social relationships, and work. But they are also basic planning questions about the appropriate mix of land uses in the

18

neighborhood, the location and delivery of services, and the level of participation of residents in defining what priorities should be. While the neighborhood unit sought to create the good neighborhood by building a refuge from the public sphere of urban life, the neighborhood as service center concept seeks to reintegrate the private and public spheres within the local environment.

REFERENCES

Ahrentzen, Sherry
forth-   "Residential fit and mobility among low-
coming   income, female-headed family households."
         In W. van Vliet, E. Huttman, S. Fava (eds.),
         Housing Needs and Policy Approaches:
         International Perspectives. Durham, NC:
         Duke University Press.

Anderson-Khleif, Susan
1981   "Housing needs of single-parent mothers."
         Pp. 21-38 in S. Keller (ed.), Building for
         Women. Lexington: D. C. Heath.

Banerjee, Tridib, and William C. Baer
1984   Beyond the Neighborhood Unit: Residen-
         tial Environments and Public Policy. NY:
         Plenum.

Bauer, Catherine
1952   Social Questions in Housing and Town
         Planning. London: University of London
         Press.

Berheide, Catherine White, Mae G. Banner, and
Fay Ross Greckel
1981   "Family types, housing preferences, and
         community services in a metropolitan
         area." Skidmore College.

Bowlby, Sophie R.
1984   "Planning for women to shop in postwar
         Britain." Environment and Planning D:
         Society and Space 2:179-99.

Brody, Elaine M., and Bernard Liebowitz
1981   "Some recent innovations in community
         living arrangements for older people." Pp.
         245-58 in M. Powell Lawton and Sally L.
         Hoover (eds.), Community Housing Choices
         for Older Americans. NY: Springer.

Brown, Carol A.
1978   "Spatial inequalities and divorced
         mothers." San Francisco: Annual Meeting
         of the American Sociological Association.

Cichocki, Mary K.
1980   "Women's travel patterns in a suburban
         development." Pp. 151-64 in G. Wekerle, R.
         Peterson, and D. Morley (eds.), New Space
         for Women. Boulder: Westview.

Connerly, Charles E.
1982   "The specialization of neighborhood use: A
         response to the community question."
         Chicago: Annual Meeting of the American
         Collegiate Schools of Planning.

Coupland, Vanessa
1982   "Mobility and access to healthcare
         facilities: The case of women and young
         children." Department of Geography,
         University of London.

Dewey, Richard
1950   "The neighborhood, urban ecology and city
         planners." American Sociological Review
         15:503-7.

Duker, Jacob M.
1970   "Housewife and working-wife families: A
         housing comparison." Land Economics
         46:138-45.

Festinger, Leon, Stanley Schachter, and Kurt Back
1950   Social Pressures in Informal Groups. Stan-
         ford: Stanford University Press.

Fischer, Claude
1976   The Urban Experience. NY: Harcourt,
         Brace, Jovanovich.

Foley, Donald
1952   Neighbors or Urbanites: The Study of a
         Rochester Residential Neighborhood.
         Rochester: University of Rochester.

Fox, Marion B.
1983   "Working women and travel." APA Jour-
         nal 49:156-70.

France, Ivy
1985   "Hubertusvereniging: A transition point."
         Women and Environments 7:20-22.

Gale, Dennis E.
1979   "Middle class resettlement in older urban
         neighborhoods: The evidence and the im-
         plications." Journal of the American Plan-
         ning Association 45:293-304.

Gans, Herbert J.
1962   The Urban Villagers. NY: Free Press.
1967   The Levittowners. NY: Vintage Books.
1984   "American urban theories and urban areas:
         Some observations on contemporary
         ecological and Marxist paradigms." Pp.
         278-308 in Ivan Szelenyi (ed.), Cities in
         Recession. Vol. 30. Sage Studies in Inter-
         national Sociology. Beverly Hills: Sage
         Publications.

Ginzberg, Eli
1978   "Who can save the city?" Across the Board
         — The Conference Board Magazine
         15:24-26.

Gunn, Jonathan P., Jacqueline Unsworth, and
Lynda Newman
1983   Older Canadian Homeowners: A Literature
         Review. Winnipeg: Institute for Urban
         Studies, University of Winnipeg.

Gutowski, Michael
1981   "Housing-related needs of the suburban
         elderly." Pp. 109-24 in M. Powell Lawton
         and Sally L. Hoover (eds.), Community
         Housing Choices for Older Americans. NY:
         Springer.

Hagerstrand, T.
1974   "The domain of human geography." Pp.
         67-87 in R. Chorley (ed.), New Directions in
         Geography. NY: Cambridge University
         Press.

Hanson, S., and P. Hanson
1981   "The impact of women's employment on

19

household travel patterns: A Swedish example." Transportation 10:165-83.

Hare, Patrick
1981 "Carving up the American dream." Planning 47:14-17.

Harman, E. J.
1981 "Capitalism, patriarchy and the city." Department of Social and Political Theory, Murdoch University, West Australia.

Harvey, David
1973 Social Justice and the City. Baltimore: Johns Hopkins University Press.

Hayden, Dolores
1981 The Grand Domestic Revolution. Cambridge: MIT Press.
1984 Redesigning the American Dream: The Future of Housing, Work, and Family Life. NY: W. W. Norton.

Hitchcock, John
1981 Neighborhood Form and Convenience: A City-Suburban Comparison. Major Report no. 19. Toronto: Center for Urban and Community Studies, University of Toronto.

Hunter, Albert A.
1975 "The loss of community: An empirical test through replication." American Sociological Review 40:537-52.
1979 "The urban neighborhood — Its analytical and social contexts." Urban Affairs Quarterly 14:267-88.

Isaacs, Reginald
1945 "The neighborhood theory, an analysis of its adequacy." Journal of the American Institute of Planners 14:15-23.

Klodawsky, Fran, Aaron Spector, and Catherine Hendrix
1983 The Housing Needs of Single Parent Families in Canada. Ottawa: Canada Mortgage and Housing Corporation.

Klodawasky, Fran and Aaron Spector
forth- "The growth of mother-led families in
coming Canada: Their potential impacts on the built environment." Women and Environments.

Knox, P.
1982 Urban Social Geography. NY: Longman.

Laska, S. B., and D. Spain
1980 Back to the City: Issues in Neighborhood Renovation. NY: Pergamon.

Lawton, M. Powell, and Sally L. Hoover
1981a Community Housing Choices for Older Americans. NY: Springer Publishing.
1981b "Housing for 22 million older Americans." Pp. 11-27 in M. P. Lawton and S. L. Hoover (eds.), Community Housing Choices for Older Americans. NY: Springer.

Leavitt, Jacqueline
1982 "Aunt Mary and the shelter-service crisis for single parents." Chicago: Association of Collegiate Schools of Planning.

1984 "The shelter plus issue for single parents." Women and Environments 6:16-20.
1985 "A new American home." Women and Environments 7:14-16.

Liebow, Eliot
1967 Tally's Corner. Boston: Little and Brown.

Mcdowell, Linda
1983 "Towards an understanding of the gender division of urban space." Environment and Planning D: Society and Space 1:59-72.

McClain, Jan, with Cassie Doyle
1984 Housing and Women. Toronto: James Lorimer.

Mackenzie S., and D. Rose
1983 "Industrial change, the domestic economy and home life." Pp. 155-200 in J. Anderson, S. Duncan, and R. Hudson (eds.), Redundant Space in Cities and Regions. London: Academic Press.

Madden, Janice F., and Michelle J. White
1978 "Women's work trips: An empirical and theoretical overview." Pp. 201-42 in Sandra Rosenbloom (ed.), Women's Travel Issues: Research Needs and Priorities. Washington, D.C.: U.S. Department of Transportation.

Merton, Robert K.
1948 "The social psychology of housing." In Wayne Dennis (ed.), Current Trends in Social Psychology. Pittsburgh: Pittsburgh University Press.
1961 "Types of influentials: The local and the cosmopolitan." Pp. 390-400 in Edward C. Banfield (ed.), A Reader in Administration and Politics. NY: Free Press.

Michelson, William H.
1973 The Places of Time in the Longitudinal Evaluation of Spatial Structures by Women. Research Paper no. 61. Toronto: Center for Urban and Community Studies, University of Toronto.
1976 Man and His Urban Environment. Reading, MA: Addison-Wesley.
1983 The Impact of Changing Women's Roles on Transportation Needs and Usage. Washington, D.C.: U.S. Department of Transportation, Urban Mass Transportation Administration.

Mumford, Lewis
1968 The Urban Prospect. NY: Harcourt, Brace, and World.

Newcomer, Robert J.
1976 "An evaluation of neighborhood service convenience for elderly housing project residents." Pp. 301-7 in Peter Suedefeld and James Russell (eds.), The Behavioral Basis of Design. EDRA 7 Stroudsburg, PA: Dowden, Hutchinson, Ross.

O'Donnell, Lydia N., and Ann Stueve
1981 "Employed women: Mothers and good

neighbors." Urban and Social Change Review 14:21-26.

Olson, P.
1982   "Urban neighborhood research: Its development and current focus." Urban Affairs Quarterly 17:491-518.

Ontario Minstry of Municiapl Affairs and Housing
1983   Study of Residential Intensification and Rental Housing Conservation. Vol. 1. Toronto: Ontario Government Printing Office.

Paaswell, R. E., and W. W. Recker
1974   "Location of the carless." Transportation Research Record 516:11-20.

Paaswell, Robert E., and Rosalind S. Paaswell
1978   "The transportation planning process." Pp. 607-32 in Sandra Rosenbloom (ed.), Women's Travel Issues: Research Needs and Priorities. Washington, D.C.: U.S. Department of Transportation.

Palm, Risa, and Alan Pred
1974   A Time-Geographic Perspective on Problems of Inequality for Women. Working Paper No. 236. Berkeley, CA: Institute of Urban and Regional Development, University of California.

Perry, Clarence
1939   Housing for the Machine Age. New York: Russell Sage Foundation.

Popenoe, David
1977   The Suburban Environment. Chicago: University of Chicago Press.

Regnier, Victor
1976   "Neighborhoods as service systems." Pp. 240-57 in M. Powell Lawton, Robert J. Newcomer, and Thomas Byerts (eds.), Community Planning for an Aging Society. Stroudsburg: Dowden, Hutchinson, Ross.

1981   "Neighborhood images and use: A case study." Pp. 180-200 in M. Powell Lawton and Sally L. Hoover (eds.), Community Housing Choices for Older Americans. NY: Springer.

Roistacher, Elizabeth A., and Janet Spratlin Young
1981   "Working women and city structure: Implications of the subtle revolution." Pp. 217-22 in Catharine R. Stimpson, Elsa Dixler, Martha J. Nelson, and Kathryn B. Yatrakis (eds.), Women and the American City. Chicago: University of Chicago Press.

Rosenbloom, Sandra
1978   Women's Travel Issues: Research Needs and Priorities. Washington, D.C.: U.S. Department of Transportation.

Rothblatt, Donald, Daniel J. Garr, and Jo Sprague
1979   The Suburban Environmnt and Women. NY: Praeger.

Rudzitis, Gundars
1982   Residential Location Determinants of the Older Population. University of Chicago:

Department of Geography Research Paper no. 202.

Saegert, Susan, and Gary Winkel
1980   "The home: A critical problem for changing sex roles." Pp. 41-64 in Gerda R. Wekerle, Rebecca Peterson, and David Morley (eds.), New Space for Women. Boulder: Westview.

Social Planning Council of Metropolitan Toronto
1980   Metro Suburbs in Transition. Part 2. Toronto.

Struyk, Raymond J., and Beth J. Soldo
1980   Improving the Elderly's Housing. Cambridge: Ballinger.

Suttles, Gerald
1972   The Social Construction of Communities. Chicago: University of Chicago Press.

U.S. Department of Commerce
1984   Statistical Abstract of the United States. Washington, D.C.: Government Printing Office.

1980a   U.S. Department of Commerce, Bureau of the Census Families Maintained by Female Householders 1970-1979. Current Population Reports. Special Studies Series P-23. no. 107. Prepared by S. W. Rawlings. Washington, D.C.: Government Printing Office.

1980b   Marital Status and Living Arrangements: March 1980. Current Population Reports. Special Studies Series P-23. no. 365. Washington, D.C.: Government Printing Office.

1980c   Household and Family Characteristics: March 1980. Current Population Reports. Special Studies Series P-23. no. 366. Washington, D.C.: Government Printing Office.

U.S. Department of Housing and Urban Development
1978   How Well Are We Housed? Female-Headed Households. Washington, D.C.: Government Printing Office.

1980   Housing Our Families. Washington, D.C.: Government Printing Office.

van Vliet, Willem
1981   "Choice under constraint: Some notes on the impact of the residential environment on employed mothers' lives." College of Human Development, The Pennsylvania State University.

Wachs, Martin
1979   Transportation for the Elderly: Changing Lifestyles, Changing Needs. Berkeley: University of California Press.

Webber, Melvin
1963   "Order in diversity: Community without propinquity." Pp. 23-54 in L. Wingo, Jr. (ed.), Cities and Space: The Future Use of Urban Land. Baltimore: Johns Hopkins.

Weiss, Robert S.
  1980   "Housing for single parents." In Robert
          Montgomery and Dale Rodgers Marshall
          (eds.), Housing Policy in the 1980s. In-
          dianapolis, IN: D.C. Heath.
Wekerle, Gerda R., Rebecca Peterson, and David
  Morley (eds.)
  1980   New Space for Women. Boulder: Westview.
Wekerle, Gerda R.
  1981   "Women in the urban environment." Pp.
          185-211 in Catharine R. Stimpson, Elsa
          Dixler, Martha J. Nelson, and Kathryn B.
          Yatrakas (eds.), Women and the American
          City. Chicago: University of Chicago Press.
  1982   "Women as urban developers." Women and
          Environments 5:13-15.
Wekerle, Gerda R., and Suzanne Mackenzie
  forth- "Reshaping the neighborhood of the future
  coming   as we age in place." Canadian Women's
          Studies.

Wellman, Barry, and Barry Leighton
  1979   "Networks, neighborhoods and com-
          munities: Approaches to the study of the
          community question." Urban Affairs
          Quarterly 14:363-90.
Wirth, Louis
  1938   "Urbanism as a way of life." American
          Journal of Sociology 44:3-24.
Whyte, William F.
  1955   Streetcorner Society. Chicago: University
          of Chicago Press.
Whyte, William H., Jr.
  1957   The Organization Man. London: Jonathan
          Cape.
Wright, Gwendolyn
  1981   Building the Dream: A Social History of
          Housing in America. NY: Pantheon.
Young, Michael, and Peter Willmott
  1957   Family and Kinship in East London. NY:
          Free Press.

Reprinted with permission from **Sociological Focus**, vol. 18, no. 2, pp. 79-95, 1985.

3 The androgenous city: From critique to practice

SUSAN SAEGERT

Historically, the physical form of urban environments, the policy priorities they reflect and the rules of operation that govern the use and creation of such environments have been based on stereotypically defined male activities, values, and goals. This paper examines what these assumptions have been, how they affect women's activities and opportunities and what changes are occurring. Two examples of planning practices and programs that take into account activities and values associated with women are described and critiqued. Then an attempt is made to formulate guidelines for the policy and practice of urban development that will improve the lives of both women and men by leading to environments that facilitate the full range of humanly valued activities.

The idea of the androgenous city arises in answer to the claim that the American city as it now exists reflects a stereotypically male bias. The physical form of urban environments, the policy priorities they reflect and the rules of operation that govern the use and creation of such environments place activities identified with men at the center of consideration (Saegert, 1980; 1982). Men are seen as breadwinners, competitors, individuals aggressively striving to get ahead whose worth is determined by their achievements. The city provides the setting for these pursuits, whether they be measured by economic gain or cultural recognition. This picture of men's pursuits and the environment for them necessarily leaves out much of the actual substance of the lives and goals of men and women in their everyday existences. The activities ignored are those stereotypically relegated to the world of women: childrearing, maintenance of social relationships, and other functions of domestic life. These pursuits for the most part are excluded from the major concerns that shape the city.

Dominant landuse and transportation patterns exemplify this gender bias reflecting the following assumptions:

(1) men will be the primary wage earners;
(2) they will have the support of women to take care of the nonwage-earning necessities of life;
(3) the environment will be organized primarily for the purposes of wage earning.

As more and more women move into wage-earning positions, we might anticipate that these kinds of assumptions would no longer hold. Three factors, however, prevent fundamental change. First, women continue to provide most of the human services people require like housekeeping, childcare, caring for the sick, preparing and serving food and doing the many menial tasks that directly support human life but are not perceived as contributing to the production of goods or investment income. Women do this without

23

pay in their own homes and neighborhoods and for low pay in service industry or public sector jobs. Second, reliance on market forces and mechanisms to meet new needs created by more women's entry into the labor force makes most of the services and environments created to resolve these needs too expensive for the majority of working women. For the most part, the target market for these amenities and services has been two-wage-earner families, especially those without children. The continuing earnings differential between men and women means that single women, especially single mothers, cannot compete with the two-job couple for goods and services, though they often need them most because their time, energy, and effort are spread the thinnest.

The third factor, and the one that links the other two, involves values. The vitality of a city is usually measured in planning and policy circles by its economic health and growth and possibly by the condition of its physical plant. The quality of life of the people living in the city is assumed to derive from these conditions. A major point this paper will examine is the extent to which this assumption is valid, especially for women. I will argue that women have had the primary responsibility for converting an environment designed and run to maximize economic values into a place that can sustain human life. They have served as a buffer between the values of the market place and values that place the creation and maintenance of human lives first. In both cases, it is important not to interpret values primarily as sentiments or personality traits. Rather, values are the weighting of outcomes that underlie the legal and informal structures of obligations and rewards associated with formal and informal social organizations. Given the history of the division of labor and differential rights of men and women, it would be impossible to assign causality to psychological dispositions or value preferences of women and men. The androgenous city would be one in which the values historically associated with women's pursuits would have equal priority in the development of city forms as those associated with stereotypically masculine values.

This paper will look first at some of the manifestations of the unequal valuation of male- and female-typed activities for different groups of women. The next section will then describe two programs that might contribute to the development of the androgenous city form. The final section advances some guidelines for programs intended to improve the lives of women and men through the development of environments that facilitate the full range of humanly valued activities.

WOMEN'S DISADVANTAGES IN THE MASCULINE CITY

The physical form of the environment and the laws and regulations that govern its use and development affect many women who work outside the home and have primary responsibility for domestic life more than they affect most men. This occurs because the organization of women's activities in time and space is more complex and demanding. When they cannot afford an adequate amount of paid help women are particularly handicapped. However, in the minority of cases where such help can be purchased, the burden is usually passed along to poorly paid women who in turn must run their own household and another woman's as well. There is little comprehensive research on the ways that the interaction of economic devaluation of the work of human caring with the physical form and temporal organization of the environment disadvantage women. However, data drawn from diverse sources suggest evidence for the lack of priority given to women, their work, and its value, within the settings where women are found. Evaluating various categories of women readily clarifies their unfavorable position in most every circumstance.

Single mothers emerge as a group that clearly has difficulty in meeting the demands placed on them, both economically and socially. If they attempt to enter traditionally male occupations, they confront a variety of barriers in an effort to win higher pay. In order to go to the top of their fields they most likely need to work long hours and be readily available to prove themselves on the job. At the same time, they are likely for most of their earning careers to suffer the same inferior pay as other women. Many single mothers enter the labor force at a disadvantage, even compared to other women. They are financially less able to pay to replace themselves with hired help, less able to depend on a spouse to replace them, and less able to drop out of the workforce during periods of maximal family demand.

The following table illustrates the large differences in household income attributable to sex of the head of the household and to number of wage earners. Women, whether maintaining their family or as the only working member of a husband-wife family, are economically disadvantaged compared to men in the same family arrangements.

The picture of women who maintain families, painted by the 1983 report from the Women's Bureau of the U.S. Department of Labor, is bleak. The number of women in this position increased steadily since the 1970s. The households of such women are more likely to live in poverty. Women in this category earn less, are usually less educated, and are more likely to have preschool children that restrict labor force participation. Nonetheless, they participate in the labor force at a higher rate than other mothers. They are overrepresented in occupations with higher unemployment rates and more adversely affected by recessions. In 1981, nearly 45 percent of female, one-parent families with children under 18 years old had incomes below the poverty level (U.S. Department of Labor, Women's Bureau, 1983). Given these statistics, the findings of Perlin and Johnson (1981) regarding marital status, life-strains and depression are not surprising. In their study, single mothers were more likely to experience serious depression. However, greater levels of depression were found only for single mothers who had more children, lower incomes, and less social support. In their study of suburban women with children living in the area of San Jose, California, Rothblatt, Garr, and Sprague (1979) found that unmarried women were less satisfied than marrieds with their housing environments, community services, and social patterns in their areas. They also scored lower on measures of psychological well-being. Unfortunately, the more systematic studies of the temporal-spatial strains on parents have excluded single mothers (c.f., Michelson, 1984).

ELDERLY WOMEN

Women also predominate in another group that is especially dependent on the immediate physical environment — that is, the elderly. Among people over 65, women outnumber men with the discrepancy increasing at older ages. In 1981, 2,773,000 women over 65 lived in poverty compared to 1,080,000 men (U.S. Department of Labor, Women's Bureau, 1983). About 70 percent of men over 65 are married, whereas two-thirds of women in that age bracket are separated, widowed, divorced, or single (Matthews, 1979).

A lifetime of economic discrimination leaves elderly women in a noncompetitive position in the housing market, often requiring them to live in less-desirable areas or in isolated, hard to maintain private homes (Myers, 1982). Yet research has shown that the well-being of elderly people can often be critically influenced by their access or lack of access to a supportive "social space" in the immediate neighborhood; that is, proximity

Table 1. Number of Earners in Families, Relationship, and Median Family Income in
1980, by Type of Family, March 1981

Number of Earners, relationship, and type of family	Number (in thousands)	Percent distribution	Median family income in 1980
Total	60,703	100.1	$21,003
No earners	8,363	13.8	8,434
1 earner	19,403	32.0	16,603
2 or more earners	32,937	54.3	27,115
Husband-wife families, total	49,316	100.0	23,263
No earners	5,903	12.0	10,187
1 earner	13,900	28.2	19,368
Husband only	11,621	23.6	20,472
Wife only	1,707	3.5	13,612
Other relative only	573	1.2	16,148
2 or more earners	29,513	59.8	28,025
Husband and wife	25,557	51.8	27,745
Husband and other, not wife	3,380	6.9	31,031
Husband nonearner	576	1.2	22,684
Other families, total	11,385	100.0	N/A
Maintained by women, (1) total	9,416	100.0	10,233
No earners	2,216	23.5	4,494
1 earner	4,612	49.0	10,350
2 or more earners	2,589	27.5	18,673
Maintained by men, (1) total	1,969	100.0	17,743
No earners	244	12.4	7,790
1 earner	891	45.3	15,577
2 or more earners	835	42.4	23,785

(1) Divorced, separated, widowed, or never-married persons.

Note: Due to rounding, sums of individual items may not equal totals.
Source: U.S. Department of Labor, Bureau of Labor Statistics.

to stores, recreational facilities, churches, and neighbors has considerable bearing on the health and quality of life of these older people. Another study (Maas and Kuper, 1974) suggests that elderly women who live in more isolated settings frequently develop lifestyles focused on disability and withdrawal.

SINGLE EMPLOYED WOMEN

A third group of women also deserve the attention of planners. They are the single, employed women who make up a large proportion of the clerical and service workforce necessary for the economic functioning of any large metropolitan area. Women are drawn to these areas by the jobs they offer (Freeman, 1980; Saegert, 1980). Yet they work in lower-paying sectors of the economy and at the same time must compete for housing with higher-paid, single men and two-paycheck households. If single, working women are forced to live in areas further from job centers, they pay a higher proportion of their incomes for transportation. They are less likely than men to own a private automobile. If a working, single woman, single mother, or elderly woman belongs to a racial minority, both her economic disadvantage and her dependence on the immediate neighborhood further increase.

Table 2: Median Income in 1981 of Year-Round Full-Time Workers, by Sex, Marital Status, Race, and Hispanic Origin

Sex, age, race & Hispanic origin	Total	Single	Married with Spouse Present	Married with Spouse Absent	Widowed	Divorced
All races						
Female 18 years and over	$12,451	$11,916	$12,340	$11,866	$13,541	$14,199
Male 18 years and over	20,708	14,337	22,006	18,691	20,752	20,535
White						
Female 18 years and over	12,672	12,113	12,425	11,937	14,480	14,412
Male 18 years and over	21,195	14,917	22,444	20,461	23,200	21,114
Black						
Female 18 years and over	11,440	10,723	11,708	11,644	9,999	12,595
Male 18 years and over	14,997	11,312	16,636	14,256	(1)	15,437
Hispanic origin (2)						
Female 18 years and over	10,922	10,704	10,862	9,772	(1)	12,244
Male 18 years and over	15,010	10,924	16,032	11,888	(1)	17,847

(1) Base less than 75,000.
(2) Persons of Hispanic origin may be of any race.
Source: Unpublished data, U.S. Department of Commerce, Bureau of the Census.

Table 2 illustrates the negative economic impact on women of being in a racial minority. It also shows that, in 1981, single, black and Hispanic women earned almost $1,500 per year less than their white counterparts. The discrepancies were smaller between married black and white women, and greatest for Hispanics compared to all others. Widowed, black women's earnings were especially low in comparison to white widows. Interestingly, divorced women in all racial groups had the highest average yearly earnings, even after the youngest age group (18--24) was eliminated from the comparison. In all marital categories, men had higher earnings within each race.

Dependence on neighborhood is reinforced both by the lesser income available for transportation and housing and by racially discriminatory housing practices.

Finally, even women in higher-income households may find it impossible to locate in environments that support both their personal development and their role as mother. My previous research (Saegert, 1980; Saegert and Winkel, 1981) revealed that many upper-middle-class, urban women with children traded off residential environments in the suburbs, seen as good for family life but limiting for personal development, for living in a central city where they had more opportunities for career development, satisfying social relationships, and cultural enrichment. However, the cramped living conditions, inaccessability of play space for young children and fear of crime particularly bothered mothers in the city. Neither urban nor suburban forms suited the needs and desires of these women.

Documentation of the disadvantages women suffer in environments created through normal market forces and planning practices has begun to accumulate. Two Berkeley geographers provided what they called "a time-geographic perspective on problems in inequality for women" (Palm and Pred, 1974) in which they analyzed the spatial location of different facilities and services in relationship to the residential settlement pattern, time schedules of women's domestic obligations, and the availability and accessibility of transportation. More recently Michelson (1984) documented the additional travel time and greater daily stress that working mothers encountered in meeting their childcare needs. He also found that both the burden of taking children to childcare and the personal stress involved were much more likely to be borne by mothers than by fathers.

In summary, many women suffer a variety of disadvantages in the masculine city. Some of these disadvantages are financial, others primarily social and psychological. Moen, Boulding, Lillydahl, and Palm (1981) looked at the many social costs women in two Colorado mining towns experienced as a result of economic development. Not only did many women, especially unmarried women, fail to share in the benefits of economic development in their towns, they also had to cope with increased prices and more social problems. Higher prices particularly affected unmarried women because they did not share in the higher pay scale that accrued to men in the new development. In interviewing women in the two communities studied, researchers found that most had been socialized to expect that they would live in growth-impacted communities because families must locate where there are good job opportunities for men. They also expected that it would be women's responsibility to accept whatever environment they were placed in and make it as pleasant as possible for their families. Since many of the social problems associated with growth directly affected the family (i.e., increased prevalence of drug and alcohol abuse, school problems, isolation), women were more likely than men to form voluntary organizations or modify existing ones to cope with these problems. For long-time residents, the mainly female networks of mutual aid were disrupted by growth and had to be modified to continue functioning. Yet the uprooting and isolation some experienced as part of the rapid immigration and changes in social opportunities, even for oldtimers, left a sizeable number of women particularly lonely and depressed.

WOMEN'S FUNCTIONS IN THE MASCULINE CITY

The past three decades have seen great changes in the place of women in U.S. communities in that many more now work outside the home. Fewer are married and more are raising children in households without men. At the same time the birthrate has steadily declined (Smith, 1979). Women's lives have continued to differ from those of men in

28

significant ways.

Despite their greater prevalence in the work force, women's employment continues to differ from male employment in specific and disadvantageous ways. In 1982, women accounted for 43 percent of the civilian workforce (U.S. Department of Labor, Women's Bureau, 1983). According to the same source, these nearly 48 million women included 53 percent of all women over the age of 16 and 63 percent of women between the ages of 18 and 64. In 1982, the median earnings annually for women were 48 percent of men's median earnings. When full-time, employed workers were considered, women's median income amounted to 59 percent of the male median, no different than in 1970 and 4 percent lower than the 63 percent of male earnings in 1956. While women have increased their participation in most types of occupations, traditional divisions of labor are still reflected in U.S. Department of Labor statistics. Women continue to account for almost the entire labor force of private household workers. This group earns the lowest median income of all full-time, employed people ($5,498 annual income in 1981). Women accounted for 80 percent of all clerical workers and 59 percent of service workers in 1981.

Data from the Department of Labor, Women's Bureau (1983) clearly reveal that women do the bulk of the paid housekeeping, nurturing, and childcare work. Women make up over 99 percent of the labor force for the following occupations: health technologists and technicians, kindergarten and prekindergarten teachers, teachers' aides, childcare workers, private household cleaners and servants, lodging quarters cleaners, practical nurses, and health aids and trainees. These and other statistics describing women's work shows that women do for pay in the market place the kind of work they have always done for free in the home and community. And the pay is poor.

At the same time women continue to do over 90 percent of the work at home, cleaning the house, caring for children, preparing meals, and doing the dishes (c.f., Geerken and Gove, 1983). Numerous researchers have documented the prevalence of women activists in projects and organizations concerned with "public housekeeping" (Gittell and Shtob, 1980; Leavitt, 1980), and good homes for the community (Birch, 1978; Lawson, Barton, and Joselit, 1980). Hayden (1980; 1984) illustrates the persistence among women activists of a household model of the good city. Bernard (1981) argues that women are primarily responsible for a function of society she calls *the integry*, an analogy to the economy. The integry creates and maintains social ties, affectional relationships, care and attention to human development. Piven (1984) relates women's traditional concern about social welfare to a political trend in which more women than men continue to support social welfare programs against cuts in the budget and as a priority that outweighs defense spending. She points out the real interest women have in a welfare state, both as major beneficiaries and as a majority of welfare workers.

Women's commitment, voluntary and involuntary, to activities and goals that support daily life without being economically profitable provide a common thread in these analyses. At present, such commitments seem to impede movement toward greater equality of opportunity and conditions for women and men. Neither free market strategies nor bureaucratically heavy and expensive public sector strategies have proven themselves. Yet we have reached the point where many women and men realize that a fully functioning community provides for the full range of human needs and activities. By focusing on programs to alter the physical *and* social environment in an integrated way it is hoped that more successful solutions can emerge. The following section will discuss and critique two projects in which I have been involved that suggest both promising directions and some barriers that must be overcome.

PLANNING A CITY FOR EMPLOYED WOMEN

The first project arose from concerns within the city government of Denver, Colorado that the course of urban growth in the 1980s was not reflecting the needs of workers and residents. Urban growth was following the standard pattern of intense commercial and office space use in the downtown area, surrounded by a horizontally spreading ring of suburban, residential construction. Our task was to develop strategies for Denver's center city growth in a manner that would take into account the needs for new urban forms and services arising from women's increased labor-force participation. We were to present possible city forms to accommodate women and men, both single and with partners, with and without children. The Denver Housing Authority took the lead by commissioning Theadore Liebman and Alan Melting, an architect and an urban planner, respectively, to suggest strategies responsive to increased labor-force participation by women, increased two-job households with children, as well as needs of single parents. In addition, the planning strategies envisioned a socially integrated community in which people of different ages, stages in life, incomes, and ethnic backgrounds all contributed to and benefited from Denver's growth. I joined the consultant's team to bring a greater focus of human needs and behavior to the planning process. This process, the research, and the recommendations produced are described more fully elsewhere (Saegert, Liebman, and Melting, 1985). A first step included analysis of existing census and planning data to determine the proportion of different kinds of households in the area and their income distribution as well as employment statistics by sex and income. While these data were too gross to be of great use they did reveal that a previous urban development plan was based on an overestimate of the number of highly-paid, single people in the workforce. Researchers had noted the rise in household incomes in the area and the increase in single, individual households. Our analysis showed that among the high-income households, the majority were male-headed households with children. A large proportion of the single individuals were elderly women and working women making relatively low salaries. Interviews with employers disclosed that many were concerned about their ability to attract and hold a clerical workforce because of the reduction in moderately-priced housing units that accompanied the office space boom. At the same time, new housing being planned was designed for childless households of persons making more than $50,000 per year. A series of group interviews with a wide variety of people already working in Denver confirmed our expectations that for many people the combination of suburban living with jobs in the downtown core taxed their human and financial resources. Yet the city as it was developing appeared an unsuitable place to raise children and an expensive, not very attractive, housing environment.

The architect, planner, and financial specialist on the team analyzed the architectural quality, landuse patterns, existing services, landmarks, and amenities. They examined patterns of landprices, vacant land, and government-owned land as a background for suggesting options that might lead to the integration of workplaces with a mixed residential community including people of different ages, incomes and household types. Decisionmakers from the governmental, financial, and developmental communities were brought together in workshops to discuss the analysis of changing housing and community needs and alternatives to address them. During these workshops, opportunity sites for development were identified on the basis of land price, governmental ownership, declining use, and access to services and facilities. Demographic and interview data were used to project the kinds of people who would be working and possibly living in Denver in the next decade. Then alternative growth scenarios were explored, including options for residential development, mixed-use development, or primarily office and commercial development. Slides of urban areas that had followed these different directions were analyzed for their applicability to the situation in Denver. One of the main tasks of the workshops involved broadening the possibilities for development that were being considered. Most of those who attended the workshops were actively contributing to downtown development either as elected officials in city government, administrators in the Department of City Planning, the Office of Community Development, the Denver Urban Renewal Authority, the Denver Housing Authority, the Mayor's Office, and so on, or as bankers, investors, developers, and leaders in civic and grassroots community organizations. Many of the decisionmakers, mainly men, were extremely skeptical about the desirability of any housing options other than single-family, suburban homes. While they were aware of the housing needs of working women living alone or those of single parents, they often saw the provision of such housing as economically unfeasible. They doubted that two-parent families would be attracted to city housing. A city seemed to many of them an unhealthy place to raise children. Despite their awareness of the large numbers of women in the workforce, they foresaw little possibility of adapting the form of the city to accommodate their needs. The unspoken assumption was that women would somehow adjust and compensate personally for any inconvenience. Single women, especially single mothers, would have a hard time, as always, but nothing could be done about it.

As the workshops progressed, more interest in alternative development strategies was aroused. Yet the standard market and governmental practices for developing housing did not seem to fit the new requirements. Many decisionmakers in both the public and private sectors felt they needed more information about the numbers of people in different income and household categories who would have some interest in city living. They also wanted to know what kind of services and amenities would be required to attract potential residents.

At the conclusion of the workshops, a plan for developing a mixed residential community was advanced. In the end, Liebman and Melting recommended strategies for downtown housing that differed dramatically from previous studies of the market for downtown housing. Their study called for 64 percent of the 10,470 units to be targeted for families. In architectural renderings of the future housing, the sizes of apartments, scale of development, mix of housing types, open-space design, and facilities responded to the needs of a diverse population. In addition, they assessed locations for development in terms of nearness to existing schools and play facilities. Finally, Liebman and Melting phased the development to provide space for 1,000 to 5,000 families during the first five years. This pace allowed for 66 percent of the units constructed during the first phase to be designed for families. Of course, they could not ensure that households with children would occupy these units. Couples or anyone who could afford the additional space could buy or rent.

But the idea of providing housing suitable for children contrasted strongly with the kind of housing being built at that time in the city's main urban residential development, the Skyline Urban Renewal Area. There most of the buildings were towers sited directly on the street with little access to services and no consideration of children's needs. The one low-rise development that gave attention to open space was affordable for only upper-income households. In contrast, the Liebman and Melting strategies designated over 75 percent of the units as affordable by middle-income households. The physical form and location of the suggested housing would change the course of Denver's development from a city that segregated places for work and adult leisure from places for domestic life and childrearing, to one that integrated these activities.

The development community in Denver was never totally convinced. The workshops did, however, lead to a demand for a more detailed study of the market for downtown housing. Initially, the Housing Authority of the City and County of Denver commissioned this research. Later, United Bank of Denver, Piton Foundation, Central Bank of Denver, Empire Savings Bank, Midland Federal Savings and Loan, Public Service Corporation of Colorado, Colorado Housing Finance Authority, and the City and County of Denver supported the final, more detailed survey of the downtown workforce, undertaken by this author. The goal was to sample representatively the downtown work force and to determine the extent of demand for different kinds of housing, including urban housing. In the survey, extensive attention was paid to the kinds of design features, activity spaces, environmental qualities, and local services different household types would require.

Through a process described in greater detail elsewhere (Saegert, Liebman, and Melting, 1985), a sample of downtown employers (businesses, institutions, etc.) was drawn from a listing categorized by location, Standard Industrial Category, and size. The sample represented employers by category in the same proportions that they occurred in the total list. The survey was administered through the personnel office or in cooperation with a designated representative in each organization. In total, 2,631 responses were returned from 53 companies and institutions in downtown Denver. This response rate included 88 percent of the companies contacted and 43 percent of the questionnaires distributed.

The results confirmed many of our expectations that single women would be disproportionately attracted to downtown housing. While single women were only 11 percent of the sample, they made up 20 percent of the population wanting centrally located housing. Single mothers added another 6.5 percent to the population attracted to city housing although they comprised only 4.3 percent of the total sample. However, these groups were not optimistic about their ability to realize their housing goals. Of all those who wanted to move to central city housing but felt blocked from doing so, 57 percent were single women. All but a few felt that they could not afford such housing. Interestingly, single mothers were the only group that cited inability to find suitable housing as frequently as financial reasons as preventing them from moving to the city, even though they would prefer to do so. These groups were also more likely to want to rent although they also were interested in buying condominiums.

The financial barriers these women experience point to the problem of relying on economic development strategies to meet the needs of women. By national standards, these women were well off. The median income for single women and single mothers fell between $20,000 and $29,000. The mean income for single mothers was somewhat higher ($33,290) than other single women ($24,140). These statistics were computed for those wanting centrally located housing only. However, they were competing for housing with married couples and same-sexed roommates earning a median income of $30,000 to $49,999. Only unmarried adults living together with children reported a lower median income, between $15,000 and $19,000. It should be noted that single men were not making more money in this sample than single women. There were, however fewer single men in the sample than single women.

The survey backed up a second expectation also. A large proportion (35 percent) of those who would like to live in centrally located housing had children under 18. Yet these households wanted housing and neighborhood amenities unlikely to be found in new city housing. These households were more likely to want lower-rise housing, especially if they had lower incomes. Parents with incomes over $30,000 saw midrise apartments as relatively good places to raise children whereas lower-income parents did not. Generally, people with

32

higher incomes expected multifamily housing to be less stressful, a better financial investment, and to feel more control over their housing than did lower-income people.

Single mothers stressed the importance of proximity to a variety of facilities. Single parents were the most interested in nearby daycare but other parents expressed almost as much concern about proximity. Single mothers were also the most interested in access to a park or open space. Along with other singles they wanted to be close to stores for daily needs. All parents gave high priority to the location of indoor recreational facilities located in the building or development. Two-parent households would accept outdoor play spaces located up to three blocks away whereas single mothers wanted them located in the building or development.

While single mothers share the interests of many people who want centrally located housing, reducing transportation costs, and maintenance, they may run afoul of others' attitudes. People without children who wanted to live downtown expressed little tolerance for living in a building or development with children. While over a third of the people who would like to live in central city housing had children, the city was almost uniformly seen as a bad environment for raising children. Respondents saw the city as offering few childcare options and poor-quality public schools. Thus, parents who wanted to move to the city were weighing proximity to work and other adult considerations more heavily than possible negative conditions for children.

Data from the survey indicated that a potential market for downtown housing existed. However, for the city to move in the direction of an integration of people varying in age, income, and lifestyles, the urban form of Denver as well as the availability of services and affordable housing would need to change in ways that required intervention in market forces.

Specifically, the research reminds us that while cities, including Denver, offer many specialized public amenities, the basic public needs for a liveable environment and support for childrearing are frequently lacking. The development process in fact tends to decrease the quality of the urban environment as a place to live and grow. The cost of land and construction as well as the probability of nonresidential construction force housing development away from economically "hot" areas. The amenities needed for childrearing and simply living in a city have no priority. This problem is one that feminists confront when they try to envision a community that would not constrain women and men socially and physically to perpetuate a gender-based division of labor, a condition that historically impoverishes women economically. While the Denver Project had few immediate consequences for women's environmental choices, the workshops and studies raised awareness of many needs that had been neglected in the planning process up until that time.

Beyond that, the major issues that need to be resolved remain: (1) the tension between market forces and the needs of all people for a supportive environment, one that serves children, older people, low-income people, and all people in their lives outside the workplace; (2) the need for a politically active constituency to support public and private initiatives that will immediately benefit women. Such a constituency in the long run contributes to the development of a new generation and a viable community.

The second project to be described contrasts sharply with the Denver study. Whereas Denver was a high growth rate city with strong economic pressures on development, the second location studied, Harlem in New York City, provided insights into how women go about meeting their needs for housing and support in the face of economic disinvestment.

WOMEN AND LOW-INCOME COOPERATIVE HOUSING

Jackie Leavitt and I have been studying residents' experiences in low-income, limited-equity housing cooperatives in New York City (Leavitt and Saegert, 1984). This research has focused on the Tenant Interim Lease (TIL) Program of the Division of Alternative Management Programs of the New York City's Department of Housing Preservation and Development. This program serves a population containing large numbers of female-headed households, most at the poverty level. At a time when public housing serving a majority of female-headed households is under attack, and other new programs in the city require incomes above the median for female-headed households, all five of the Division of Alternative Management Programs seem to have special importance for women. In addition, the social organization required to develop and maintain housing cooperatives especially draws on the skills and values of women. The cooperative form of ownership proposed can be seen as an extension of a household style of organization. Indeed, we found that the women leaders we interviewed viewed their buildings as a family and gave them the same kind of twenty-four-hour-a-day attention. Their social ties provided both a network from which to organize and a glue to hold the organization together over time. However, not all leaders or active tenants were women. Women were in the majority but in a number of buildings men, most often men who had retired from their jobs, played a key role. While this paper focuses on women, our findings suggest that even though women may more frequently seek to extend their efforts to create and maintain secure homes, men, especially older men who were more likely to focus their energies close to home, can and do play important parts improving low-income cooperatives. In fact, we think that the combination of a program that taps women's value priorities and skills with a program that clearly can benefit both sexes and incorporate the energies and talents of men is particularly desirable.

We interviewed 46 TIL tenants in 14 buildings in Harlem. Our sample of buildings represents 64 percent of the TIL buildings in Community Boards 9 and 10. Of the residents interviewed, 36 were black, 7 Hispanic, and three white — an ethnic distribution comparable to the population of the community. Thirty-five respondents were women and 11 men. The majority were leaders in their cooperatives. Of these leaders, 62 percent were black women. In addition to finding a majority of women in leadership positions, we also found that elderly people occupied critical leadership roles in 10 of the 14 buildings.

This study confirmed that the program was indeed serving very low-income women. Beyond that, the cooperative ownership form involved them in positions of leadership. They used the program not only to establish security of tenure but also to create a housing environment that supported people socially rather than merely providing shelter. In all buildings we found that more able tenants aided those with physical handicaps or frail elderly in a variety of ways. Yet the spirit in the buildings contributed to a sense that all were engaged in a joint endeavor. In many cases, relatively housebound older people were significant contributors to the success and security of the cooperatives. We also found a strong connection between people's sense of identity and social connectedness and their buildings and apartments. The buildings had often been the site of their experiences of family and friends for over 30 years. The apartments contained momentos of these years, housed relatives from down South, grown children, grandchildren, and other visiting relatives for different periods of time. These homes functioned as both reminders of and resources for their occupants' involvement in supportive social networks. Many residents had fond memories of their building as it had been in former days of grandeur when Harlem was a better place to live, a wellspring of hope and vision for the

34

future. The security of tenure plus the experience of control and efficacy arising from cooperative ownership seemed to buttress these earlier connections. As in families, these supportive ties and relationships coexisted with frequent and sometimes serious conflicts. Yet the cooperative structure provides a way that disagreeing residents can bring their divergent needs and opinions to light in order to try to work them out. Increased technical assistance in managing cooperatives would most likely be an inexpensive and very helpful way to make limited-equity cooperative programs more widely applicable.

LESSONS FOR THE ANDROGENOUS CITY

The case of the Harlem low-income cooperatives provides a striking contrast to the Denver planning study. In Denver one of the stated purposes of the work was to develop a plan for downtown development that would support both work in the economic sector and the requirements of domestic life. Yet the combination of economic priorities that made a good living environment, especially one that supported childrearing, appear unfeasible. A lack of political leadership and a constituency with sufficient influence to bring about such major changes resulted in inaction. In the Harlem case, the limited-equity cooperatives we studied were not intended to have any special bearing on the needs of women. Yet the inactivity of the market and the structure of the TIL program combined with female leadership and participation in the cooperatives led to the creation of environments that supported domestic life. These cooperatives could be seen as failing to contribute to the economy since they were not profit-making. On the other hand, they did provide affordable housing for working men and women at the low end of the salary scale, otherwise dependent on publicly-owned housing. The support networks and opportunities for the pursuit of noneconomic values that characterized these cooperatives are examples of the kinds of changes in the operating of environments that would be required in the androgenous city.

In order to correct the masculine biases seen in most existing cities and living environments, some feminist guidelines can be offered that grow out of the low-income cooperative example. First, programs must be structured so that they are accessible to households in the income brackets in which large numbers of minority, elderly, and single-women households are found. Second, programs that build on existing social ties and commitment to existing places and communities are more likely to both attract women and draw on their leadership skills. Third, programs that facilitate group cooperation rather than individual competitive advantage will attract women, support them in the many different roles they must play and help women to continue to contribute to the healthy social development of communities that include children and elderly people.

While the programs we studied do seem to work well for older women and women without young children, single mothers of young children are often too burdened to be active in cooperative development. After cooperatives are functioning they seem to provide good places for such mothers to live. Yet the many demands of limited-equity cooperative ownership of old buildings suggests that some infusion of social services such as daycare, job training, and so on into a network of tenant cooperatives would make them more accessible and attractive to single mothers.

This observation leads to a fourth principle of feminist planning: the integration of supports for human development and well-being into housing and economic development projects. The existing division between housing development, economic development, and social services runs directly counter to the demands women face in daily life. It also replaces effective, informal structures of care and support with inefficient, impersonal, bureaucratic services that place women in a client rather than a leadership role. The key to such integration lies in making resources available to women through programs which require that they exercise leadership and authority. In addition, a focus on housing and neighborhood locations for necessary services would be more compatible with the daily demands women must cope with, especially when they have children or are elderly. The goals of such programs would be to move toward community environments that serve the needs of women rather than perpetuating urban forms and services biased against women. By pursuing this direction however, we hope to arrive at an androgenous city, one that provides places and supports for the full range of human activities without biasing access on the basis of gender.

REFERENCES

Bernard, J.
1981   The Female World. New York: Free Press.
Birch, E. L.
1978   "Women-made housing: The case of early public housing policy." Journal of the American Institute of Planners 44:130-43.
Freeman, J.
1980   "Women and urban policy." Signs: A Journal of Women and Culture 5 (Supplement):1-19.
Geerken, M., and W. T. Gove
1983   At Home and at Work: The Family's Allocation of Labor. Beverly Hills, CA: Sage Publications.
Gittell, M., and T. Shtob
1980   "Changing women's roles in political volunteerism and reform of the city." Signs: A Journal of Women and Culture 5 (Supplement):567-78.
Hayden, D.
1980   "What would a non-sexist city be like?" In C. R. Stimpson, E. Dixler, M. J. Nelson, and K. B. Yatrakis (eds.), Women and the American City. Chicago: University of Chicago Press.
1984   Redesigning the American Dream: The Future of Housing, Work, and Family Life. New York: W. W. Norton.
Lawson, R., S. Barton, and J. W. Joselit
1980   "From kitchen to storefront: Women in the tenant movement." Pp. 255-72 in G. R. Wekerle, R. Peterson and D. Morley (eds.), New Space for Women. Boulder, CO: Westview Press.
Leavitt, J.
1980   "The history, status and concerns of women planners." Signs: A Journal of Women and Culture 5 (Supplement):226-30.
1983   Aunt Mary and the Shelter-Service Crisis for Single Parents. New York: Columbia University, Division of Urban Planning.
Leavitt, J., and S. Saegert
1984   "Women and abandoned buildings: A feminist approach to housing." Social Policy (Summer):32-39.
Maas, H. S., and J. M. Kuper
1974   From Thirty to Seventy. San Francisco, CA: Jossey Bass.
Matthews, S. H.
1979   The Social Worlds of Old Women: Management of Self-Identity. Beverly Hills, CA: Sage Publications.
Michelson, W.
1984   "Maternal employment, community contest and pressures: The case of child care." Women and Environments 6:9-11.
Moen, E., E. Boulding, J. Lillydahl, and R. Palm
1981   Women and the Social Cost of Economic Development: Two Colorado Case Studies. Boulder, CO: Westview Press.
Myers, P.
1982   Aging in Place: Strategies to Help the Elderly Stay in Revitalizing Neighborhoods. Washington, DC: The Conservation Foundation.
Palm, Risa, and Allan Pred
1974   "A time-geographic perspective on problems of inequality for women." Working Paper No. 236 Berkeley, CA: Institute of Urban and Regional Development, University of California.
Perlin, L. I., and J. S. Johnson
1981   "Marital status, life-strains, and depression." In P. J. Stein (ed.), Single Life: Unmarried Adults in Social Context. New York: St. Martin Press.
Piven, F. F.
1984   "Women and the state: Ideology, power

and the welfare state." Socialist Review 14:13-22.

Rothblatt, D. N., D. J. Garr, and J. Sprague
1979   The Suburban Environment and Women. New York: Praeger.

Saegert, S.
1980   "Masculine cities and feminine suburbs: Polarized ideas, contradictory realities." Signs: A Journal of Women and Culture 5 (Supplement):93-108.
1982   "Toward the androgenous city." In G. Gappert and R. K. Knight (eds.), Cities and the 21st Century. Beverly Hills, CA: Sage Publications.

Saegert, S., T. Liebman, and A. Melting
1985   "Planning the city for working women: The Denver experience." In E. Birch (ed.), The Unsheltered Women. New Brunswick, NJ: Rutgers University, Center for Urban Policy Research.

Saegert, S., and Gary Winkel
1980   "The home: A critical problem for changing sex roles." Pp. 41-61 in G. R. Wekerle, R. Peterson, and D. Morley (eds.), New Space for Women. Boulder, CO: Westview Press.

Smith, R. E.
1979   "The movement of women into the labor force." In R. E. Smith (ed.), The Subtle Revolution. Washington, DC: The Urban Institute.

U.S. Department of Labor, Women's Bureau
1983   Time of Change: 1983 Handbook of Women Workers. Washington, DC: U. S. Government Printing Office.

Reprinted with permission from **Sociological Focus**, vol. 18, no. 2, pp. 161-176, 1985.

PART II
SUBURBAN ENVIRONMENTS

4 Coping with the suburban nightmare: Developing community supports in Australia*

RUTH EGAR, WENDY SARKISSIAN,
DOROTHY (BRADY) MALE, and LESLEY HARTMANN

Australian suburbs are generally characterized by low-population densities in exclusively residential areas. Community services and facilities are often lacking or inaccessible. The isolation of women in these environments is exacerbated by inadequate public transportation. This article describes a federally-funded neighborhood development program which stresses a process-oriented approach based on self-help initiatives by local women. In the Adelaide suburb where the program was implemented, significant improvements in community life have resulted.

This article is about a "missing link" in the lives of Australian suburban women who have expressed dissatisfaction with their situation. What is needed and what has been found to work is much *more* than community development by facilities planning: it is women working with other women — the *human* resource. While it is important to continue the struggle for planning which acknowledges women's needs and provides the facilities and services they require, other measures are urgently needed. This article examines the Family Support Scheme (FSS), an innovative federally-funded neighborhood development program in Salisbury North, an isolated suburb of Adelaide, Australia. In the first three years of operation, this program has encouraged a number of local community initiatives. The FSS strives to combat the social isolation which emerges as the greatest single problem for women in suburbia. It puts women in touch with each other — and with the resources

*Earlier versions of this paper were presented at the International Interdisciplinary Congress on Women and Society, Haifa, Israel, 29 December 1981, and at the 52nd. Congress of the Australian and New Zealand Association for the Advancement of Science, Macquarie University, Sydney, Australia, 14 May 1982. The authors gratefuly acknowledge the help and support of the Corporation of the City of Salisbury, the Land Commission of New South Wales and particularly Frank Wyatt, Bob Wilkinson, Gwen Lines, Pat O'Loughlin, Harry Pateman, and Jean Slade. Leonie Sandercock, Barbara Adams, Don Perlgut, and David Wilmoth provided valuable comments on an earlier version. Bob Wilkinson contributed greatly to the final sections of this paper and provided guidance throughout. Vicki Bevan and Beverley Waters typed many drafts, while Monica Allebach did a great job preparing the final version.

39

of the community. Ultimately, as the community grows in self-determination, it may also change the physical face of suburbia.

BACKGROUND

Australia is the world's most urbanized country with about 90 percent of its population in a string of coastal cities. The major cities — Sydney with 3.5 million, Melbourne with nearly 3 million, Adelaide, Perth, and Brisbane each with nearly one million — all have large, low-density, residential areas of detached, single-family houses with spacious front and rear gardens. In Adelaide, capital of South Australia, with a carefully planned central area, carbon-copy suburbs stretch for 80 km between hills and the coast.

Life in Adelaide's Salisbury North area, the site of the work described in this paper, represents in microcosm a humble version of the Australian "post-war suburban dream." The area has 1,000 houses on about 190 hectares at an average of 3.6 persons per dwelling. From Adelaide's Central Business District, the distance is about 30 km; from the nearest district center, about 5 km. By bus, Adelaide is 45 minutes away. About half the houses are semidetached, single-story, public rental houses first occupied in the 1950s and 60s; nearby are recently built owner-occupied, single-story, brick houses built by private builders "on spec."

In the owner-occupied houses, incomes are generally higher and more households are headed by two adults, sometimes with two incomes. Despite the higher gross household and family incomes, mortgage payments are very high; many owner-occupiers are in financially perilous situations. Renters come to live in Salisbury North because of housing availability, despite its stigma, isolation, inadequate public transit, and poor range of activities. Community services and poor facilities are simply not adequate to meet demands.

SUBURBAN LIFE AS A WOMEN'S ISSUE

Women's opinions of suburbia in Toronto have been found to differ substantially from those held by men: "women moving from city to suburban houses are least satisfied with this choice and view their isolation from downtown and commercial locations as a major compromise. . . ." (Michelson, 1977). Research in New York City and surrounding suburbs supports the findings cited above and further highlights the differences between male and female evaluations of suburbia:

> . . . many of the wives who actually moved experienced serious emotional difficulty in adjusting and expressed a lack of personal fulfilment in the situation. . . . Almost all wives. . . felt they had more options and were personally happier in the city; most husbands preferred the suburbs for reasons of economic investment, status and increased activity options. (Saegert, 1977:140)

Women as a user group most heavily bear the penalties of suburban development. There is a need for "enriched" neighborhoods which provide "a more balanced setting for the home environment, while encouraging the widening of women's roles and therefore the range of environments in which women operate" (Wekerle et al., 1980:29). Choice is essential, even for those women who express contentment with their suburban lives.

The answer to this question is that many, though certainly not all, fare poorly. For many Australian women, suburbia is not a dream but a nightmare. And the situation, far from improving, is rapidly deteriorating with cuts in government funding for social programs, services, and facilities at every level. Bryson and Thompson (1972) and Brennan (1973) were among the first to outline the detrimental social consequences of low-density, fringe development. In 1973, the Australian Institute of Urban Studies published a study on "Housewives in a N.S.W. Suburb" (Wearing and Wearing, 1973), and initiatives of the Federal Labor Government (1973-75) provided the impetus for consulting reports (Keys Young Planners, 1975) and a generally broadened interest in the social implications of suburban development for women.

A 1974 survey of 1,073 households in Melbourne suburbs is particularly illustrative of the problems faced by suburban women (Anderson, 1975). These problems have been aggravated by increased female participation in the workforce and a higher incidence of family breakdown, resulting in fewer women being at home during the day, a greater demand for childcare facilities, and more female-headed households living in or close to poverty.

PHYSICAL AND SOCIAL ISOLATION

The most alarming finding in the above study is the extent of physical and social isolation. Of 834 women interviewed, 18 percent left the house in daytime less than once a fortnight. Nearly 40 percent left the house only once a week or less. Over half had only infrequent or no contact with neighbors; those who wanted more contact lacked confidence, were shy, or were afraid that they might not be welcomed by their neighbors. More than half did not visit neighbors, their contact extending only to chatting if they met, or just greeting. The problem was exacerbated by the lack of public transport.

Anderson's findings of isolation were confirmed by another large study of women in Sydney (Keys Young Planners, 1975) which examined attitudes to a range of issues: employment, social contact, recreation, transportation, shopping, accommodation, and the local environment. Overall, fewer than 20 percent of the 1,200 women interviewed had frequent contact with their neighbors, and more than one-third had no friends within ten minutes' walking distance of home. More than two-thirds had no relatives within ten minutes' walking distance. Approximately 40 percent never went out without their husband when he was working. Depending on marital and employment status, between 40 and 50 percent said that they would like to meet more people.

Recent research in an outer-suburban Sydney public housing estate is also illustrative of the extent of women's social isolation (Sarkissian and Doherty, 1984). Of 200 women interviewed, 47 percent reported they were lonely; only 11 percent knew their neighbors "very well"; and 78 percent had no close family within 10 minutes' walk. These studies confirm that women need much more than services and facilities. These women's experiences have structured their reality in which they have come to perceive themselves as helpless. They lack motivation, skills and supportive environment to help them change their lives. The suburban woman

. . . is lonely, has no interests of her own and experiences a lack of achievement and sense of failure. As she is isolated from other women in the same circumstances, she believes she is alone in her problems and so must assume that her frustration and lack of satisfaction is due to her own failure. After all, it would appear that she has everything to make her happy so naturally she assumes her problem is with her. (Anderson, 1975:31)

These observations applied acutely to the women we worked with in Salisbury North. Many of them were suffering from depression and a lack of self-esteem, were addicted to TV soap operas, and characterized by an inability to take steps towards making themselves known in the neighborhood or welcoming newcomers. Indeed, the neighborhood itself was perceived as a very threatening and hostile environment. Young mothers were isolated from family and friends. Neighborhoods were devoid of services. Few opportunities existed for women to share their experiences and support each other throughout some of the most demanding years of their lives. Women who had previously held challenging, exacting jobs, who were independent and reasonably secure, lacked the support of other women and of husbands who were away at work. The lack of meeting places and inadequate public transport greatly restricted opportunities for social interaction. The supermarket was the most common meeting place. This isolation made in difficult for women to develop an understanding of their collective situation and many remained unaware, and therefore uncritical, of the structures and processes that shaped their lives in this suburban community. The family support scheme, described below, was intended to identify those factors.

THE FAMILY SUPPORT SCHEME

In 1978, the City of Salisbury received a three-year Federal grant for a "Family Support Scheme" (FSS) in an underprivileged, isolated neighborhood of 1,000 homes (3,600 people). Initially it was characterized by an emphasis on child-parent relationships, child development, parent-self-awareness, and integration of agencies through a closer involvement with a core group of parents. Eventually, a much more broadly-based neighborhood social development program developed.

A model was found in the approach of Joseph Cardijn, a Belgian priest, who worked with small groups of young factory workers in the 1920's based on a belief in the uniqueness of every person, and in the workers' dignity. The workers evaluated priorities and were expected to undertake practical action to alter their situation, either individually or collectively. The movement flourished within the Catholic Church in Belgium in the 1920's, in Europe in the 1930s, and in most countries after World War II. Other social movements, including international movements for young farmers, students, sailors, and middle-class workers, adopted its principles. Paolo Freire, also influenced the development of the FSS. In Freire's literacy and agrarian reform programs, reflection has been a key principle, leading to a "dialogical encounter" with others and focusing on previously inconspicuous phenomena. Contemporary liberation philosophies, indebted to Cardijn and Freire, inspired the Adelaid "Christian Life Movement" and resulted in the development of movements for workers and students. From these small groups developed a model for working with the isolated suburban women in Salisbury North.

In 1978, Salisbury Council employed, with Federal funding, three Home Visitors for the FSS, one full-time and two part-time. All were local women who worked on the premise (1), that the women needed each other's support to create changes that would transform their families, homes, and neighborhoods: and, (2), that, considering transportation difficulties, accessible opportunities for developing social action had to be created within walking distance of the women's homes.

The Home Visitors began by door knocking, followed by an informal chat. The aim was to leave people with a task, a challenge for action, e.g., finding out about availability of childcare arrangements, or the location of the local rubbish dump, or investigating Council regulations on some matter. No action could be too small or insignificant. Follow-up continued until the women had taken a more independent stance or were supported within a neighborhood group. Seemingly insurmountable problems thus assumed "everyday" qualities. Indeed, far from being crisis-oriented, the FSS focuses on "everyday" lives. Crises and "the spectacular" are too rare for sustained community development. In general terms, the method involves a process of discovery through identifying the issues surrounding an event, evaluating priorities in a situation; and acting, i.e., finding the next action which will be consistent with knowledge and evaluation.

Initially, small women's groups were created. The next step was relatively simple: to encourage one woman to talk to another, to invite neighbors and friends to join small "review" groups. Resourcefulness and creativity began to be shared, leading to action to alleviate some community problems. Knowing that others were experiencing similar situations raised the women's awareness and provided new motivation, not simply for "coping" better, but for changing their responses. The first signs of the vitality of the FSS appeared when neighbor groups began to meet in the street. New play groups were formed. A meeting was held to examine public transport issues. A first group of mothers began a phase of well-coordinated thinking, planning, and acting to organize a daycare facility. Within a year, another group held regular public meetings providing information and urging women to identify concerns and to work with the group for change. Various groups and individuals approached Council for information on such things as: availability of grants, services offered, local government bylaws, and ways of supporting community facilities. A new policy for leasing a sports facility to a community recreation group was also negotiated. During the first three years of the FSS, the actions succeeded in improving the neighborhood as a place to live. Changes included, for example, the reorganization of arrangements for the use and control of sports fields and locker rooms and increased preschool facilities. Equally important, however, were changed relationships and friendships which made the neighborhood a much more supportive and enriching place. For many women it was a major breakthrough. The discovery of a common collective experience was as essential as the actions which resulted.

The most effective structure which emerged was a network of small groups. The appropriate process was a sequence of action-reflection-action on the women's expressed needs, leading towards a more realistic analysis of social, political, economic, and physical factors in their community. Reflection was a key principle. Often it was necessary to develop or create structured opportunities for reflection. This emphasis on the need for reflection and reflective sharing is supported by other studies of women's needs in suburbia (Anderson, 1975).

WHY LOCAL GOVERNMENT?

The Salisbury FSS is operated by the local council which has provided a supportive base from which to work. The scheme has gained credence and legitimacy from belonging to local government. This has also resulted in acceptance of the scheme and its team members by professionals with whom the women work. This support and the contact with the leadership in Salisbury North were important in the effectiveness of the scheme's operations. As "shareholders," residents enjoy participating in efforts which represent "their taxes and work." The development of the FSS has directed the Council into new responsibilities, and the presence of elected members has helped residents to see issues in the context of their local community.

The Salisbury experience shows convincingly that efforts, subsidized by local government, can develop women's political and organizational skills and strengthen decentralized decision making. As Elise Boulding has argued, "women's wide experience at the local level will become increasingly important in the development of 'self-help' systems that must replace functioning centralized systems" (quoted in Wekerle et al., 1980: 28).

An emphasis on a process-oriented approach, acknowledging the value of conflict, is essential to the effectiveness of the FSS. Unlike casework or group work, the FSS model develops a form of community organization known as "community development," which presupposes that community change may be pursued optimally through broad participation of a wide spectrum of people at the local community level in goal determination and action (see Rothman, 1970:21). Development of "indigenous leadership" is seen as essential. The FSS, like other locality development approaches, concentrates on "process goals," aimed at establishing "cooperative working relationships among groups in the community, creating self-maintaining community problem solving structures, and improving the power base of the community..." (Rothman, 1970:25). Getting local people together to determine and reflect on "felt needs" and solve their own problems is the basic change strategy, as opposed to the data gathering strategy of planning, or the mass action strategies of the "social change" approach (Rothman, 1970:27-28). Above all, the approach is the antithesis of the "rational-comprehensive" planning model (Grabow and Heskin, 1973). It shuns elitism and centralism and is change-oriented. No final vision of a perfect community is being aimed for, rather, the approach is open-ended, involving the progressive formulation of common goals, determination of priorities, and selection of means of implementation. For the most part, it is something everyday, piecemeal, gradual.

CONCLUSION

The scheme described in this paper has qualities which make it appropriate for local government in countries where local control of community development is accepted. Where municipalities have few powers or view their responsibilities in a more limited way, a more appropriate sponsor may be a private agency or nonprofit group. Central government is too remote from women's everyday experiences and is therefore not an appropriate sponsor, at least in Australia. In the suburb described here, the FSS provides the link between otherwise isolated women and the wider community. It encourages development and more extensive use of services and facilities and promotes self-help initiatives, at the same time facilitating social development. Working within a supportive municipal government, the scheme has encouraged women to help that level of government become more accountable and more responsive to their needs.

REFERENCES

Anderson, Robin
  1975   Leisure — An Inappropriate Concept for
          Women? Canberra: Australian Government
          Publishing Service.
Brennan, Tom
  1973   New Community: Problems and Policies.
          Sydney: Angus and Robertson.
Bryson, Lois, and Faith Thompson
  1972   An Australian Newtown: Life and Leader-
          ship in a New Housing Suburb. Ringwood,
          Victoria: Penguin.
Grabow, S., and A. Heskin
  1973   "Foundations for a radical concept of plan-
          ning." Journal of the American Institute of
          Planners 106:108-14.
Keys Young Planners
  1975   Women and Planning: Women's Attitudes.
          Report for the cities commission. Surry
          Hills, N.S.W.: M. S. J. Keys, Young
          Planners.
Michelson, W.
  1977   Environmental Choice, Human Behavior,
          and Residential Satisfaction. New York:
          Oxford.

Saegart, Susan
  1977   "Towards better person-environment rela-
          tions." Pp. 139-43 in P. Suedfeld, J. R.
          Russell, L. Ward et al. (eds.), The
          Behavioral Basis of Design. Volume 2.
          Stroudsburg, PA: D.H. and R.
Rothman, Jack
  1970   "Three models of community organized
          practice." Pp. 20-37 in F. M. Cox et al.
          (eds.), Strategies of Community Organiza-
          tion. Itasca, IL: F. E. Peacock.
Sarkissian, Wendy, and Terry Doherty
  1984   Living in Public Housing: A Report of a
          Tenants' Evaluation of Medium-Density
          Public Housing in Suburban Sydney.
          Sydney: NSW Housing Commission.
Wearing, R., and A. Wearing
  1973   Housewives in a N. S. W. Suburb.
          Canberra: Australian Institute of Urban
          Studies.
Wekerle, Gerda, R. Perterson, and D. Morley
  1980   New Space for Women. Boulder, CO:
          Westview.

Reprinted with permission from **Sociological Focus**, vol. 18, no. 2, pp. 119-125, 1985.

45

5 Residential preferences in the suburban era: A new look?*

SYLVIA F. FAVA

The intersection of gender, residential preference and suburban dominance is examined with data from a national sample of adults from a survey conducted by the Louis Harris organization. The data show a gender gap in residential preferences and challenge the conventional wisdom about women's residential preferences for the city. There are important implications: the migration of women to suburbs and the "fit" of women's residential preferences with those of men.

This paper deals with the intersection of three emergent themes in urban sociology. First, the introduction of women's worlds into the study of cities and suburbs resulting in major questions about the generalizability of conclusions drawn mainly from male perspectives. Second, the shift in residential patterns such that the largest portion of the population of the United States now live in suburbs. This resulted, among other things, in a "suburban generation," — the cohort of young people who were born and raised in the suburban landscape which came increasingly to dominate the United States after the Second World War. Third, the change in cities themselves. Urban change with job and population loss, fiscal crises, and decaying infrastructure is well known but it has not been considered before in conjunction with women's worlds and the suburban generation. Suburbs are changing, too. They are increasingly differentiated, with many suburban areas having reached the "critical mass" of density, jobs, shopping, and support services that women need.

The analysis of urban and suburban life from the point of view of women's roles dates only to the mid-1970s. A pioneering effort was the conference on women and planning sponsored by the Department of Housing and Urban Development in 1973 (Hapgood and Getzels, 1974). Critiques of the sexist assumptions of urban and suburban sociology appeared shortly thereafter (Fava, 1980; Lofland, 1975). The low-density suburbs of single-family homes segregated from nonresidential activities provide a setting suitable only for the traditional wife-mother role. Higher density and more mixed settings, which are mainly but not exclusively urban in the United States, provide a greater availability of services closer to home. Despite women's greatly increased labor force participation they still have major responsibility for household tasks and rely more on public transportation than men. Access to workplaces, shopping, childcare, medical, recreational, and other facilities is therefore crucial for women because it reduces time pressures, enabling them to integrate their various roles.

*Material was gathered during a stay as Visiting Scholar at the Center for Urban Affairs and Policy Research, Northwestern University in Spring 1982. The Center's assistance is gratefully acknowledged.

47

The conventional wisdom — if I can apply that term to so new a conception — is that cities are better for women than suburbs.[1] Indeed several studies support this contention. Loneliness was reported by over half the women in a planned suburban community and a somewhat smaller proportion reported boredom (Keller, 1981); lack of support networks of relatives for social interaction and mutual assistance were a major problem for less affluent and blue-collar women in suburbs (Berger, 1960; Gans, 1967; Popenoe, 1977), while among more middle-class women informal networks developed to provide childcare, hairdressing services, tailoring, transportation to shopping and dentists, and other services not available in or near their suburb (Genovese, 1980). Most telling were the studies comparing suburban husbands and wives: husbands were less local in their contacts than wives (Fischer and Jackson, 1976); husbands were more satisfied than wives with suburban life (Mackintosh, 1977; Michelson, 1973).

These studies of suburbia have typically dealt with women (and men) who have moved to the suburbs from the city. Sometimes this was explicitly in the research design, as the authors sought to determine the impact, if any, of suburbs on movers' behavior and attitudes (Berger, 1960; Gans, 1967; Mackintosh, 1977; Michelson, 1973). Indeed this orientation to suburban research was characteristic of (and suitable to) the period after the Second World War when large streams of urbanites migrated to the suburbs. In 1950, according to the United States census, only about a quarter of the residents of the United States were suburbanites (that is, lived in metropolitan areas but outside the central cities); by 1960 suburbanites still accounted for less than a third of the United States population. However, by 1970 suburbanites had risen to 38 percent, making suburban residents the most numerous residential group, outnumbering central city residents (31 percent) for the first time. By 1980 suburban residents accounted for 45 percent of the total United States population, and central city residents for only 30 percent. (The remainder of the United States population, 25 percent, lived in nonmetropolitan areas.)

Suburbs are no longer appendages to the city — suburbs are increasingly self-sufficient and autonomous, at least on a daily basis, providing an ever-widening array of educational, medical, cultural, and other services, as well as an expanding job market and a virtually complete range of retailing. However, the women and men portrayed in the available studies of postwar suburbs moved *to* these places and they were comparing them with their own experience of growing up and living in large cities.

For the "suburban generation" who were born and raised in postwar suburbs, there is no direct experience of living in cities. The recognition of the new suburban group is just emerging (Newitt, 1984; Fava, 1983; O'Connell, 1979) and there have been few attempts to test the gender relevance of the new suburban setting. Cities also changed greatly in the period after the Second World War, so that comparison for the new suburban generation is of different kinds of urban and suburban places than for the "decentralized suburbanites" who moved *to* suburbs in the immediate aftermath of the Second World War. The geographer Peter Muller has described the structure of the American metropolis in the period after the Second World War as "a monocentric city with suburbs," but characterizes the period from the 1970s as a "polycentric city" with a *declining central city*, an *inner suburban ring*, an *outer ring of suburbs* with "minicities" — multipurpose concentrations of shopping, jobs, and entertainment that were formerly found only in the downtown central city; and an outlying *urban fringe* (Muller, 1981).

Three aspects of urban and suburban change are particularly relevant for women: public transportation, the location of jobs, and safety. At the close of the Second World War in 1945 annual transit ridership was 23 billion trips, but dropped 30 percent by 1950 to 17 billion and fell to only 6 billion trips in the late 1970s, while freeway construction,

48

largely underwritten by the 1956 federal Interstate Highway Act, produced more than 13,000 miles of freeways by 1969, serving to make outlying parts of the metropolis more accessible (Muller, 1981). Automobile ownership increased substantially; in 1960; 21.6 percent of the households in the United States did not own a motor vehicle, but by 1980 the percentage had dropped to only 12.9 (Long and DeAre, 1984). Although ownership was less prevalent in urban areas, the growth of urban vehicles outpaced urban population and household growth (Long and DeAre, 1984), indicating the replacing of public transit by the private automobile in cities. The change has not necessarily benefited women, for they rely on public transportation more than men and are also less likely to drive and to have access to a private automobile (Mazey and Lee, 1983).

During the 1960s many cities, especially the largest, began to lose population — and between the 1970 and 1980 census declines of 10 percent or more were common. Jobs also moved to suburbs and by 1973 suburban employment nationwide surpassed the cities' job total for the first time (Birch, 1975; Muller, 1981). As important is the fact that the job "mix" has changed in central cities, with blue-collar jobs in manufacturing declining while white collar jobs, especially in finance, insurance, real estate, and professional services have expanded. The job shifts vary from city to city and the consequences for women, where they have begun to be analyzed, are varied. In New York City, comparison of job gains for white, black, and ethnic subgroups of women with the corresponding male groups present a complex picture (Bailey and Waldinger, 1984; Mollenkopf, 1984).

Fear of crime in cities constricts their activities, women report (Gordon et al., 1980), including the use of mass transit (Richards, 1978). Compared with men, the women studied in Chicago, Philadelphia, and San Francisco were more fearful of crime and engaged in a variety of precautionary strategies, such as going out only in the daytime, that seriously limited their (women's) activities, amounting to adopting lifestyles which prevented them from becoming victims (Gordon et al., 1980). The operative factor is the *perception* of crime since research indicates women often inaccurately judge (both overestimating and underestimating) the actual incidence of crime in various city neighborhoods (Gordon et al., 1980). In fact, contrary to widely accepted beliefs, analysis of the more accurate crime data derived from victimization surveys shows that except for "property crimes with contact" (robbery, personal larceny) there is no relationship between density and victimization, that is to say, between densely populated cities and "true" crime rates (Decker et al., 1982). The belief that cities, especially large cities, have much more crime than other kinds of places is nevertheless almost universal among Americans, no matter where they live. A national survey of adults found that 91 percent believed large cities had the highest crime rates (Louis Harris, 1978). The belief is real and has real consequences, especially for women.

RESIDENTIAL PREFERENCES IN THE AGE OF SUBURBIA

In light of the three themes above, our research examines difference in the residential preferences of men and women who live in the United States, where suburban residence is the norm, and where cities are experiencing deindustrialization, substantial job and population losses as well as declines in urban services such as mass transit. Many of the adults are themselves part of the "suburban generation," that is, they have actually spent all their lives in suburbs.

The intersection of gender, residential preference, and suburban dominance has not been posed before as a research question and no data combining all three components exist. However, national data dealing with various subcombinations are available. Through

Table 1. Gender and Residential Preference

Residential Category	"What Is Your First Choice of Places to Live?"		"When They Grow Up I Want My Children to Live In ..."[a]	
	MALE %	FEMALE %	MALE %	FEMALE %
Large City (250,000+)	16.3	15.9	4.7	5.5
Medium-Size City (50,000-250,000) in the Suburbs	10.4	11.9	14.0	19.5
Medium-Size City (50,000-250,000) not in the Suburbs	7.3	9.2	10.8	10.8
Small City, Town or Village (under 50,000) in the Suburbs	15.2	15.6	19.1	17.6
Small City, Town or Village (under 50,000) not in the Suburbs	22.1	23.2	13.6	20.0
Rural Area	27.0	22.8	33.8	23.3
Not Sure	1.7	1.4	4.1	3.4
	100.0	100.0	100.0	100.0

[a] Responses only of those who wanted their children to live in places different from where respondents currently lived
SOURCE: Louis Harris and Associates, Inc., The 1978 HUD Survey of the Quality of Community Life. A Data Book, pp. 563, 573.

them we can discern an emerging picture that differs from the accepted idea that women prefer urban life because it facilitates the management of multiple roles — especially employment, home management, and childcare — by concentrating many activities in a relatively small space with easy access among the specialized activities and support services. A new look suggests that what women prefer in the city, the density and diversity which simplify the coordination of multiple roles, are now increasingly available in many suburban areas. Women's residential preferences begin to reflect these metropolitan changes. Women's preferences for suburbs are augmented by the fact that a large proportion of the women have grown up in suburbs and prefer similar settings, being unable to adjust readily to the public spaces and residential life of cities.

50

Nevertheless the city exerts a "pull" on suburban women as a place they may work and live in relatively briefly for their own personal fulfillment and advancement, before returning to suburban areas to "settle down," especially for childrearing. Women's residential preferences may have changed (there are no earlier surveys that disaggregate the data by gender)[2] but there is still a gender gap. Men prefer smaller-size places and especially rural areas more than women.

Our conclusions have been previewed above. They are derived largely from a 1978 survey conducted by Louis Harris and associates for the Department of Housing and Urban Development (Louis Harris, 1978). In a national representative sample of the United States population aged 18 and over, 7,074 individuals were asked 250 items related to community life. The survey did not analyze responses by gender, but since the responses were disaggregated by gender it has been possible to construct the following tables, and add our own analysis. When presented with the question, "What is your first choice of places to live?" the responses of the men and women, indicated in Table 1, showed few major differences, except that men preferred rural areas (27.0 percent) more than women (22.8 percent). The other differences are small but not in the expected direction: women prefer the large city (15.9 percent) slightly *less* than the men (16.3 percent), and women prefer the medium-size city, whether in the suburbs (11.9 percent) or not (9.2 percent) slightly *more* than men (10.4 and 7.3 percent, respectively). Both men and women have as their most frequent preference the small-size places, either suburbs or small towns: the percentages are 15.2 and 22.1 for men and 15.6 and 23.2 for women.

The differences in residential preference between women and men are clearer when they are allowed to project their preferences. The data are shown in the right-hand columns of Table 1. In reply to the question, "When they grow up I want my children to live in . . . ," the large city is the big loser among both men and women; the percentages drop to 4.7 and 5.5, respectively, although it is interesting that the women express a greater preference for the large city for their adult children than do the men. The big gainer among the women are the medium-size cities in suburbs, which 19.5 percent choose as the place they would want their adult children to live in. For their children men also increase their preference for the medium-size city in the suburbs — to 14.0 percent.

There is a revealing contrast between the child-projective responses, that is the view of the future metropolitan amenities reflected in the two right-hand columns of Table 1, and the current views reflected in the two left-hand columns; for both women and men the preference for "medium cities in the suburbs" gains (but more sharply for women than men) making this the third-highest preference category, whereas it was next to the last, that is fifth choice for both women and men in the left-hand columns. The preference for large-city residence for one's children drops to last place among both women and men compared to the third place it held among both sexes in the left-hand columns.

Comparison of the two sections of Table 1 suggests a widening gender gap in residential preferences between women and men. Almost all of the differences in women's and men's preferences are greater in comparing the two right-hand "future" columns than in comparing the two left-hand columns. The most marked contrast is the increased male preference for low-density, rural-type areas, rising to 33.8 percent, while women's preference, at 23.3 percent is virtually unchanged. There is also a wide gap between men's preference for small, nonsuburban towns and cities in nonmetropolitan areas (13.6 percent) and women's preferences (20.0 percent). It is not possible to determine from the data but this may reflect women's preferences for somewhat more clustered residential areas — small towns — in open country in contrast to male preferences for unclustered residential areas — rural areas — in open country.

Table 2. Reasons Rated Very Important or Important in Decision to Move to
Present Residence

	MALE	FEMALE
	%	%
Being near friends/relatives	30.1	37.2
Convenience of shopping	25.6	31.4
Neighborhood safety	64.1	69.1
School quality	49.0	52.5
Quality of mass transportation	16.6	19.8
Ethnic/racial background of residents	20.5	22.4
Neighborhood appearance	59.3	62.8

SOURCE: same as Table 1, adapted from pp. 593, 601, 609, 617.

"Medium-size cities in the suburbs" is surely a mixed residential bag, but these survey results are consistent with our revisionary view of cities and suburbs. The suburban cities — larger, denser, and multipurpose — may provide the infrastructure women need, while cities may now provide it less often. It is important to remember that it is not city or suburb that is important to women, but the characteristics of the residential setting. A carefully designed case study focused on suburban women in the San Jose area who had at least one child living at home found that most of the women no longer wanted a single-family house in the suburbs but preferred low-maintenance, multifamily housing near town (Rothblatt et al., 1979).

> We found that either older inlying neighborhoods of single-family homes or new, outlying, planned, higher density residential areas provide more satisfying housing for women than conventional suburban developments, new, low density areas of single-family homes built in small, less planned increments near the edge of the metropolitan area. While it seems clear that residents of smaller suburban political units do enjoy greater satisfaction with community services compared to their central city counterparts, we also discovered that older inlying neighborhoods can provide superior social rewards, such as a rich friendship pattern and a deep sense of belonging. (Rothblatt et al., 1979:165)

The greater importance to women of the characteristics of the local residential area in regard to local support and services is indicated in Table 2, which is based on the national Louis Harris survey. In response to questions on the considerations involved in choosing their present residence, women differed from men in placing greater importance on the presence of friends and relatives, convenient shopping, neighborhood safety, school quality, quality of mass transportation, ethnic/racial background of residents, and neighborhood appearance.

52

There is one overriding factor in residential choice — where one grew up. The Louis Harris survey found, as have earlier national surveys (Zelan, 1968), that the kind of place one's childhood was spent in was associated significantly with choice of a place to live. Thus, in each of the six residential categories used in the Harris survey, respondents chose most frequently by far as their first choice of place to live, that category which had been their "longest childhood location." The results of the cross-classification are substantial and unvarying. Thus, of those who had grown up in large cities, 43.3 percent said their preference for a place to live was large cities; of those raised in medium-sized cities in suburbs, 34.1 percent said their preference for a place to live was medium-sized cities in suburbs; similar results obtained for the remaining four residential categories (Louis Harris, 1978: 558-59). The implications are clear. As detailed earlier, the United States has become increasingly suburban since the Second World War. Consequently more and more people will have grown up in suburban places and are most likely to choose to live in similar places when they are adults.

Small-scale interview studies of young adults who have lived all their lives in suburbs have begun to reveal how the process operates (Fava, 1984; Kling, 1984; Fava and DeSena, 1983). These surburban-reared young adults had seldom visited cities when they were growing up — having been taken by their parents to the cultural or recreational attractions of the city as youngsters or, as young adults, going on their own to special urban events or shopping or entertainment. Suburban-reared adults live an almost totally suburban life, carrying out their daily routines within the suburban rings. Very few choose to live and work in cities when they leave the parental "nest" (Fava and DeSena, 1983), and even fewer indicate any permanent commitment to cities (Fava, 1984; Kling, 1984; Fava and DeSena, 1983). Young suburban migrants to the city saw it as a place for career advancement, personal development and fulfillment, and almost all said they would choose other types of places for "settling down," and especially for raising children. They were *not* attracted to the city as a place where they could contribute to solving urban problems (Fava, 1984). They acknowledged the problems were there; in fact, they saw them as an integral part of urban life — poverty, dirt, decay, fear of crime — but these were not "their" problems.

A tantalizing and, at this point, unanswered question is whether the gender gap in residential preference is increasing among young adults raised in suburbs. Is this group contributing disproportionately to the gender gap noted in the right-hand columns of Table 1: the increasing male preference for "rural" residential areas, essentially low-density, nonfarm housing, while women prefer high-density, suburban areas?

The city, especially the large city, still has its attractions even in the period of suburban dominance. The Louis Harris survey found that Americans were ambivalent about their large cities — valuing them highly as places of culture, entertainment, employment, and special services — but rejecting them as places to live, especially to raise children (1978). While it is important to note that the survey dealt with preferences, not actual residential behavior, our analysis of the data yielded provocative, even if not definitive, findings. The intersection of gender with residential preference and suburban dominance suggests that we need to take a new look at what the built environment of present-day cities and suburbs offers women.

NOTES

1. For a comprehensive bibliography see Wilson and Ridgeway's classified, annotated guide (Wilson and Ridgeway, 1982).

2. See, for example, the noninclusion of gender variables in the comprehensive discussion of residential preferences in U.S. Commission on Population Growth and the American Future (1972).

REFERENCES

Bailey, Thomas, and Roger Waldinger
1984 "A skills mismatch in New York's labor market?" New York Affairs 8:3-18.

Berger, Bennett
1960 Working-Class Suburb, Berkeley: University of California Press.

Birch, David L.
1975 "From suburb to urban place." Annals of the American Academy of Political and Social Science 422:25-35.

Decker, David L., David Schicher, and Robert O'Brien
1982 Urban Structure and Victimization. Lexington, MA: Lexington Books, Heath.

Fava, Sylvia F.
1980 "Women's place in the new suburbia." Pp. 120-50 in G. Wekerle (ed.), New Space for Women. Boulder, Colo.: Westview Press.
1984 "Residential preferences of Northwestern University students." Unpublished manuscript.

Fava, Sylvia F., and Judith DeSena
1983 "The chosen apple: Young suburban migrants." Pp. 305-22 in V. Boggs, G. Handel, and S. Fava (eds.), The Apple Sliced: Sociological Studies of New York City. S. Hadley, MA: Bergin and Garvey.

Fischer, Claude, and Robert Max Jackson
1976 "Suburbs, networks, and attitudes." Pp. 279-308 in Barry Schwartz (ed.), The Changing Face of the Suburbs. Chicago: University of Chicago Press.

Gans, Herbert J.
1967 The Levittowners. New York: Pantheon Books.

Genovese, Rosalie G.
1980 "Women's self-help network as a response to service needs in the suburbs." Signs 5 (Supplement): S248-56.

Gordon, Margaret T. et al.
1980 "Crime, women and the quality of urban life." Signs 5 (Supplement): S144-60.

Hapgood, Karen, and Judith Getzels
1974 Planning, Women and Change. Chicago: American Society of Planning Officials.

Keller, Suzanne
1981 "Women and children in a planned community." Pp. 67-76 in S. Keller (ed.), Building for Women. Lexington, MA: Heath.

Kling, Sandra Schoenberg
1984 "Questionnaire results from Hofstra students." Personal communication.

Lofland, Lyn
1975 "The 'Thereness' of women: A selective review of urban sociology." Pp. 144-70 in Marcia Millman and Rosabeth Moss Kanter (eds.), Another Voice. Garden City: Doubleday Anchor.

Long, Larry, and Diane DeAre
1984 "Where the cars are." American Demographics 6:18-22.

Louis Harris and Associates, Inc. for the Department of Housing and Urban Development
1978 The 1978 HUD Survey of the Quality of Community Life, A Data Book. Washington, D.C.: United States Government Printing Office.

Mackintosh, Elizabeth et al.
1977 "The middle income family's experience in an urban highrise complex and a suburban single-family home." Graduate Center of the City University of New York, unpublished manuscript.

Masey, Mary Ellen, and David R. Lee
1983 Her Space, Her Place. Washington, D.C.: Association of American Geographers.

Michelson, William
1973 "Environmental change." Research Paper #60. Centre for Urban and Community Studies, University of Toronto.

Mollenkopf, John
1984 "The post-industrial transformation of the political order in New York City." In J. Mollenkopf, Ira Katznelson, and Thomas Bender (eds.), Power, Culture, and Place: Essays on New York City. Unpublished manuscript.

Muller, Peter O.
1981 Contemporary Suburban America. Englewood Cliffs, New Jersey: Prentice Hall.

Newitt, Jane
1984 "Where do suburbanites come from?" American Demographics 6:24-28.

O'Connell, Brian
1979 "Where have all the children gone?" New York Affairs 5:84-87.

Popenoe, David
1977 The Suburban Environment. Chicago: University of Chicago Press.

Richards, Larry G. et al.
1978 "Perceived safety and security in transportation systems as determined by the gender of the traveler." Pp. 441-78 in Sandra Rosenbloom (ed.), Women's Travel Issues: Research Needs and Priorities. Conference Report of the United States Department of Transportation. Washington, D.C.: United

States Government Printing Office.

Rothblatt, Donald, Donald Garr, and Jo Sprague
1979   The Suburban Enviroment and Women.
        New York: Praeger.

U.S. Commission on Population Growth and the
American Future
1972   Population Distribution and Policy. Sara
        Mills Mazie (ed.), Vol. 5 of the Commission
        Research Reports. Washington, D.C.: U.S.
        Government Printing Office.

Wilson, Hugh, and Sally Ridgeway
1982   Women in Suburbia: A Bibliography.
        Chicago: Council of Planning Librarians.

Zelan, Joseph
1968   "Does suburbia make a difference: An ex-
        ercise in secondary analysis." Pp. 401-8 in
        S. Fava (ed.), Urbanism in World Perspec-
        tive. New York: Crowell.

Reprinted with permission from **Sociological Focus,** vol. 18, no. 2, pp. 109-117, 1985.

6 The social construction of the physical environment: The case of gender*

KAREN A. FRANCK

Ideas about gender and family help determine the physical design and location of dwellings, places of work, and other designed environments. These settings then support the ideas of gender and family that generated them. This paper examines how the built environment in contemporary American society supports a particular sex/gender system characterized by a differential assignment of activities and relationships to women and men. This division helped generate a separation of spatial domains for men and women most fully articulated in the design of the prototypical suburban house and community. This situation is analyzed in terms of three social functions the designed environment fulfills and the problems created for women, children, and men. Recent changes in household composition and suburban design are presented with attention given to what changes are needed to support a system of gender integration rather than gender separation.

Houses and communities are as much social contructions as the concepts of gender and family. Both types of construction direct and order activities, relationships, and feelings of identity in profound ways. The quite different types of constructs have an important mutually determinant relationship with each other. At any particular time in history ideas about gender and family help determine the physical design and location of dwellings, places of work, open spaces, and other designed settings. These environments then support and reinforce the ideas of gender and family that generated them. The design of environments translates into physical form society's expectations of what activities should take place where, who should pursue those activities, and how they should relate to one another. These expectations often differ for men and women, family and nonfamily, young and old, and design translates those differences into physical parameters. Sometimes, as is happening now, the expectations attached to the concepts of gender and family change more quickly than the physical form of our surroundings, making it difficult to enact these new expectations without considerable hardship.

The "social construction of reality" (Berger and Luckman, 1966) can thus encompass both the ongoing production and modification of concepts like gender and family and the ongoing production and modification of the designed environment. This general idea of the social construction of the physical environment has been used by anthropologists in analyzing the social and spatial arrangements pertinent to gender relations (Ardener,

*The preparation of this paper was supported by Grant CEE-830721-B from the National Science Foundation. I am grateful to Maria DeIsasi, my research assistant for her help. An earlier, abbreviated version of this paper was presented at the Annual Meeting of the American Collegiate Schools of Architecture, Charleston, South Carolina, March 1984.

1981). The present paper takes a similar approach, exploring how differential expectations about the activities and relationships appropriate for men and women generate and then are reinforced by the design of the physical environment. In pursuing this objective concerns and concepts are adopted from feminist sociology and anthropology as well as from environment-behavior research. The focus is on contemporary, middle-class circumstances in the United States.

This introduction continues with a short discussion of the concepts of sex and gender, family and household and concludes with a review of three social functions the designed environment fulfills. These functions are then used to guide the subsequent discussion. The central and major portion of the paper explores how the design of the prototypical suburban house and community supports and reinforces a particular sex/gender system, creating problems for women, children, and men. Following that is a review of recent changes in the composition of American households and of desirable and actual changes in the design of suburban homes and communities.

SEX AND GENDER

Sex is often defined as the biological dichotomy between male and female which is determined by chromosomes (Gould and Kern-Daniels, 1977). Gender is considered the division, again dichotomous, between behaviors and attitudes society deems appropriate for males and females, respectively. Gender takes a set of biological, observable differences and transforms them into a set of expected social differences, which children are taught to follow. Not only is gender socially constructed and socially maintained, it is also socially alterable in that expectations of what is appropriate can and do change.

One reason for studying expectations for sex and gender is that they are important in the organization and conduct of our daily lives. At the same time, however, we need to analyze sex and gender with concepts that are not simply duplicates of the perspectives of the actors being studied. Two problems arise in this regard: the unselfconscious adoption of the gender concept, and coupling gender with role theory. Focusing on gender, without questioning its importance to the research at hand, serves to support its misunderstood status as something given and unalterable (Matthews, 1982). One solution is to use the concept of gender only when it is truly relevant to the discussion or research and only when it stands for a structural feature of the social situation.[1]

Recently, feminist sociologists have begun to recognize problems inherent in the application of the concept of role to gender research (Eichler, 1980; Gould and Kern-Daniels, 1977; Lopata and Thorne, 1978; Thorne, 1982). The concept of role focuses attention more on individuals than on social strata and more on socialization than on social structure. The roles referred to are described and analyzed as if they exist rather than as analytical constructs developed as a tool to describe what exists.

One alternative to role theory as applied to gender is Rubin's sex/gender system which is "the set of arrangements by which a society transforms a biological sexuality into products of human activity and in which these transformed sexual needs are stratified" (Rubin, 1978:155). As reviewed by Thorne (1982), the sex/gender system includes in one form or another:

(1) the social creation of two dichotomous genders from biological sex, involving an exaggeration of differences and a suppression of similarities between women and men;

(2) a particular sexual division of labor, which divides men and women and also exacerbates differences.[2]

58

This approach has several advantages over the use of "sex roles" or "gender roles." It emphasizes the systematic links between the creation of two genders and the sexual division of labor. It focuses attention on relations between genders, social process and social change rather than on fixed, unchanging positions of single individuals. It allows for the consideration of power and conflict and it is clearly an analytical construct and thereby less likely than roles to become reified. It makes it nearly impossible to consider one gender in isolation from the other: "system" indicates the interrelations of both.[3]

Applying the sex/gender system to an analysis of the design of physical environments encourages consideration of the spaces and activities of women and men and of the relations between these activities and these spaces. It also encourages consideration of different household types and different age groups. Any variant of a systems perspective seems to stimulate a more complete, less fragmented view of social circumstances.

HOUSEHOLD AND FAMILY

Family, like gender, is a socially created concept and is more descriptive of what should be than of what is. It takes observable biological relationships and transforms them into socially prescribed relations, thus dictating how people who are related to one another should behave. These ideas, like gender and other social concepts, change over time and differ between cultures.

With respect to dwellings, "family" refers more to who should live together whereas the more general, less normative term "household" refers to people who do live together (Rapp, 1979). Thus "household" can refer to those who share living quarters and "family" to a particular kind of household where members also share kinship ties. The definition of household is not always simple because the sharing of living quarters may be difficult to define operationally. Kobrin (1978) suggests three criteria: privacy as defined by separate access; use as indicated by the presence of cooking equipment; and the number of unrelated persons present. "Group living quarters," including hotels, dormitories, barracks, and institutions, have been excluded from the census's count of households because they do not meet the kinds of criteria Kobrin lists. Lodging and boarding houses fall into a gray area: the census has alternately included and excluded them in the household count. Following the census definitions, people live in family households, nonfamily households, or group quarters. Family households consist of two or more persons sharing a dwelling unit who are related by birth or marriage. Nonfamily households consist of one person living alone or two or more unrelated persons sharing a dwelling unit.

SOCIAL FUNCTIONS OF THE DESIGNED ENVIRONMENT

One way to explore how the designed environment supports the enactment of a particular sex/gender system is to first delineate the social functions of the designed environment and then to examine how these functions have different implications for men and women in existing environments. For the purposes of this paper three functions are delineated: providing a setting for particular activities; creating a social system and network of communications; and expressing self identity.[4] These functions are briefly described below and are then used to analyze the sex/gender system that is supported by the American suburban house and community.

A designed environment provides a setting for particular activities and tasks, often to be carried out by particular people or particular kinds of people. For instance, a kitchen in the United States today is intended to be a place for storing, preparing, and cooking food; for storing, cleaning, and drying equipment needed for food preparation and consumption; and sometimes for eating the food. Each of these activities involves several distinct and related tasks. The spatial and physical arrangements of places, including the presence and layout of furniture and equipment, makes certain actions easy to carry out, others more difficult, and still others impossible. Similarly, one type of user, a full grown, healthy adult, may be able to carry out the tasks easily while another, a small child, may not.

This first function, providing a setting for particular activities, is described by Ittelson et al. (1976), Steele (1973), Gutman (1975), and Broadbent (1975). Michelson's congruence model (1970), which suggests that some forms of behavior are more "congruent" with a particular setting than other forms, speaks to this function as does most of the research on user needs and design guidelines (Cooper, 1975; Howell, 1980; Newman, 1972).

The second function of the designed environment pertinent to this paper is its physical manifestation of a social system. The designed environment supports and even concretizes in physical form expected social relationships between individuals and between groups of people. Design arrangements also can encourage certain kinds of social interaction and indicate the status of people vis-a-vis other people. This function has been described by Gutman (1975) as "establishing a communication net," by Steele (1973) as the function of "social contact," and by Ittelson et al. (1976) as "social system." Research that focuses on this second function includes: the studies on spatial proximity and friendship formation (Festinger et al., 1950; Festinger, 1951); and the research and writings about physical design and sense of community (Chermayeff and Alexander, 1963; Jacobs, 1961; Newman, 1972, 1980). Other studies dealing with this function include office furniture arrangement and type of social interaction, chair arrangement and class participation (Sommer, 1974), and the design of courtrooms in different cultures (Hazard, 1972).

The third function of interest here is the potential the designed environment has to express self identity. This function, as described by Ittelson et al. (1976) and Cooper (1976) suggests some of the ways our surroundings fulfill this function. The residential setting in particular may fulfill this function: the choice of dwelling and the decoration of its interior and exterior are ways people express their identities through manipulation of the physical environment. Newman (1972) points out how residence in public housing imposes a poor self identity on residents through the stigmatizing effects of its physical design. One way institutional settings deprive inmates of their individuality is by preventing the expression of self identity through manipulation of the environment. Research on the effects of environmental change demonstrates how homes, neighborhoods, and places of work figure prominently in people's sense of who they are as individuals and as members of a larger group (Fried, 1972; Hareven and Langenback, 1981; Marris, 1974).

THE SUBURBAN HOUSE AND COMMUNITY

The American suburban house and the larger suburban community support and reinforce an age and gender system that divides the activities of men and women and of adults and children. This division of activities is accompanied by a division of social relationships and a difference in the degree of support the residential environment provides for the self-identity of men and women. While these social divisions predate the suburban setting, they made its design both possible and popular. The suburban environment translated into physical form the divisions of age and gender. Furthermore, suburban settings strengthened and extended these divisions by separating and distancing the spaces where the activities of men and women occur. Social divisions became physical divisions and separations.

Social scientists and feminists, even in the nineteenth century and long before the suburban expansion of the 1950s, recognized the disadvantages of the spatial and social separations for women (Hayden, 1982). It has only recently been suggested, however, that men may have experienced disadvantages as well (Bernard, 1981; Ehrenreich, 1983). Similarly, we now recognize the difficulties that suburban settings pose for wives or mothers who are employed and for other household members who do not follow the traditional division of activities by gender. But it is not so obvious that the divisions also pose problems for the idealized household of wage-earning father and homemaking mother, the very people for whom the suburban setting was intended. Some of the problems experienced by members of this household type are explicated below in the discussion of the suburban settings as the most extreme spatial arrangement so far devised for separating residential and wage-earning spaces and for enforcing a division of activities and relationships by gender.

SEPARATION OF ACTIVITIES AND SPACES

The division of activities according to gender centers on the expectation that women will pursue homemaking and childrearing activities and men will pursue wage-earning activities. Moreover, these two sets of activities are to occur in different and separate spaces. The assignment of wage earning to men and homemaking to women and the creation of separate spatial domains for each set of activities, and thus for each gender, developed during the nineteenth century with industrialization and the movement of men into the labor force (Cowan, 1983). While women also joined the labor force (Kessler-Harris, 1982), society's ideal was that only men would do so and that women's proper place was in the home. At the same time, industrialization eliminated the housework that had been assigned to men and children, without changing much of the work women had to do in the home (Cowan, 1983). Both of these developments, the need for a paid labor force working outside and at some distance from the dwelling and the elimination of household chores for men and children, allowed the "separate spheres" ideal to become possible. From then until very recently it was simply assumed to be the given and, moreover, the ideal situation.

During the nineteenth century when the separation of spheres developed, the dwelling was still often located in urban areas where many households goods and services were delivered to the household and where many others were offered for sale within a short walk of the dwelling (Cowan, 1983). Friends, relatives, and others who were not members of family households themselves were often able to live in family households or within a short distance of families. This allowed for a greater overlap of activities and a greater opportunity for different people to contribute to the family's daily life than is now possible in suburban situations.

It was also during the nineteenth century that the image developed of the dwelling as a refuge and a retreat from the competitive spirit of the city and the workplace. It was this powerful social and physical image that fueled the popularity of the suburban house and community, first among upper and middle-class families and then in the working class. The ideal, in image and in actuality, was intended for the nuclear family only, for two parents and their own children, young enough to be living at home. The detached single-family house achieved a high degree of privacy in two senses: it was physically private and it was socially private since the definition of who was to live there was limited to two parents and their children (Franck, 1985).

The single-family detached house, located in a setting having more natural amenities than the city, was considered an ideal place to raise children. Some of the characteristics of the suburban setting were an improvement over urban conditions, such as the availability of safe, open spaces to play in, but these attributes were almost invariably linked to a host of other characteristics that were not helpful for children or adults. These characteristics include: the separation of residential space from commercial, educational, and other facilities and services; exclusionary zoning permitting only single-family detached homes and allowing no more than three unrelated persons to share a house; sizeable distance between dwellings and places of wage work; absence of public transportation; absence of shared open space; and the unique design of the house itself.

The design of the house requires each homemaker to take sole responsibility for many homemaking tasks that might otherwise be shared with other homemakers or performed by a commercial service. The absence of any facilities to support the latter alternatives require that all housekeeping tasks be performed by each homemaker separately from all other homemakers and for her household only. Each does the same tasks over and over that other homemakers are also doing, often at the same time and with the same equipment. These tasks are often performed in isolation from other household members as well.

Since the residential units are separated and at some distance from necessary services such as stores, schools, medical care, places for entertainment or athletics, the homemaker is required to spend considerable time transporting herself and others to these different services simply to fulfill her homemaking obligations. Cowan's (1983) historical analysis of American household technology illustrates vividly the time and energy consumed by transporting goods and people. By the middle of the twentieth century the time saved by electrical applicances and other household amenities and by the replacement of homemade goods with consumer goods as taken up by driving, shopping, and waiting for services.

Many of the characteristics of suburbia actually made the tasks of homemaking more difficult than they have been previously and certainly more difficult than they had to be. Fava (1980:133) suggests that "suburbia as a built environment, at least as presently built, is conducive to and facilitating of only one female role, that of housewife and mother." Yet in many respects the suburban environment does not facilitate even that role. Another difficulty it posed for the homemaker, through exclusionary zoning, was the enforced absence of other types of householders who might be able to assist in homemaking and childrearing, examples being elderly people, single people, or couples without children.

While the suburban home was chosen for its benefits for raising children, it has had some negative consequences in that regard as well. One problem, now recognized but unresolved, is that suburbs do not provide facilities for teenagers. Another is that participation in any activities at any distance from the dwelling for all children require that they be transported there by adults. This creates an otherwise unnecessary dependency of children on adults. Also, the distance in suburbs between dwellings and places where children might go for sports or entertainment probably contributes to feelings of dissatisfaction and boredom. In comparing teenagers' evaluations of their neighborhoods in urban and suburban Toronto, van Vliet (1981) found that urban children often listed access to places as a good aspect of their neighborhoods, whereas suburban children cited poor access as a disliked characteristic.

In terms of activities, suburban spatial arrangements make it difficult for children to take on any substantial household responsibilities. The mother, when not employed

62

outside the home, is often the sole adult available to oversee the child's work, which tends to defeat the purpose of allowing the homemaker to share household responsibilities. Many tasks require transportation to other locations, meaning the mother would have to drive the children, again defeating the purpose. This inability to share household responsibilities contributes to children's dependence on adults, encourages them to be passive members of the household, and discourages the development of any sense of contributing to the household among children.

The relative infrequency of children helping in household work is common to urban, rural, and suburban settings. We cannot blame this phenomenon on suburban design. Boocock (1981) reports in her research on children of various income levels and in various types of communities that less than half the children in any setting claim to do any household tasks at all, including cleaning up their own rooms. She does note that urban children were more restricted in their exploration of physical surroundings than suburban or rural children (Boocock, 1981:111). Previous research reviewed by van Vliet (1983) and findings from his own study are consistent with this conclusion. Children living in suburbs have a wider spatial range of activities than children living in cities. At the same time, however, the separation in suburbs of residential space from commercial space and from all other places of wage work serves to separate children from a knowledge of the workday life of society. Not only is it infrequent that children in any community in the U.S. work in the home, it is also infrequent that they have the opportunity to observe or to contribute to work outside the home.

The one member of the idealized family who has been widely recognized as benefiting considerably from suburban living is the wage-earning husband and father. Saegert and Winkel (1980) review research that indicates men found the retreat and recreational aspects of the suburban home more satisfying than did women. They point out that men are able to maintain their involvement with urban life, the stimulation, relationships, and activities it offers, while also living in the suburbs and enjoying its benefits. Women who spend their entire time in the suburbs do not enjoy this combination of benefits. Similarly, Michelson's (1977) study of the experiences of new residents in downtown apartments, downtown single-family homes, suburban apartments, and suburban single-family homes shows that, of the four groups, women in suburban houses were the least satisfied with how they spent their time and men in suburban houses were the most satisfied.

While suburban men's satisfaction with their activities may be high, they also experience the burden of commuting to and from work and, in the traditional household, of being financially responsible for maintaining a suburban "retreat" which they have less time to enjoy than do other members of the household. This may generate more dissatisfaction among suburban husbands and fathers than has yet been uncovered. This possibility is supported by recent analyses of men's dissatisfaction with their idealized role of "good provider." Some, like hobos and tramps in times past, reject the role altogether; others simply can not live up to it; and others overperformed by becoming workaholics (Bernard, 1981). Ehrenreich (1983) presents a provocative argument that the male breadwinner ethic has collapsed and that this "male revolt," supported by expert opinion and public sentiment, will continue to grow and to present hardships for women with children and for women who wish to have children.

SEPARATION OF SOCIAL RELATIONSHIPS

Before industrialization, men were more likely to work in or near the dwelling itself, thus spending their working time in close proximity to other household members, including their wives. In addition, household work required their contributions. Cowan (1983) describes how in the preindustrial circumstances of eighteenth-century America the work of cooking and homemaking generally required the contributions of adults of both sexes and children:

> ... the daily exigencies of agrarian life meant the men and women had to work in tandem in order to undertake any single life-sustaining chore. The relations between the sexes were reciprocal: women assisted men in the fields, and men assisted women in the house. (Cowan, 1983:38)

With the coming of the industrialization not only were husbands and fathers removed from the home for wage-earning purposes but, in addition, their household chores of slaughtering, tanning, and wood chopping were eliminated. Men's working lives are now spent at some distance from the dwelling and they no longer participate in household tasks. This separation of activities and spaces may have generated a social and emotional distance between husbands and wives. Bernard (1981) describes this possibility and suggests that

> when men and women are in close proximity, there is always the possibility of reassuring glances, the comfort of simple physical presence. But when the division of labor removes the man from the dwelling for most of the day, intimate relationships become less feasible. (Bernard, 1981:3).

The opportunities for being intimate may also be decreased by the opposing needs of the wage earner and the homemaker. At the end of a working day, the former is likely to want a certain amount of quiet and relaxation while the latter, having been alone or with children all day, may desire adult conversation and more active pastimes. Given such different realms of needs and experiences, wage earner and homemaker may have less understanding of one another's problems than was the case in earlier times when their activities and experiences were regularly observable to one another and were even shared.

By creating physical distance between wage-earning spaces and homemaking ones, suburban settings simply strengthened the experiential differences between wage earner and homemaker and created different arenas for the relationships of each. In addition to distancing husband from wife, suburbia may have distanced the wife from potential friends. Saegert and Winkel (1980) report from their research that women in the city had more friends within walking distance than did men, whereas men in the suburbs were more likely than women to live near their friends. Among the respondents, urban women reported more neighboring than any other group. This tendency for suburban women to be relatively socially isolated is consistent with Friedan's (1963) early interviews with middle-class suburban women.

Children's relationships are also affected by suburban circumstances. Boocock (1981) reviews findings from several studies showing that children in low-income, densely settled neighborhoods had the richest social contacts. Lesser parental involvement with children was balanced by more frequent contact with other adults. Compared to urban children, suburban children had overall less varied social contacts but did more things with their mothers (Boocock, 1981:101). There is a possibility that suburban children have more difficulty establishing relationships with other children than do urban children. Van Vliet (1981) found in his study of teenagers in Toronto that those from low-density, suburban neighborhoods reported having fewer friends and that neighborhoods where respondents reported a lack of friends had significantly lower densities of children. Boocock suggests that

. . . the low density suburban areas and the privacy of suburban homes and yards, combined with lack of common land where children can find each other, severely limits the development of children's play groups; by contrast children in crowded urban areas have greater opportunity to meet greater numbers of adults and children and develop skills in social relations. (1981:113)

DIFFERENTIAL SUPPORT FOR SELF-IDENTITY

There seems to be longstanding cultural expectation that the dwelling is woman's domain and the outside public world is man's (Loyd, 1975; Tognoli, 1979). This is certainly consistent with the separation of activities and relationships described above. To the extent that individuals experience these expectations of women's domain and men's domain in their own lives, men may feel more at ease in public places than do women, whereas women may feel more at ease at home than do men. Rapoport (1982) suggests this is true among working-class households in Australia where places of work and taverns are considered men's spaces and the dwellings, women's. He describes how the spaces are decorated accordingly: houses with lace curtains and doilies, taverns with little decoration at all.

The traditional sexual division of activities would contribute to, even account for the differences in feelings of ease. One might also expect differences in the amount of support for self-identity men and women derive from the dwelling. There is evidence that women derive more of such support than do men. Hayward (1977) studied the meaning of home among young, married couples. Women were more likely to think of the home as an expression of their identity, as a personalized place, whereas men were more likely to view the home simply as a physical place. The greatest differences between the sexes in the meaning of home occurred between men who were employed outside the home and did not share the housework and women who were mainly homemakers. Women who were primarily homemakers seemed to derive more identity support from the home than did women among task-sharing couples. These findings suggest that the sharper or the more complete the division of labor between women and men as a couple, the greater the difference between them in the degree of support for self-identity they derive from the home. At the same time, however, even when men do housekeeping activities, they do not derive as much support for self-identity from the home setting as do women.

Saegert and Winkel (1980) in their interviews with couples found that women felt it was more important that the home express their personalities than did men. This was true in urban and suburban locations. Women also found it more important that a home be a place to display belongings. Neither of these studies suggest whether or not men derive support for self-identity from other physical settings, such as their places of work. It is possible that men are less likely to derive identity support for any physical setting than are women.

In their research on the meanings of domestic objects for people of different ages, Csikszentmihalyi and Rochberg-Halton (1981) found that men value objects of action (TVs, stereo sets, sports equipment, vehicles, and tropies), whereas women valued objects of contemplation (photographs, sculptures, plants, plates, glass, and textiles). In exploring the symbolic meaning of home for women and men these authors found that fathers talk extensively about the work they have done to the house such as building a new kitchen or putting in new plumbing: "Work invested in the physical structure itself seems to be the most salient tie between the self of the adult and his home" (1981:131). Women tended to see the house primarily as a place where people interact. When they talked of work they had done to the house, it was usually of the decorative kind such as putting up new wallpaper or putting in new furniture. Men also tended to give fewer positive affective responses in their descriptions of their homes and more neutral ones than did women.

Among children this sex difference did not appear, indicating to these authors that attachment to the home continues to be strong among women whereas "men essentially cool out in their relationship with the home" (1981:129).

It is not clear whether this is a hardship for men or benefit to women, although all the researchers reporting these differences imply that deriving self-identity from the home is advantageous. It is possible that after retirement or when making additions to the home is no longer possible men feel more at a loss than do women who can continue to derive support from a home setting and from objects of contemplation. This research also tells us nothing about the experiences of single people. When women are not married or part of a couple, they may feel less comfortable about deriving support for self-identity from their homes and they may be less encouraged to do so by friends and family. Similarly, women with careers, married or single, may feel some conflict about the meaning their places of residence have for them. The division of activities, feelings, and space according to gender seems likely to pose problems for any person who does not fit into the stereotype of a married, employed man or a married, homemaking woman.

CHANGES IN HOUSEHOLDS AND HOUSES

As shown in Table 1, the composition of American households has changed dramatically since 1970. The outstanding changes are an increase in the proportion of married couples with children, an increase in the proportion of single-parent families and in the proportion of households composed of people living alone. Significantly, it is women more often than men who are single parents with children under 18 and it is women more often than men who live alone. Most importantly with respect to the suburban house and its intended household, only 11.7 percent of all households in 1983 were composed of a wage-earning father, a homemaking mother and dependent children (U.S. Department of Census, 1984:169). Conversely, the proportion of all households where husband and wife both work and have children under 18 was 16.1 percent in 1983. The increase in the labor force participation of women overall has been another significant change: from 1960 to 1980 the proportion of all women who were in the labor force grew from 34.5 to 51.4 percent (Hacker, 1983:133).

Table 1. Household by Type of Household: 1970 and 1983

Type of household	1970[a]	1983[b]
Family households	81.2%	73.2%
Married couple,own children under 18	40.3	29.0
Female householder,own children under 18	4.5	6.8
Male householder,own children under 18	.5	.9
Family, no own children under 18	35.8	36.4
Non-family households	18.8%	26.8%
Living alone	17.1	23.0
Not living alone	1.7	3.9
Total households	100.0%	100.0%
N	63,401,000	83,918,000

a   U.S. Department of Commerce, Bureau of Census, Current Populaton Reports Series P-20 #388, Household and Family Characteristics, Table A (1983:2).
b   U.S. Department of Commerce, Bureau of Census, Current Population Reports Series P-20 #388, Household and Family Characteristics, Table A (1984:2).

The increase in employment among wives and mothers does not mean they have given or even seriously reduced their homemaking responsibilities, even when husbands are present. Empirical studies consistently show that women continue to perform all or a very large portion of all housekeeping tasks (Berk, 1980; Hartman, 1981; Miller and Garrison, 1982; Vanek, 1974). Based on her review of time budget research Hartman concludes that about 70 percent of all housework time is contributed by wives and that women who work for wages are not given more help by their husbands than women to do not work for wages. Other research suggests that women who are employed do receive somewhat more help from their husbands but not very much more (Miller and Garrison, 1982). One study (Berk, 1980) compared the proportion of household tasks completed by wives, husbands, and children. Wives completed the overwhelming proportion of tasks within all categories, roughly 80 to 95 percent of the sixty discrete household tasks studied. The only category where husbands made a substantial contribution was outside the house — running errands. Moreover, the contributions made by husbands or children are "help"; the managing and planning remain with the wives. The research on household work demonstrates quite clearly that the sexual division of activities within the house has not changed despite the decline in the sexual division of activities outside the house. Both men and women are now engaged in wage earning, but only women are engaged in homemaking.

Changes in the composition of American households are far more dramatic than any changes in the physical design of suburban housing and communities or in the social arrangements needed to support these new types of households. Many commentators agree that the best social and spatial arrangements for women with children, whether or not they are married or employed, are high-density, mixed-use communities inhabited by other households with children, by elderly, and by young singles and couples without children. These communities would have commercial, educational, and other facilities and services close to the dwellings and to places of work, and would provide public transportation. One might also add shared outdoor spaces and arrangements for collective or cooperative recreational and homemaking activities.

Wright (1981) notes that young people are moving into cities and communities having some of these attributes, called "urbanized suburbs." Yet the traditional suburban homes and communities still exist.[5] Over three-fourths of American households own their own homes and most of these are in suburbs (Wright, 1981:270). People, including single and employed mothers, are likely to want to stay in their own homes if at all possible. Existing traditional suburbs need to be transformed to provide public transportation, stores that are open all night, and daycare centers. Changes in zoning laws are required to allow these additions and to allow multi-unit housing, accessory apartments, elder cottages, use of homes for wage labor, and the opportunity for more than three unrelated persons to share a single-family house.

Hayden (1980) presents a plan for transforming 40 suburban detached single-family houses into a community that would provide employment, collective facilities, and support services such as daycare and home care for the sick. Residents could find employment and needed services in on-site laundry, grocery store, dial-a-ride and cooked food services. Her proposal is primarily for households with children: out of 40 households, only four would be childless. But there would be a mixture of single-parent, one-worker, and two-worker households. Outdoor spaces, previously completely private, would be redesigned to consist of private and collective spaces, the latter including a vegetable garden and play area. Significantly her plan breaks down the traditional suburban separations between private and public, residential and commercial spaces, and home and workplace.

It seems fairly clear that mothers, children, and single people without children would all benefit from changes of this type. Husbands and fathers would probably benefit as well, although that is less clear. Research reviewed earlier suggests that the traditional suburban arrangements were most satisfying to these members of the household. Moreover, many of the suggested changes given in the literature, such as Hayden's plan, seem to assume that the set of activities traditionally expected of husbands and fathers will not be changing. The needs addressed by the suggested physical and social changes are primarily those of the employed or single mother who now takes on wage earning and homemaking responsibilities. These altered settings would support this combination of responsibilities but the father could continue pursuing his single class of responsibilities, wage earning, take on homemaking responsibilities, or take off altogether and continue earning wages but for himself alone, as Ehrenreich (1983) describes. If Enrenreich is correct, helping mothers and children become more self-sufficient would support and encourage men's flight from family commitments.

Designing new environments that have that effect is not desirable. We need to recognize all the changes in household composition and the changes in patterns of activities for various types of households and for all household members. While women's needs and the needs of single parents are particularly pressing, it is important in research and design to consider men and children. This will be difficult to do since it is not clear how or whether men's activities are changing. Nor is it clear what society now expects of men vis-a-vis families. Even if many fathers are not longer living with their own families, what kinds of physical and social arrangements can be designed to incorporate them into family and community life, even when it is not their own family?

Just as our expectations of the responsibilities of men need to be examined in a world where the activities and responsibilities of women have changed considerably, so do our expectations of children need to be examined. In single-parent and two-worker families particularly, children can contribute to household work. To this end, the designers of kitchens and storage units should consider all household members as potential homemakers.

The point has been made in this paper that the suburban house and community divide and separate the spaces, activities, and relationships of women and men. In doing this, it separates residential spaces from commercial and wage-earning spaces and from all support facilities and services. It also creates other divisions and separations: between age, life style, and income groups and even between private homes by spreading them out and providing no public transportation between them. Divisions between public and private, home and work, are intrinsic to suburban design (Hayden, 1984). Observers also believe that surburbs are maintaining their homogeneity and boundedness (Schwartz, 1980). Schwartz suggests "If there is a god of suburbia, it must be Terminus, the superintendent of boundary lines" (1980:646).

All of the suggested changes to suburbs described above would require the softening, even the dissolving, of these divisions and separations that are so central to the suburban ideal and to its current configuration. In order to build environments that support a sex/gender system of gender integration rather than separation, we need to build ones that support integration at many different levels — of people, of activities, and of spatial domains. It is not at all clear that such profound changes are likely to happen, particularly given the predictions of Schwartz (1980) and others.

The changes that can be detected so far are of a more modest sort. Unrelated individuals are sharing single-family houses in increasing numbers. They often locate one another through programs designed to match suitable persons. Often the homeowner is an elderly person who benefits from the rent, company, and help extended by those who

68

share the dwelling. One matching program in Portland, Oregon has placed 350 tenants in private homes over its two year existence. Most of the homeowners are elderly and most of the tenants are under 35. Other examples of housesharing involve several elderly, several young people or several of each (Hayden, 1984). Homesharing is of direct assistance to elderly and to young people; it will also lead to greater age integration of suburban areas.

Another development of a more physical kind is the addition of accessory units to existing single-family homes, which is taking place in many urban and suburban communities in violation of local zoning ordinances (Hare, 1982) and in other places, such as California under recent revisions to ordinances. Such units provide rental income to homeowners, provide tenants with housing options other than complete houses, and allow members of the household such as grown children or elderly parents to live close to the family but with independence. This change, while often fiercely fought for fear of lowering property values and increasing density, brings with it the integration of unit types, age groups, and household types but not the integration of work and home or of residential and commercial spaces.

New suburban housing tracts in California are routinely including a new floor plan intended for single, unrelated copurchasers of the house. This development recognizes the increase in the number of one-person households and the need among such households to pool resources to afford the purchase price of a house. The plan, containing two complete master bedroom suites, is also suitable for a single parent with an older child or other types of households (Franck, 1985). The modification is useful but makes a little dent in the primary divisions and separations of the suburban setting.

In my research on spatial and social innovations in housing the one building I have found that seeks to cross divisons between work and home of suburbia, and between residential and commercial spaces is a cooperative house in a suburb of San Diego. Called the "Go Home," it was invented and designed by Ted Smith, a young architect determined to make "a city based on combinations instead of separations." The four units in the house are small, not more than 500 square feet on two levels, and are intended for single people who wish to use part of their units for work space. The house is in a transition zone between commercial and residential areas but the lot on which it is built is zoned R-1, which requires that it be a single-family house, meaning that only one kitchen is allowed. Hence the four units share a kitchen. The work spaces and the parking face the commercial district; the living spaces face the residential area. The kitchen is purely utilitarian: there is no space or furniture for residents to eat together. Smith reports that his intention was "to make a single family house and use the loophole of the R-1 zone. It was not meant to be a beautiful communal space. . . . Most of the Go Home is workspace."

These recent changes recognize the existence of households not traditionally housed in suburbia: elderly, single persons, two unrelated copurchasers of a house, or single people who wish to pursue their work in their living spaces. With the exception of the Go Home, the only integration occurring is of age groups and household types. This integration, although welcome, makes no dent in the other separations of residential from commercial or of private from public spaces.

SUMMARY

Buildings and other designed spaces are intended to support society's expectations of what activities should take place where, who should pursue those activities, and how they should relate to one another. In these ways the designed environment is a physical manifestation of social concepts. Some of the expectations concern the activities and relationships deemed appropriate for men and women. Thus, gender and designed environments is a special case of the more general idea that the physical environment is socially constructed.

This paper has shown how the design of American suburban homes and communities was generated by, and in turn reinforced, a particular sex/gender system characterized by a differential assignment of activities to women and men. The design developed that system further by creating physical distances between the spaces where those activities are to take place. This phenomenon was analyzed in terms of three functions designed environments fulfill and the problems it has created for women, children, and men in the traditional suburban household of wage-earning father, homemaking mother and dependent children.

While the composition of American households is changing dramatically and the proportion of households for whom suburbs were originally intended is declining, the physical form of suburbs is changing only slightly. Moreover, it is clear that for the suburbs to reflect a sex/gender system of gender integration, various kinds of integration must take place in social and spatial terms. Whether this can happen is uncertain. A few modest changes were described. These developments do not, for the most part, alter the predominant suburban separations of work from home, residential from commercial, and private from public that need to be bridged for a system of gender integration to be supported.

NOTES

1. Glennon (1983) argues against adopting the gender concept at all because of the dualism it entails, which research will reinforce. Instead she proposed a paradigm of synthesism that will generate a nonpostivist approach to research and a new social organization where specialized roles will be replaced by a continual "becoming."

2. Another alternative to sex roles is proposed by Eichler (1980): that is, the concept of the double standard. In order to show that a double standard exists, we need to determine that the behavior performed by the two sexes is the same but that it results in different consequences.

3. Rubin's (1978) analysis is more extensive than what is described here. She sees the oppression of women as rooted in kinship institutions where women are a commodity given and taken in marriage with implications for genealogical status, lineage names, rights, and relationships. This "exchange of women" had political and economic functions that exist no longer and yet continue to organize our lives.

4. Other functions of the designed environment include: provision of shelter (Steele, 1973), creation of an artificial ambience (Gutman, 1975), being a filter (Broadbent, 175): having symbolic identification (Steele, 1973), reinforcing values and goals (Gutman, 1975), having cultural meaning (Broadbent, 1975): constituting a capital investment (Broadbent, 1975): being an emotional territory (Ittelson et al., 1976) giving pleasure (Steele, 1973), creating a mood (Gutman, 1975): promoting growth (Steele, 1973): and changing the microclimate (Broadbent, 1975).

5. While suburbs are changing in some ways, they remain predominantly white, more affluent, and more oriented toward childrearing than urban centers (Schwartz, 1976, 1980). Moreover, the physical form of suburban houses and communities that have already been built and the segregation of land uses have not changed and cannot change without changes to the zoning ordinances that govern many aspects of physical form and land use.

70

REFERENCES

Ardener, Shirley
1981   Women and Space: Ground Rules and Social Maps. New York: St. Martin's.
Berger, Peter, and Thomas Luckmann
1967   The Social Construction of Reality. Garden City, N.Y.: Anchor.
Berk, Sarah H.
1980   "The household as workplace." Pp. 65-81 in G. Wekerle, R. Peterson, and D. Morley (eds.), New Space for Women. Boulder, Co: Westview.
Bernard, Jessie
1981   "The good provider role." American Psychologist 36:1-12.
Boocock, Sarane S.
1976   "Children in contemporary society." Pp. 414-36 in A. Skolnick (ed.), Rethinking Childhood. Boston: Little Brown.
1981   "The life space of children." Pp. 93-116 in S. Keller (ed.), Building for Women. Lexington, Mass.: Heath.
Broadbent, Geoffrey
1975   "Function and symbolism in architecture." Pp. 75-95 in B. Honikman (ed.), Responding to Social Change. Stroudsburg, Pa.: Dowden, Hutchison, and Ross.
Chermayeff, Serge, and Christopher Alexander
1963   Community and Privacy. Garden City, N.Y.: Doubleday.
Cooper, Clare
1975   Easter Hill Village. New York: Free Press.
1976   "The house as symbol of self." Pp. 435-48 in H. M. Proshansky, W. H. Ittelson, and L. G. Rivlin (eds.), Environmental Psychology. New York: Holt, Rinehart, and Winston.
Cowan, Ruth S.
1983   More Work for Mother. New York: Basic.
Csikszentmihalyi, Mihaly, and Eugene Rochberg-Halton
1981   The Meaning of Things. Cambridge: Cambridge University Press.
Ehrenreich, Barbara
1983   The Hearts of Men: American Dreams and the Flight from Commitment. Garden City, N.Y. Anchor.
Eichler, Margrit
1980   The Double Standard: A Feminist Critique of Feminist Social Science. New York: St. Martin's.
Fava, Sylvia
1980   "Women's place in the new suburbia." Pp. 129-49 in G. R. Wekerle, R. Peterson, and D. Morley (eds.), New Space for Women. Boulder, Co.: Westview.
Festinger, Leon, Stanley Schacter, and Kurt Back
1950   Social Pressure in Informal Groups. New York: Harper.
Festinger, Leon
1951   "Architecture and group membership." Journal of Social Issues 7:152-63.
Franck, Karen
1985   "Together or apart: Sharing and the

American household." Paper presented at the Annual Meeting of the American Collegiate Schools of Architecture, Vancouver.
Fried, Marc
1972   "Grieving for a lost home." Pp. 229-48 in R. Gutman (ed.), People and Buildings. New York: Basic.
Friedan, Betty
1963   The Feminine Mystique. New York: W. W. Norton.
Glennon, Lynda M.
1983   "Synthesism: A case of feminist methodology." Pp. 260-71 in G. Morgan (ed.), Beyond Method. Beverly Hills, Ca.: Sage.
Gould, Meredith, and Rochelle Kern-Daniels
1977   "Toward a sociological theory of gender and sex." American Sociologist 12: 182-89.
Gutman, Robert
1975   "Social functions of the built environment." Pp. 37-49 in A. Rapoport (ed.), The Mutual Interaction of People and Their Environment. The Hague: Mouton.
Hacker, Andrew (ed.)
1983   U.S.: A Statistical Portrait of the American People. New York: Vintage.
Hare, Patrick
1982   Accessory Apartments. Chicago: Planning Advisory Service.
Hareven, Tamara, and Randolph Langenback
1981   "Living places, work places, and historical identity." Pp. 109-23 in D. Lowenthal and M. Binney (eds.), Our Past Before Us. London: Temple Smith.
Hartman, Heidi
1981   "The family as the locus of gender, class, and political structure." Signs 6:366-94.
Hayden, Dolores
1980   "What would a non-sexist city be like?" Pp. 167-84 in C. R. Stimpson, E. Dixler, M. J. Nelson and K. B. Yatrakis (eds.), Women and the American City. Chicago: University of Chicago Press.
1982   The Grand Domestic Revolution. Cambridge, Mass.: MIT Press.
1984   Redesigning the American Dream. New York: W. W. Norton.
Hayward D. Geoffrey
1977   Psychological Concepts of Home Among Urban Middle Class Families and Young Children. Doctoral dissertation. City University of New York.
Hazard, John N.
1972   "Furniture arrangement as a symbol of judicial roles." Pp. 291-98 in R. Gutman (ed.), People and Buildings. New York: Basic.
Howell, Sandra C.
1980   Designing for Aging. Cambridge, Mass.: MIT Press.
Ittelson, William H., Karen A. Franck, and Timothy O'Hanlon
1976   "The nature of environmental experience."

Pp. 187-206 in S. Wapner, S. Cohen, and B. Kaplan (eds.), Experiencing the Environment. New York: Plenum.

Jacobs, Jane
1961   Death and Life of Great American Cities. New York: Random House.

Kessler-Harris, Alice
1982   Out to Work: A History of Wage-Earning Women in the United States. Oxford: Oxford University Press.

Kobrin, Francis E.
1978   "The fall in household size and the rise of the primary individual in the United States." Pp. 69-81 in M. Gordon (ed.), The American Family in Social-Historical Perspective. New York: St. Martin's.

Lopata, Helena Z.
1976   "Review essay: Sociology." Signs 2: 165-76.

Lopata, Helena Z., and Barrie Thorne
1978   "On the term 'sex roles'." Signs 3: 718-21.

Loyd, Bonnie
1975   "Woman's place, man's place." Landscape 20:10-13.

Marris, Peter
1974   Loss and Change. New York: Pantheon.

Matthews, Sara H.
1982   "Rethinking sociology through a feminist perspective." American Sociologist 17:29-35.

Michelson, William
1970   Man and His Urban Environment. Reading, Mass.: Addison-Wesley.
1977   Environmental Choice, Human Behavior and Residential Satisfaction. New York: Oxford University Press.

Miller, Joanne, and Howard Garrison
1982   "Sex roles: The division of labor at home and in the work place." Annual Review of Sociology 8:237-62.

Mostoller, Michael
forth- "Life in a single room." In E. L. Birch
coming (ed.), The Unsheltered Woman. New Brunswick: Rutgers University Press.

Newman, Oscar
1972   Defensible Space. New York: Macmillan.
1980   Community of Interest. New York: Doubleday.

Rapoport, Amos
1982   The Meaning of the Built Environment. Beverly Hills, Ca.: Sage.

Rapp, Rayna
1979   "Household and family." Feminist Studies 5:175-81.

Rothman, Sheila
1978   Women's Proper Place. New York: Basic.

Rubin, Gayle
1978   "The traffic in women." Pp. 154-66 in A. M. Jaggar and P. R. Struhl (eds.), Feminist Frameworks. New York: McGraw-Hill.

Saegert, Susan, and Gary Winkel
1980   "The home: A critical problem for changing sex roles." Pp. 41-63 in G. R. Wekerle, R. Peterson, and D. Morley (eds.), New Space for Women. Boulder, Col.: Westview.

Schwartz, Barry (ed.)
1976   The Changing Face of the Suburbs. Chicago: University of Chicago Press.
1980   "The suburban landscape." Contemporary Sociology 9:640-50.

Sommer, Robert
1974   Tight Spaces. Englewood Cliffs, New Jersey: Prentice Hall.

Steele, Fred I.
1973   Physical Settings and Organization Development. Reading, Mass.: Addison-Wesley.

Thorne, Barrie
1982   "Feminist rethinking of the family." Pp. 44-68 in B. Thorne and M. Yalon (eds.), Rethinking the Family. New York: Longman.

Tognoli, Jerome
1979   "The flight from domestic space." Family Coordinator: 599-609.

U.S. Bureau of the Census
1983   Current Population Reports Series P-20 #388: Household and Family Characteristics. Washington, D.C.: U.S. Government Printing Office.
1984   Current Population Reports Series P-20 #388: Household and Family Characteristics. Washington, D.C.: U.S. Government Printing Office.

Vanek, Joann
1974   "Time spent in housework." Scientific American 231:116-20.

van Vliet, Willem
1981   "Neighborhood evaluations by city and suburban children." American Planning Association Journal 47:458-66.
1983   "Exploring the fourth environment." Environment and Behavior 15:467-88.

Wright, Gwendolyn
1981   Building the Dream. New York: Pantheon.

Reprinted with permission from **Sociological Focus**, vol. 18, no. 2, pp. 143-160, 1985.

PART III
HOUSING TYPE

7 A window on her world: The relevance of housing type for the urban Japanese housewife

ANNE E. IMAMURA

BACKGROUND

Much has been written about the effect of housing and architectural style on human behavior. For the mobile urban resident, housing design is argued to play a major role in helping or hindering social contacts (Mehrabian 1976). Specifically, housing that maximizes privacy may inhibit social interaction (Mehrabian 1976; Hoshino 1964). High population density exacerbates this effect. As crowding increases, individuals establish barriers and stake out territories. Carried to the extreme, this can lead to social isolation in one's neighborhood.

The effect of housing type appears to vary depending on whether the individual is a "localized" resident (home much of the day), or not (Zito 1974). Fulltime housewives who are home or in the neighborhood much of the day, and who are living in a densely populated urban situation, may thus be more affected by housing type than those who spend little time in or near home.

Japan is one example of a modern urban society with high population density. Although women are increasingly becoming involved in work and other activities outside the home, gender roles tend to keep housewives home-centered. At the same time, the greater part of urban community integration is left up to the housewife (Imamura 1980). While studies have been made of the effect of individual housing types (e.g., Kiefer 1974), no attempt has been made to compare several types in a single neighborhood.

This paper examines the housing milieu of urban Japanese housewives in order to ascertain what dimensions of housing type affect their patterns of interaction in the wider community. It provides data for comparison with developed and developing urban communities.

Data, unless otherwise indicated, come from a larger study of Japanese urban housewives. They were collected in 1977-1978 in a single suburban city in the Santama area of greater Tokyo. The suburb, which is conveniently located for commuter travel to Tokyo, grew from a population of 54,198 in 1950 to 149,113 in 1970. At the time of study, the growth rate had declined to about 1 percent annually. The population was slightly younger than that of the nation. In 1976, 68 percent was under forty and 28 percent under twenty. For the nation, the figures were 63 percent and 31 percent respectively.

Nationwide, a slight majority of people -- 59 percent in 1975 -- own their homes. In the Santama city, the situation was just reversed. A slight majority -- 60 percent in 1975 -- were renters. In spite of this, a city government survey found that 75 percent of the residents wished to reside permanently in that city, although not necessarily in their current residences (Mitaka-Shi). At the time of this study, the city government was actively working to build community spirit. They had completed one community center which provided recreational facilities and offered some government sponsored adult education and recreational programs. During the year of research, a second community center was opened, and a third constructed.

Data were collected in three ways: (1) 4 months' participant observation in the only community center functioning at the time; (2) in-depth interviews with 56 house-wives selected through introductions to include 10 women from each of five housing categories (described below); and (3) a survey of 228 housewives aged 25 and above. For the survey, the sample was city-wide, randomly chosen and stratified by population distribution in the various subdistricts of the city.

Of the 56 interviewees, seven were leaders of various voluntary groups. The remaining 49 consisted of ten residents each of owned homes, owned condominiums, **danchi** (public housing), and company housing (**shataku**). Nine lived in rented apartments. Data for survey respondents are presented in table 1.

Table 1
Housing Categories of Survey Respondents

Owned house	56.3
Owned condominium	1.3
Rented house	7.0
Rented apartment	18.4
Danchi (public housing)	8.8
Company, gov't housing	7.9
Total	100.0% (N=228)

THE JAPANESE HOUSEWIFE

The Japanese family has undergone many changes since World War II. Rapid industrialization and urbanization have been accompanied by an improved position for women. The Constitution of Japan prohibits discrimination by sex (although it exists in practice), and women have entered virtually all occupations. On the other hand, protective legislation and different on-the-job training means that, in fact, the route to the corporate top is much less accessible to women than to men with equal qualifications.

The contemporary Japanese woman typically chooses to marry and work until the birth of her first child. Longevity and a low birthrate have contributed to give her a long "free period" from about her mid-forties until her mid-fifties (when her husband retires). This has in turn resulted in her increased activity outside the home. As her children grow, she becomes increasingly involved in classes, charitable work or other community activity and/or returns to paid employment. This latter usually is as a part-time or temporary employee.

Once a Japanese woman marries and has children, she is expected to treat her role as wife and mother as a profession (Imamura 1980; Vogel 1978), demanding the same degree of commitment that her husband gives to work. Although she may combine other roles with motherhood, she must not allow them to compete. Her role responsibilities include: managing the family finances; taking complete care of her husband when he is home (Imamura 1980; Lebra 1984; Salamon 1974); and being almost completely responsible for her children. This latter includes seeing that they do well in the extremely competitive school entrance examinations. She must accordingly become knowledgeable about after-school tutoring and prep schools; participate in Parent Teacher Associations (PTA) in order to keep up with relevant information and convince teachers she is sincere about her children's education; and maintain a home atmosphere in which children can study. She must also maintain a good image in the neighborhood. This is particularly important if the family expects to reside there at the time of their children's marriage. Especially in the case of a daughter, investigators may ask neighbors to vouch for the family character before marriage agreements are made (Imamura 1980). Lastly, after her children are launched, she takes on the role of caretaker for her retired husband. For some women, the role of wife includes caring for (usually) her husband's aged parents.

This series of obligations over her life course tends to keep the housewife close to home. She chooses her work and other activities with care so that they can be done in the time she has free from wife/mother responsibilities. In general, this limits her to activities which are close to home and can be done in short periods of time or started and dropped as she moves through different stages in her life course.

HOUSING

Japan urbanized rapidly. Her urban population increased from 25 percent in 1930 to 68 percent in 1980 (Fukutake 1982). As a consequence, adequate housing is a severe problem. This is especially true of Tokyo and the Kyoto-Osaka-Kobe and Nagoya metropolitan areas which combined accounted for 47.8 percent of Japan's population in 1980 (Fukutake). A few years ago the Japanese public expressed outrage at a European characterization of Japanese homes as "rabbit hutches." Rabbit hutches or not, Japanese dwellings are extremely small and expensive:

*"The price of land and housing has gone out of the
reach of the average citizen. The average price of ·
a house in 1977 in the sphere of Japan's three
largest cities (Tokyo, from 30 to 50 kilometers
from its center; Nagoya, from 30 to 40 kilometers
in radius and Osaka, from 20 to 40 kilometers out
in all directions) was: for an independent house
(86 square meters in area)... about $82,000... and
for a unit in a medium- to high-rise building (66
square meters of floor area)... about $68,000... The
income of the average worker was... about
$14,500. If possible savings and loans are added...
This is only 51.4 percent of the amount needed for
the detached dwelling and 62.6 percent for the
apartment dwelling unit (Hayakawa, p. 5)"*
*"Although there is public housing, the ratio of public
ownership is only 6.9 percent, with an average floor
space of 400 square feet (37.2 square meters)
(Hayakawa, p. 5)."*

       This study deals with five different types of housing found commonly in urban
Japan: privately rented apartments; public housing (danchi); company housing (shataku);
condominiums (apartment buildings in which units from one room and up are purchased
by residents); and privately owned homes. The basic assumption is that ideally, Japanese
aspire to own independent homes (Hayakawa 1983; Koyano 1978). The least desirable
category of housing is privately rented apartments. This is because lacking government
or company subsidies, renters pay much more for space. It is important to note that living
in either company housing or danchi does not necessarily mean having more space or
better quality housing than in private apartments. It does mean lower rents, and hopefully, the ability to save for one's own home in the future. Condominiums also range in
size and quality. Unit size varies from one room and up. Residents tend to be those who
cannot afford an independent house, but who do not wish to spend money on rent.
Naturally, they must also be able to afford the down payment, which is roughly one third
of the cost of the home. Young condominium residents see themselves as temporary and
plan to move to either an independent house or to a better condominium in the future.
Older condominium residents typically plan to stay and see the condominium as their
place of retirement.

       Danchi refers to public housing. Originally constructed to meet housing
shortages after World War II, danchi continue to be built to meet housing needs today.
They are typically high rise structures with little to distinguish one building from another.
Although rents are much lower (if housing quality and location are considered) than
privately owned apartments, residents are restricted to those whose monthly incomes are
at least 5.5 times the rent. Demand for choice locations is high and apartments are
allocated by lottery. Young couples without the option of company housing hope to move
into danchi in order to save and buy their own homes. Not all residents attain this dream;
some remain permanently in danchi, and some danchi offer a proportion of apartments for
purchase.

76

Because of the lottery factor in danchi, and because of the provision of company housing in some cases, one cannot strictly equate housing type with socioeconomic status. Another factor entering into the "choice" of housing type is the probability that husbands will be transferred to other locations. In such cases, families may live in company housing until close to retirement, then purchase something of their own.

HOUSING AND SURVEY RESPONDENTS

The majority of survey respondents have lived in a different type of housing in the past, and the majority of all except danchi dwellers and home owners expect to move in the future. Residents of danchi and owned homes tended to be slightly older than those in other categories. Stem or extended families lived only in danchi (15 percent) or owned homes (37.2 percent). Home owning also correlated with progress along the family life course. Home owners increased from a low of 35.4 percent of those with preschool children to a high of 88.5 percent of those with college age children. Other details are given in table 2.

Apartment dwellers: Japanese apartment buildings tend to be small, two to three story buildings, with small apartment units inside. Since they are unsubsidized, they are more costly per square foot of rented space than public or company housing and attract single or newly married people with no other alternative. Renters are usually hoping to win the lottery to enter public housing or to move to their own home as soon as possible.

In a typical low rise apartment building, outside stairways lead to the upper floor(s) and individual units open directly onto an outside corridor. One enters the apartment through the kitchen. Interviewees' apartments were all of what is most likely the common type today 2DK (two rooms and a dining-kitchen). In size, these also usually approximated the 400 square feet (37.2 square meters) of public housing. Newer units have baths, although in some cases landlords will cut construction costs by installing baths only in ground floor units. Other units will rent for less, and residents will use a neighborhood public bath.

Women apartment dwellers not involved in the community were extremely difficult to locate for interviews, and obtaining introductions was next to impossible. Finally, some apartment dwellers were located through a woman who distributed educational materials for the city and thus knew all the local residents.

Apartment dwellers saw themselves as isolated, but temporary. They were not interested in initiating friendships that would not be permanent, and were reluctant to spend even minimal amounts of money on women's or community activities. For example, one apartment resident argued that she did not want to visit others nor invite them in because it would cost money for refreshments. She was quite sociable by nature, but preferred to chat outside with neighbors. Clearly, these women were all very budget conscious because of high rent, and they were hoping to save money to move to a place of their own.

Apartment residents also indicated that the buildings tended to be empty during the day. With the exception of a few mothers with small children, everyone was busy working, and resident turnover was great. Since rents rise every second year, and housing quality is relatively poor, no one willingly stays long. This leads to lack of trust among residents and unwillingness to open up to one another.

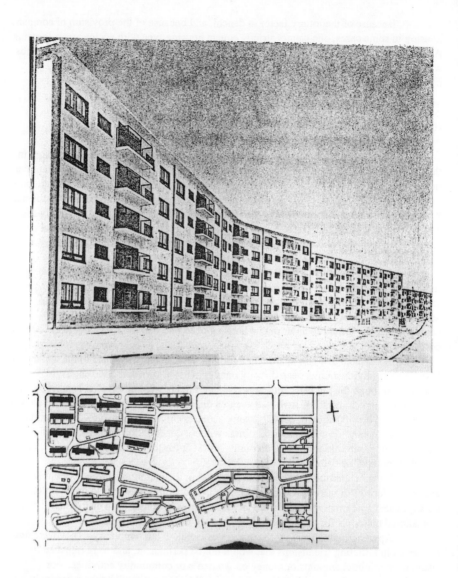

Fig. 1 Typical high rise *danchi*

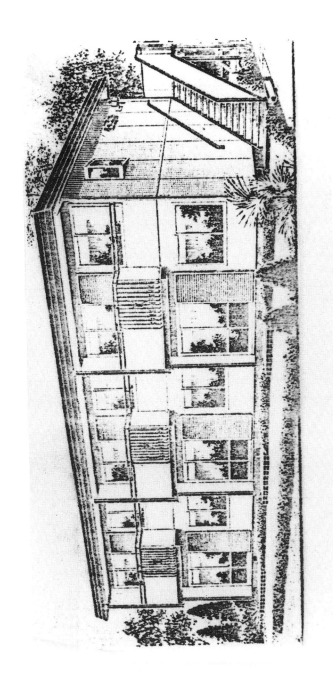

Fig. 2 A typical low-rise apartment building containing small privately rented units (Photo: Yomiuri Shinbun, February 25, 1985).

Table 2
Selected characteristics of residents of various housing types

a. Housing type by age of respondent

Housing type	35 yrs. or less	over 35
Company hsg. (shataku)	58.3%	41.2%
Apartment	78.6	21.4
Condominium	100.0	0
Danchi	35.0	65.0
Own house	24.0	76.0 (N=211)

b. Housing type by family income*

Housing type	4 million yen** or less	4.5 million plus
Company hsg.	47.0%	53.0%
Apartment	66.6	33.4
Condominium	33.3	66.7
Danchi	70.0	30.0
Own house	34.2	63.7 (N=211)

* Average annual income for an employed individual in 1975 was 2.2 million yen.
** 250 yen = approximately $1 US.

c. Housing type by husband's education

Housing type	High sch. or less	Jr. col. or more
Company hsg.	47.0%	53.0%
Apartment	52.4	47.6
Condominium	0	100.0
Danchi	55.0	45.0
Own house	37.0	63.0 (N=209)

80

d. Housing type by respondent's education

Housing type	Compulsory	High sch.	Jr. col. or more
Company hsg.	29.4%	35.3%	35.3%
Apartment	16.7	61.9	21.5
Condominium	—	—	100.0
Danchi	35.0	50.0	15.0
Own house	16.3	51.2	32.6 (N=211)

e. Housing type by husband's job

Housing type	Wht. col.	Mg./Pro.	Self-emp.	Blue col.	Part time/Oth
Company hsg.	52.9%	17.6%	0	29.4%	0
Apartment	33.3	9.5	21.4	35.7	0
Condominium	100.0	0	0	0	0
Danchi	30.0	20.0	20.0	30.0	0
Own house	43.3	~ 16.3	23.3	16.3	0.8 (N=211)

f. Housing type by intention to stay in present residence

Housing type	Stay	Move
Company hsg.	18.8%	81.2%
Apartment	0	100.0
Condominium	0	100.0
Danchi	57.9	42.1
Own house	82.5	17.7 (N=206)

g. Housing type by length of residence

Housing type	1-5 yrs.	5-10 yrs.	over 10 yrs.
Company hsg.	76.5%	17.6%	5.8%
Apartment	66.6	23.8	9.5
Condominium	100.0	0	0
Danchi	40.0	40.0	20.0
Own house	22.5	16.3	61.5 (N=211)

Danchi dwellers: Even a casual visitor to Japan is struck by the sight of danchi: several high rise ferro-concrete structures each with a number written in black paint on its side, cluster around some green space and, in the case of new danchi, parking areas.

Danchi are physically distinct from "apartments" because of their size, uniformity of construction, and the numbering on them, although in some cases company housing may be physically the same. Newer danchi tend to include 3DK as well as 2DK units and to be better insulated than immediate postwar ones. They are also located further away from the center, increasing commuting time. New danchi also may have their own shopping center in the complex. Those with more than four stories have elevators and individual units, like apartments, are entered from an outside corridor through the kitchen. Newer danchi have play areas in their green space, and during the day, these are filled with mothers and their young children. Danchi also may include a common room where lessons, meetings and other activities may be held.

Although most residents hope to move to their own homes someday, relatively low rents make mobility less of a factor than in apartments. Some units may be purchased, and some families live their entire lives in danchi (Oyabu 1975).

Early danchi residents looked forward to relatively impersonal surroundings. Assuming themselves to be temporary, they hoped to be free from community involvements:

> "When we first moved into this danchi (30 years ago) we well liked the idea of privacy. We did not want the old (traditional) sticky types of relationships. But after a while we got lonesome" (63 year old graduate of the prewar higher school for women).

Once a danchi is fairly settled, too much visibility and maintaining distance become problematic.

> "Of course, I say hello to women on my stairwell, but I don't go so far as to invite them in."

This may be fostered by the attitudes encountered when moving in.

> "When (we) moved in...I was asked a lot of questions (by the neighbors)...how much my husband makes...very personal things...(by) the people who live on my stairwell" (35 year old university graduate).

After settling in, the feeling of visibility may act as a constraint on activity (cf. Salamon for further discussion of this point).

> "(In a danchi) whenever we go out there is always someone in the hallway...In a house, if you want to let people in you can...if you don't you don't have to. Here people have no privacy because everyone knows what goes on in the home..." (63 year old high school graduate).

82

Fig. 3 *Danchi* with some green space in front (Source: The Japanese Embassy, Washington, DC, USA).

Fig. 4 A newer *danchi*, the Harumi Apartment House, Tokyo, which was the first high-rise apartment building with elevators built by the Japan Housing Corporation, and the first such building of its scale ever designed by Japanese architects.
Source: David Paulson

Fig. 5 *Danchi* with play areas for children

There is a great deal of speculation by non-danchi residents about danchi life. Women who lived in their own homes mentioned rumors they had heard about arguments among danchi neighbors; about the cramped apartments and how difficult it must be to live in them. On the other hand, they stressed that they had friends who lived in danchi and that their children played with danchi children. However, when asked to enumerate their danchi friends and how they met, with the single exception of a woman active in Christian church affairs, none could name one. They were certain that their children must know someone in a danchi because danchi children went to the neighborhood school. They also remarked that surely someone from their Parent Teacher Association (PTA) related group must be from a danchi. Once again, although these women stated that they invited their PTA friends home occasionally and went to these friends' homes, they, for the most part, had never visited anyone living in a neighborhood danchi.

The danchi residents explain that they live in quarters too cramped to invite in women who live in their own "big" homes. The women were very conscious of this difference and not willing to be too exposed to outsiders. One woman said she had invited PTA friends home once but that they had not come, suggesting instead that they meet in the larger home of one of the members.

The desire to own a place of their own too plays a role in the activity choices of the danchi wives. Active participants in women's groups commented on the lack of danchi members. A city official familiar with patterns of participation of women in local city sponsored activities pointed out that it was not the danchi women who lived directly opposite the city facility in question who made use of it, but rather women in their own homes who lived farther away. This particular official stated that danchi women "preferred to work" -- part time or piece work, a "preference" for work which may, of course, reflect the desire to save for a home of one's own. It may also reflect a situation in which piece work is brought to the danchi, and women encouraged to join those already involved:

> "In this danchi...piecework
> (naishoku)...assembling radio parts...there is a lot
> of that kind of work...housewives can do at home.
> They bring it in trucks and cars from nearby
> factories...If you make ten pieces you earn 100 yen
> (about 40 cents)...The truck comes daily or every
> other day...and (wives who want to do the work)
> collect it...(to me, as a university graduate)...it
> (seems like) boring work...to wind (something
> around something else). If that's all, it's better to
> read a book...It also takes time away from cooking.
> (The women who do it) use instant food and carry
> outs. (They use all their earnings) on carry out
> food." (35 year old university graduate).

A woman living in her own home, long active in her community, pointed out that unless a woman is living in her own home she does not have the noneconomic reserves to engage in volunteer and other activities. Women not in their own homes are unsettled, she argued, and cannot think beyond the needs of their own families. This argument was

86

seconded by the 30-year danchi resident quoted above who pointed out that younger women were not interested in involving themselves in any community service activities, centering all around their individual homes and families.

Although most of the danchi women interviewed did not work, they did not seem to have the necessary motivation or energy to improve their present situation in life. With the exception of the apartment of the one woman who worked, the danchi visited were depressing in the extreme. Even women who had lived in their danchi for over ten years made no effort to make the apartments cheery. Many had torn "fusuma" (paper sliding doors) patched with newspaper. Gummed paper for recovering such doors is available in supermarkets and is inexpensive, but these women seemed to be in a state of inertia about improving the situation. Many also could have improved things by clearing out the stacks of newspapers and magazines. The apartment of the working woman, by contrast, was bright and cheerful, decorated with inexpensive curtains and potted geraniums. Things were neat and inviting but not costly.

The primary activities of danchi women interviewed were related to children's school or to religion -- several were either members or attended meetings of one of the evangelistic "New Religions" -- and they were likely to indicate few real friends in either the danchi or the wider neighborhood. Rather, they would make acquaintances in the child's kindergarten or school, and use these outside meetings for information gathering, especially on child care and/or education. Occasionally, they would invite other danchi women in for tea, but usually limited their relationship to talking in the danchi compound or on the stairs. They felt strongly that they had to treat all neighbors equally and sought to avoid "trouble."

The poor construction of danchi contributed to the problem of privacy and some of the rumors of arguments within apartment units.

For example, in one danchi, residents on lower floors could hear all the water coming down the pipes from the apartment above and wanted to restrict bathing and even toilet flushing to before 10 p.m. Since residents on the upper floors pointed out that this would mean many husbands would never be able to take a bath, the idea was dropped. As a result, residents on the upper floors felt that they should not flush the toilet too often at night, creating a strain on a family with small children.

Another example of this type of "trouble" involved a situation that arose when one of the residents had washed her carpet in the yard using an outside faucet. Since each household shared the water bill and not every household had a carpet to wash, it was decided by the residents' association that no one would be allowed to wash carpets or other large items such as cars using the outside faucet.

A third example of trouble occurred when one family heard rumors about their financial problems. They realized that the discussion on which the rumors were based had been held between husband and wife in the family bath in order to keep it from the children's ears. The thinness of the walls had carried the conversation to their neighbor's ears and thence to others.

The danchi women see themselves as separate from women living in private homes, yet unable to form a community among themselves. Unlike the women in apartments, they are more likely to form casual friendships within their complexes. This is probably due to the larger number of people from whom to choose and the presence of play areas for children so that mothers of small children may come to know one another. Such friendships do not develop among co-residents of a single floor or stairwell. Rather, they are between persons who live in separate buildings or on different floors. They clearly recognize distance as a necessary physical buffer to preserve privacy. They also recognize the disruptive nature of forming friendships with some close neighbors but not all. The large number and variety of residents allow them to form some friendships while preserving a certain amount of privacy. This presents a very different situation from the women in company housing.

Company housing dwellers: Company housing (shataku) is impossible to identify by physical appearance alone. It resembles the danchi in figure 6, but with fewer buildings. Depending on its needs, a company will either build a danchi-like structure, or rent private apartments or houses for its employees. Size of allocated residence was related to rank in company rather than family size, and rent was usually calculated as a percentage of husband's salary. Unlike danchi, company housing is necessarily temporary. Some companies placed a ten to fifteen year limit on employee residence. All required they vacate on retirement. Every company housing resident then had to plan to acquire alternative accommodation in the future. The two major factors affecting resident women were this expectation of temporality and the work relations of their husbands.

> *"As soon as a woman moves into a shataku*
> *(company housing) she starts planning to move out*
> *(because of interpersonal relations)." (40 year old*
> *day care professional). "When I was young and*
> *living in the shataku (she is now a home owner) it*
> *was very enjoyable, we were all friends and went*
> *back and forth with our children. I am so glad that*
> *I never got involved in shataku 'trouble.'"*

Women in company housing were eager to avoid getting too close to women in the same company housing complex because "trouble" (usually, as in the case of danchi, related to children or rumors) could affect their husbands.

> *"(When we lived in company housing) I made sure*
> *my children greeted everyone politely. If they*
> *didn't my husband might have heard about it..." (47*
> *year old high school graduate).*

They also thought they might find themselves living with one or more of their present neighbors in another shataku in the future. It would be terrible, they said, if they made an enemy and that person should precede them to a new transfer. In such a case, their new environment would be prejudiced against them before they arrived.

Another reason these women were especially wary of close involvements was that this group had the highest degree of mutual visibility.

> *"(If they get too involved)...people worry their*
> *income and other (personal) things will become*
> *known...so we never mention*
> *personal...things...there are people who will ask*
> *political questions or for political support...so (we*
> *company housing residents) avoid controversial*
> *topics." (32 year old high school graduate).*

They knew when one another's husbands had entered the company and the ranks of the husbands and could predict income very accurately.

In order to avoid the possibility of "trouble," several interviewees indicated they had deliberately made an effort to find friends outside the shataku. For that very reason, one had joined a ping pong class and started basket weaving. Furthermore, women who had tried to make friends or form groups in shataku found that too much activity left them open to criticism which might even come back to their husbands at work (Morishita 1983). So they moved their sphere of activity outside where there was less visibility.

One such woman said that her home library activities were considered "pink" by some of the shataku residents and that the children who came were from outside that particular complex of independent homes. She also said that when they moved there from a danchi, her husband told her not to ask any of the wives to babysit because they were either in positions above or below her, based on their husbands' positions. Those above could not be asked to perform such favors while those below would have difficulty refusing.

Because the housing was managed by the company, wives were reluctant to ask for needed improvements. To do so gave the appearance of criticizing what the company had provided:

> "When I moved in, there was a big hole in the
> fence leading out into the road. A neighbor's child
> went right down the hill on his bicycle through the
> hole and was hit by a car. I worried that my son
> would be next and called the office managing the
> company housing. They told me they needed a
> resident petition. So I went around to get
> signatures...people here had never done that...They
> told me I was "Red" and I didn't get signatures.
> Finally, last summer (the office) put up a fence.
> Not because of what I did" (39 year old university
> graduate).

Finally, many women in shataku indicated that they were faced with constant uncertainty about being transferred, having already moved a lot. For such women, outside work was difficult, unless they had specific skills such as tutoring or were interested in piece work. Of course there were usually part time jobs in the neighborhood stores, but women expecting to move at any moment tended to put off looking.

Owned home and condominium dwellers: Condominiums range from fairly simple apartment-like structures to elaborate buildings with elevators and security systems. Unit size ranges from a single room and up. Interviewees indicated a unit with four rooms and a living-dining-kitchen (LDK) was most desirable, but a check of real estate advertisements indicates that 2LDK and 3LDK units are most common -- undoubtedly due to cost.

Individual houses vary in size, also. Their important physical features are small gardens, which all condominiums residents desired; high fences to preserve privacy; and the problem of closing up the house when empty.

Older homes have sliding doors which may be locked but easily opened. All homes have shutters over glass veranda doors and windows. The independent house provides the wife with privacy but may also be isolating:

> *"In company housing human relations are*
> *difficult...you have to relate (because of) husbands'*
> *relations. In a condominium you can associate if*
> *you want to, but you don't have to. In an inde-*
> *pendent house you don't have the chance to meet*
> *as many people" (36 year old high school*
> *graduate, condominium resident).*

Women in separate houses and in condominiums were more likely to be concerned about neighborhood relations than women in other housing categories, the only exception being the few danchi women who do not expect to move. A major motive for this concern was their children's welfare. Good neighborhood relations are important in case the children want to stay in the house in the future, and when investigators check into the family character before a daughter is married.

This category of women tended to be involved in activities such as the home library or charity work. Motivation for participation varied with age: older women who had just moved into condominiums were looking for friends, whereas younger women made friends through children's kindergartens and either joined "circles" together or formed them in order to have a reason to meet. They tended to stay in certain activities such as crafts and study groups for a long period of time and thus maintain friendships over the years.

Women who were living in houses rather than condominiums seemed more settled. Interviewees from condominiums were of two types: younger women planning to raise their presently completed families; and older women who had moved to the condominium after living in a series of shataku, danchi or apartments.

The two groups were very different. The younger women did not see them-selves as permanent, the older women did. The younger women expected to make friends in the condominium and the wider neighborhood through their children, and the older women expressed hesitation about how to go about finding friends of their own age. They also perceived the condominium as "young" and saw they had little contact with younger women. One might expect that higher visibility within a condominium -- as compared to a private house -- might lead some of these older women to actively seek each other out. This does not seem to be the case unless, as one older woman put it, they happen to run into another older woman whose "daily rhythm is the same."

In other words, if two older women take out the garbage or run errands at the same time, the condominium stairs and elevator may serve as a place of contact. Merely living in the same complex is not enough. Younger women spend more time in public spaces because of their children, and are therefore more likely to meet one another. Both groups have an unsettled quality. Older women, including those who expected to stay in their condominium permanently, wanted to move where they could have a bit of a garden and all the younger women expected to move.

All condominium women saw their condominium as a unit and spoke of activities for children or classes for themselves within the condominium. They also spoke

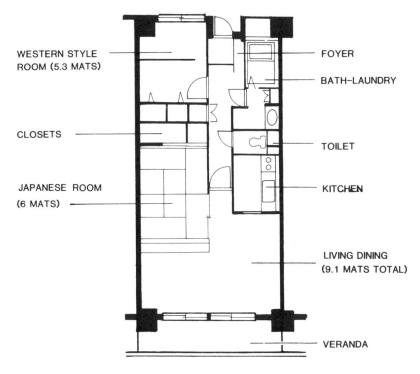

WESTERN STYLE ROOM (5.3 MATS)

FOYER

BATH-LAUNDRY

CLOSETS

TOILET

JAPANESE ROOM (6 MATS)

KITCHEN

LIVING DINING (9.1 MATS TOTAL)

VERANDA

Fig. 6 A typical, fairly large condominium

91

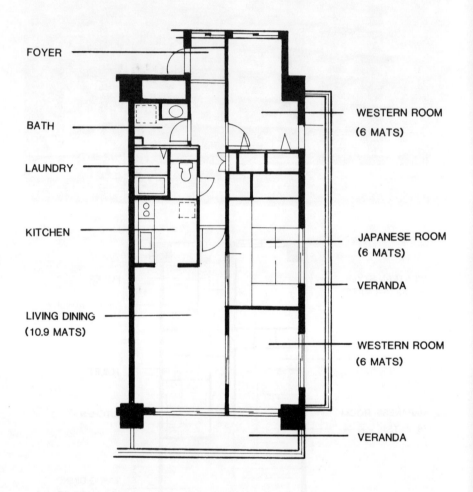

FOYER

BATH

LAUNDRY

KITCHEN

LIVING DINING
(10.9 MATS)

WESTERN ROOM
(6 MATS)

JAPANESE ROOM
(6 MATS)

VERANDA

WESTERN ROOM
(6 MATS)

VERANDA

Fig. 7 An average 3 LDK apartment in a condominium, between 62.5 and
73 M². Source: Weekly Housing Report, Nov. 14, 1984.

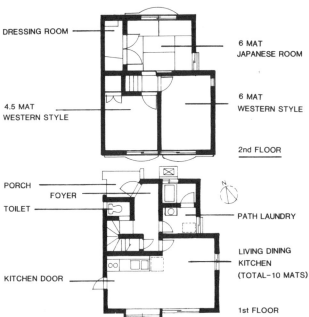

DRESSING ROOM

6 MAT
JAPANESE ROOM

4.5 MAT
WESTERN STYLE

6 MAT
WESTERN STYLE

2nd FLOOR

PORCH

FOYER

TOILET

PATH LAUNDRY

LIVING DINING
KITCHEN
(TOTAL–10 MATS)

KITCHEN DOOR

1st FLOOR

Fig. 8 An independent house of the 3 LDK type (70.14M2). This house
has one unusual feature—a "dressing room."

93

of the condominium mood, as friendly or not. One middle aged woman, a cooking teacher, spoke of the loneliness of the older women who had no friends, little to do, living in these "concrete boxes." She said that when she meets such women in the hall, she invites them to come to her cooking classes.

> *"If I look around...there are many lonely wives*
> *here...the wife next door has no children and she is*
> *always alone when her husband is at*
> *work...everyone says a condominium is lonely*
> *when you are old" (47 year old high school*
> *graduate teaching cooking in her condominium).*

Women in their own homes have a sense of permanence. If they are young, they worry about maintaining good neighbor relations for the sake of their children. If they are older, they stress the importance of good long term relations.

DISCUSSION AND CONCLUSIONS

Residents of different housing types participate differently in the wider community. This research as well as perceptions of women active in community centers indicate that the majority of regular participants are residents of individually owned homes. Apartment dwellers, on the other hand, are attracted to one-time activities.

Survey respondents active in a variety of groups (study, leisure, political, consumer and charitable) disproportionately came from residents of their own homes (table 3).

Table 3
Percent of members of various groups by housing type

Type of group	Comp. hsg.	Apt.	Condo.	Danchi	Own home	N
Leisure	9.6%	9.5%	3.2%	3.2%	71.4%	63
Child-Rel.	7.1	28.6	7.1	3.6	53.6	28
PTA (active)	5.4	18.2	0	14.5	56.4	55
Study	15.8	5.3	0	0	68.4	19
Consumer	0	11.8	0	17.6	64.7	17
Charitable	0	0	11.1	0	88.9	9 (N = 201)

Three dimensions of housing affect the housewife's social interaction: architecture, co-residents, and ownership.

Architectural features such as size, lack of sound-proofing, access routes (e.g., elevators, stairways and halls), fences and gardens, and intercoms affect the degree of personal effort required to maintain privacy. They also affect means by which territoriality can be established. In Japan, the traditional barrier was not a locked door, but the foyer (genkan) area in which shoes were removed. Locked doors and intercoms represent recent additions to this barrier. The genkan is still a definite social barrier. Invitations to

94

cross that barrier and enter private (family) space are quite selective. Also related to architecture is the desire expressed by housing complex residents for public halls. They expected co-resident interaction to increase when it did not involve violation of private space.

Co-residents also affect social interaction. Danchi residents indicated a need to treat everyone on their hall or stairwell equally. This encouraged them to look for friends among women in other buildings or on other stairwells or floors. Shataku residents were most concerned about maintaining the little privacy they had, and not causing trouble that might pursue them over their husbands' careers. These concerns even drove them out of the shataku to search for activities that would keep them out of "trouble."

Ownership is related to expectations of permanence. Women in their privately owned homes are perceived as settled with more energy to turn to local activities. They are also more concerned with keeping up the neighborhood and maintaining a good image in it. Long term residents may develop networks of friends with whom to share common experiences over the life course. In this sense they may develop relations approximating those found in small towns, where women who spent their years as "young wives" in near proximity to one another and watched one another's children grow are able, as grand-mothers, to sit over tea remembering their shared pasts.

In the suburban situation, women attending an exercise class at the community center included a number in their forties with children in middle school. All of these women had lived in the area since their children were in grade school and all lived in their own homes. They went back and forth and out together frequently. They knew if decorating changes had been made, and their posture and eating habits indicated casual familiarity. Their conversations also had continuity. They were able to discuss one another's children, the PTA, and other women in the PTA in the past. Although their homes were in the immediate vicinity of a danchi and they said they knew danchi women who were also long term residents of the neighborhood, it was the women in their own homes who went back and forth. They were not necessarily living in closer proximity to one another than they were to the danchi.

Space to provide a relaxed atmosphere for talking in a comfortable situation, and perhaps the quiet that pervades a home -- in contrast to the "people noise" of housing complexes -- added to the ability of these women to relax with one another. Because each home was separated from the outside world by a fence, and had an entrance hall so that opening the door did not mean showing the visitor the entire dwelling, these women felt free to go back and forth. They could preserve privacy when they desired and open their homes when they wished. Cooperative living, regardless of type, carries the danger of too much visibility and barriers are set up to preserve privacy.

Ownership establishes a kind of territoriality. It is also an achievement, and even the smallest owned home is more worthy of showing off than a rented dwelling. Increased space, being settled and the accomplishment of ownership may all relate to the greater involvement of home owner wives in their local community.

For the first generation of urban residents, the housing situation can present a severe contrast with that of the countryside or small town. On the positive side, Japanese women noted that they were able to maintain greater privacy from their neighbors. They were relieved to escape the "sticky," "country" type of relations in which they were rarely able to refuse a request. Older rural housing styles permit less privacy, involving the young wife both with in-laws and with neighbors whose family networks go back many generations. From this point of view, the urban women welcomed being able to lock the doors of their apartments and keep out the world. They also welcomed the opportunity to pick and choose personal friends, noting that "country" relations were more family to family and urban ones more individually directed. Although family reputation was still an important consideration, family to family interactions were much less frequent or nonexistent in the urban setting.

On the minus side, once children were raised, these women missed some aspects of the long term relations of the country. This was particularly felt as they aged or if they had to move into a new neighborhood after the children were grown. They also found it difficult to cope with being shut up in a concrete box. These women wanted neither the traditional "sticky" bonds nor the lack of neighborhood integration in urban areas.

Another dimension which is particularly urban is the lack of husband integration in the neighborhood (Imamura 1980). In the rural/small town situation the husband grew up and went to school with his neighbors and is likely to work with some of them. In contrast, with the exception of local shopkeepers, the urban man typically works outside his neighborhood and has no meaningful contact with other residents. Most urban housing types allow little if any space for the husband to pursue any personal interest or to invite friends to visit. The focus of men's involvement is a combination of "old boy" and work related ties with almost all interaction taking place outside the neighborhood.

Last but not least, the consumer preference for independent homes, however small, has led to mini development (mini kaihatsu). There is growing public concern that scarce land will be parcelled out into infinitesimal lots and also recognition that the quality of housing is extremely low, considering Japan's economic position. The Japanese government is emphasizing improving housing to improve the quality of life and to conserve some of her scarce land as green space.

For Japanese wives, but not for their husbands, urban neighborhoods come close to community "...in the classic ecological sense, that is locations where all the significant activities of life...take place" (Mehrabian 1976). They offer opportunity for close to home social interests for transient and permanent residents. At the same time, the urban elements of lack of husband-neighborhood integration and perception of temporary residence influence the degree of hold the community has on residents, and the degree to which privacy may be maintained. Within this setting, housing type acts as a window through which the housewife perceives opportunities for interaction and through which neighbors can view her.

ACKNOWLEDGMENTS

Data collection in Japan was made possible by funding from the U.S. Department of Health, Education and Welfare (HEW), Fulbright and the Japan Foundation. I am indebted to Sylvia Fava and to Kenneth E. Corety for comments. All responsibility for content is my own.

REFERENCES

Fukutake, Tadashi (1982), **The Japanese Social Structure: Its Evolution in the Modern Century** (Tokyo, University of Tokyo Press).

Hayakawa, Kazuo (1983), "Housing poverty in Japan," EKISTICS, vol. 50, no. 298, pp. 4-9.

Hoshino, Ikumi (1964), "Apartment life in Japan," **Journal of Marriage and the Family,** no. 26, pp. 312-17.

Imamura, Anne Elizabeth (1980), "Kanai or Kagai? The Japanese urban housewife -- her image of and involvement in her community," unpublished Ph.D. dissertation.

____(n.d.), "Time lag or different visions: Gender roles and the urban Japanese housewife."

Kiefer, Christie W. (1974), "The danchi zoku and the evolution of the metropolitan mind," in Austin Lewis (ed.), **Japan: The Paradox of Progress** (New Haven, Yale University Press), pp. 279-300.

Koyano, Shoogo (1978), "Thought patterns and their change among the collective housing dwellers in Tokyo," unpublished paper presented at the 9th World Congress of Sociology, Uppsala, Sweden.

Lebral, Takie Sugiyama (1984), **Japanese Women: Constraint and Fulfillment** (Honolulu, University of Hawaii Press).

Mehrabian, Albert (1976), **Public Places and Private Spaces: The Psychology of Work, Play, and Living Environments** (New York, Basic Books).

Mitaka-Shi Shakai Chosa Kenkyu-Sho (1977), "Mitaka-shi Kohon Keikaku Sakutei no Tame no Anketo Chosa Hokoku-sho" (3 gatsu, Showa 52 nen. Mitaka-shi, Tokyo).

Morishita, Ritsuko (1983), **Ookoku no Tsumatchi: Kigyoo Jookamachi Nite** (Tokyo, Komichi Shooboo).

Oyabu, Juichi (1975), "Danchi: Furusato," **Asahi Shinbun** (November 21).

Robbins-Mowry, Dorothy (1983), **The Hidden Sun: Women of Modern Japan** (Boulder, Colorado, Westview Press).

Salamon, Sonya Blank (1974), "In the intimate arena: Japanese women and their families," unpublished Ph.D. dissertation.

____ (1975), "The varied groups of Japanese and German housewives," **The Japan Interpreter,** no. 10, pp. 151-170.

Vogel, Suzanne H. (1978), "Professional housewife: The career of urban middle class Japanese women," **The Japan Interpreter,** XII, pp. 16-43.

Zito, Jacqueline M. (1974), "Anonymity and neighboring in an urban, high-rise complex," **Urban Life and Culture,** 3, pp. 243-63.

Reprinted with permission from **Ekistics** 310, Jan./Feb., 1985, pp. 34-44.

8 Housing type and the residential experience of middle-class mothers

ALAN BOOTH and HARVEY CHOLDIN

Low-density suburban housing is thought to reduce women's access to jobs, childcare, and other community services and facilities. High-density housing is often proposed as a solution. We explore possible effects of high-density housing on women. Using interview data from an urban sample of 561 white middle-class women with dependent children, the residential experiences of single-family dwelling inhabitants are compared with those living in townhouses. duplexes, and apartments. Only apartment dwellings seem to have adverse effects. To explain the link between apartment residence and the quality of women's residential experience we examine four intervening variables: the respondents' floor level, the number of residential units in their building or complex, whether or not community facilities exist on the premises, and preference for other housing types. A multivariate analysis reveals that each of the intervening mechanisms associated with apartment living has one or more adverse effects. People who live on higher floors communicate less with their neighbors, but people on the lower floors are more troubled by noise. People in larger complexes seem to be less integrated in their neighborhood and to have more noise problems. Community facilities create noise which is bothersome; at the same time they do not seem to facilitate neighborhood interaction. Finally, the apartment dweller's preference for another housing type seems to affect all aspects of the quality of neighborhood life studied.

W omen's increasing self awareness, rising expectations and changing roles have led to a reexamination of various aspects of home, neighborhood, and their effect on women. Some investigations have focused on the interior design of the home (e.g., Jeth, 1976). Others have been concerned with effects of density and land use (e.g., Hapgood and Getzels, 1974). Most observers agree that suburban low-density housing has been costly for women. The segregated land use and absence of services has limited women's access to childcare facilities, jobs, friends, educational opportunities, healthcare, governmental services, housekeeping and maintenance assistance, as well as cultural events and recreational facilities (Palm and Pred, 1977; Lapata, 1980). Excellent reviews of this work include Wekerle (1980), and Fava (1980).

With the rising demand for inexpensive housing, high-density housing is now making substantial inroads into suburban areas. More than one-third of the existing suburban housing stock is multiple-family dwellings (U.S. Bureau of the Census, 1982). As a result, land use is becoming less segregated and services more abundant. While these trends should be less costly for women, the fact remains that our knowledge about the effects of multiple-dwelling habitation on women is limited (van Vliet, 1983).

The women and housing literature tends not to mention possible drawbacks of multiple dwelling residence. In a recent study by Edwards et al., (1982) women in high-density residence were more likely to feel a lack of privacy and report marital discord than those in single-family dwellings. While these were modest effects, they do suggest that there may be trade-offs in moving into high-density housing. Also, in the literature there is a tendency to view multiple dwellings as a single category of residence type. However, they are not. Townhouses, duplexes, and apartments may have quite different impacts on their inhabitants.

In this study, we examine a few of the possible costs of multiple-dwelling residence in a sample of Chicago women with children. Specifically, we examine the frequency and quality of neighborhood interaction, noise problems, and overall satisfaction with the neighborhood. First, we compare various types of multiple dwellings and single-family dwellings to see whether any negative effects are selective or apply to all multiple dwellings alike.

This analysis is followed by an examination of the possible causes of any adverse effects found. Booth (in press) has proposed that the adverse effects of multifamily housing may be due to four particular variables:

(1) the floor level on which the dwelling was located;
(2) the number of residential units in the building or complex;
(3) whether or not community facilities exist on the premises; and
(4) preference for a housing type other than a multiple dwelling.

We examine how apartment living affects neighboring, recognition of noise problems, and neighborhood satisfaction and, further, whether the aforementioned variables explain any of the relationships we find.

Why these four variables? In considering this question we need to keep in mind that women invest more labor in the home, spend more time there, and receive more satisfaction from the home setting than do men (Saegert and Winkel, 1980). Moreover, they are more likely than men to interact with neighbors and have primary responsibility for childcare and supervision. These differences in role behavior occur whether or not women are in the paid labor force. Thus, home environment characteristics such as floor level, number of units, presence of community facilities, and housing preferences have special meaning to women.

For example, it is more difficult to supervise small children from several stories up than from the ground floor which may lead to dissatisfaction. In addition, persons living on higher floors are more likely to share floor, ceiling, and walls with neighbors. This increases the likelihood of being disturbed by noise as well as irritating the neighbors with one's own clatter. Such factors may increase neighborhood friction and lead to a decline in neighborly relations.[1] On the other hand, the proximity of households enhances opportunities for contact with neighbors which, in turn, could stimulate integration and mutual aid.

The number of units in the building potentially influences the number of people with whom a mother interacts. While such contacts may be socially enriching, they may also lead to excessive stimulation (cf. Milgram, 1970; Simmel, 1950). In response to excessive stimulation, women may engage in activities that limit interaction and thereby decrease the quality of neighborhood relations. Again, women could be especially affected. In addition, the larger number of units could create more occasions for neighbors to annoy one another with noise, and, thereby lower people's satisfaction with the quality of neighborhood relations.

The availability of community areas such as play areas and recreation facilities may be substitutes for amenities the single-family dwelling resident enjoys; thus, their absence may be a source of frustration that lowers people's evaluation of their environs. In addition, access to community areas may facilitate social interaction and thereby enhance neighborhood relations. On the other hand, such areas could be a source of noise that lowers the quality of neighborhood interaction.

Michelson (1977:377) has shown that people in households with a particular composition and lifestyle prefer particular types of housing. He found, for example, that most intact families with dependent children prefer single-family dwellings. Michelson (1977:273-302) also demonstrated that when actual conditions depart from personal preferences, dissatisfaction resulted (except when there was the prospect of moving in the near future to the preferred dwelling). We propose that people residing in multiple dwellings are much less likely to be living in the housing they prefer and that this will cause them to be less sanguine about their neighborhood environment, even to the point of diminishing the quality of neighborly relations.

Our basic hypothesis is that apartments and other multiple dwellings, compared to single-family dwellings, have qualities that diminish neighborhood relations and lower evaluation of the neighborhood as a place in which to live. These qualities are: residence on a higher floor, numerous units, the absence of community areas, and residence in a nonpreferred housing type.

We use multivariate techniques on interview data from a Chicago-area sample of women with children. We examine the extent to which each quality of multiple-family structure explains any relationships we observe between type of residence and diminished neighborhood involvement and satisfaction.

DATA

SAMPLE

The source of information for the analysis is a sample of 561 telephone interviewed mothers with dependent children residing in the Chicago metropolitan area. Somewhat over half the sampled households were in suburbs, the rest were in an "outer city," residential area. The sample was predominantly middle-class, all female, white, and all households had children. With 54 percent of the households in multiple-unit structures and 46 percent in single-family detached houses, the sample design maximized the analytical opportunity to examine differences by type of residence.

VARIABLES

The following analysis examines the relationship between living in a multiple-unit structure (as an independent variable) and neighboring, problems with noise, and expressing neighborhood satisfaction (as dependent variables). Four specific properties of multiple-unit structures will be posited as intervening variables.

To tap the quality of neighborhood relations, two questions were asked: "How often do you chat with your neighbors? Is it often, sometimes, seldom, or never?" And "How often do you exchange things like tools, recipes, etc.? Is it often, sometimes, seldom, or never?" Those selecting the "often" category were coded 1, all others 0.

101

To assess constraints imposed by noise we asked: "When you're at home, how often are you bothered by too much noise from the neighbors; often, sometimes, seldom, or never?"; and "How often do you feel that you can't do something that you want to do because it might disturb the neighbors; often, sometimes, seldom, or never?" Again the "often" response was coded 1, the others 0.

To measure satisfaction we asked: "In general, how satisfied are you with your neighborhood?" "Are you very satisfied, satisfied, not very satisfied, or not at all satisfied?" Those responding very satisfied or satisfied were coded 1, all others 0.

INTERVENING VARIABLES

Respondents lived in basement apartments and on each floor up to those on the sixth floor. Basement apartment dwellers were recorded as living on the first floor. Those living in single-family dwellings were also coded in this way. The number of apartment units ranged from three to 120. Single-family dwelling residents were coded as one unit. Because of their distributional properties, both floor level and number of units were recoded with log transformations, but as the results were the same, we show the effect of the unlogged measures. The presence of community areas was a dummy variable in which those having a play area for children were coded 1. Single-family dwellings were assigned a code of 0 in this variable. To assess housing preference, respondents were asked: "Would you prefer to live in a single family house, an apartment, or something else?" Their preference was compared with the type of dwelling in which they lived. If they were residing in something other than their preference, they were coded 1, otherwise 0.

CONTROL VARIABLES

Because both stage in the life cycle and socioeconomic status could affect both the independent and the intervening variables, age and education were statistically controlled throughout the analysis.

ANALYSIS AND FINDINGS

HOUSING TYPE AND QUALITY OF NEIGHBORHOOD LIFE

We began our analysis using Multiple Classification Analysis (Andrews et al., 1976) to examine the impact of housing type on the dependent variables. The dependent variable means are calculated for each of four housing types: single-family, duplex, apartment, and townhouse, while controlling for the age and education of the woman. Mobile homes and other living arrangements were omitted from the analysis due to the small number of cases.

The proportions shown in Table 1 indicate that the residential life is consistently poorer for mothers in apartments on all variables; the exception was women living in duplexes, who report lower levels of interaction with neighbors then those living in apartments. The quality of life for townhouse residents seems to be very similar to that of single-family dwelling residents, with one exception: the latter are more likely to be bothered by noise from neighbors. Thus, these data confirm the earlier findings that some aspects of multiple-dwelling residence are stressfull to inhabitants. It should be noted that the effects of multiple-dwelling residence on residential life are modest; the differences among types of dwellings rarely exceed 20 percentage points.

Table 1. Type of Housing and Quality of Neighborhood Life[1]

Selected Residential Experiences	Detached Single Family	Duplex	Apartment	Townhouse	Significance Level Using F Test
Chat with their neighbors often	53%	43%	41%	56%	.07
Often exchange things with their neighbors	27	13	20	25	.04
Bothered by too much noise from their neighbors	45	38	63	55	.01
Often feel they can't do things because they might disturb their neighbors	42	45	64	42	.01
Satisfied with neighborhood	89	92	79	87	.03
N	257	100	117	73	

[1]Adjusted for age and education of respondent.

Half of the women in the sample were in the labor force. As employed mothers spend less time in the home and may prefer the amenities that go with high-density housing, it is possible that labor force participation might influence the relationships found. Employment status was added to the equations and we checked for possible interactions. Only one interaction was found. Townhouse women not in the labor force tended to be less satisfied with their neighborhood ($p < .03$). Perhaps the noise problem associated with townhouse residence noted above produces more stress among those who are at home for extended periods. This stress may be translated into lower levels of satisfaction with the neighborhood. Further research is needed to establish the exact mediating process at work.

Because suburbs are thought to be especially problematic for women, we added a variable to the analysis reflecting the outer city-suburban residence dimension of the sample. No significant interactions were found. Thus, suburban residence did not enhance or decrease any of the adverse effects of multiple-dwelling residence observed in our sample.

POTENTIAL CAUSES OF LOWER QUALITY NEIGHBORHOOD LIFE

We turn now to the characteristics of multiple-dwelling residence that may account for the adverse influence of apartment residence. We omitted duplex and townhouse residents because we had only limited information on the intervening variables for them. Apartment residents were coded 1, single-family unit dwellers 0. Path analysis was used to assess the extent to which the effect of housing type on the dependent variables could be reduced by floor level, number of units, community area, and housing preference.

The mode of analysis is represented diagramatically in Figure 1 and draws on procedures developed by Alwin and Hauser (1975). The basic relationship between the independent and dependent variable is shown in Panel A where the unstandardized

103

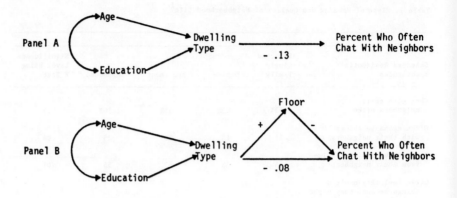

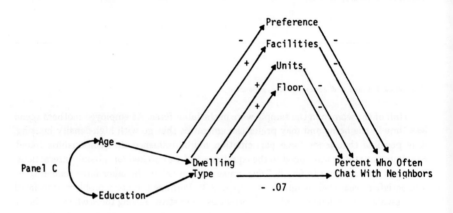

Figure 1. Illustrative Path Model for Dwelling Type-Quality of
Neighborhood Life Analysis.

regression coefficient −.13 represents the relationship between dwelling type and percent who often chat with their neighbors after controlling for age and education. Column I of Table 2 contains this and the other coefficients reflecting the relation between dwelling type and the dependent variables.

Panel B of Figure 1 shows the model when an intervening variable is added to the equation. In this illustration, when floor level is added to the equation, the direct effect of dwelling type on percent who often chat with their neighbors is reduced to −.08 after controlling for age and education. The unstandardized coefficients representing the relationship between dwelling type and the dependent variables after each intervening variable is added to the equation are shown in Column II-V in Table 2.

Finally, Panel C of Figure 1 shows the model when all of the intervening variables are added to the equation at the same time. In this illustration, when floor level, number of units, community areas and preference are in the equation, the direct effect of dwelling type on percent who often chat with their neighbors is −.07 after controlling for age and education. The unstandardized coefficients representing the relationship between dwelling

TABLE 2

Unstandardized Regression Coefficients Showing Relation Between Type of Dwelling and Dependent Variables Before and After Intervening Variables Are Included in the Equations.

	I	II	III	IV	V	VI
		Effect of Living In An Apartment After Controlling For				
	Effect of Living in an Apartment[1]	Floor Level[2]	Number of Units[2]	Living in a Complex with a Community Facility[2]	Preferring To Reside In Some Other Type Of Dwelling[2]	Effect of Living in an Apartment, Controlling For All Intervening Variables[3]
Percent who chat with their neighbors often	-.13*	-.08	-.07	-.08	-.18	-.07
Percent who often exchange things with their neighbors	-.10*	-.07	-.09	-.09	-.01	.01
Percent who are bothered by too much noise from neighbors	.17*	.27*	.12	.07	-.18	-.12
Percent who can't do things because they might disturb neighbors	.22*	.27*	.17*	.17*	.07	.08
Percent who are satisfied with their neighborhood	-.10*	-.10*	-.01	-.06	-.05	-.02

N = 358

*Significant at .05 level

[1] Direct effect of housing type after controlling for age and education.

[2] Direct effect of housing type after controlling for intervening variable, age and education.

[3] Direct effect of housing type after controlling for floor, units, facilities, preference, age and education.

type and the dependent variables when all of the intervening variables are included in the equation are shown in Column VI of Table 2. We now consider the results for each intervening variable in turn.

Floor Level. It is evident that floor level is one aspect of apartment dwelling which explains lower levels of communication with neighbors. Women/mothers living on higher floors are less likely to chat with or exchange things with others in the vicinity. Floor level suppresses the relationships between dwelling type and being bothered by neighbor's noise and constraining one's activities so as not to disturb neighbors. Those who live on the lower floor find noise to be more of a problem.[2] Further analysis using MCA reveals, however, that those living on higher floors still have significantly greater noise problems than single-family dwelling residents. Interestingly, floor level has no effect on the relationship between dwelling type and one's overall satisfaction with the neighborhood; perhaps because the social interaction and noise factors balance each other.

Number of Units. The number of units in the building or complex has the same impact as floor level on women's neighboring behavior. Women who reside in larger buildings or complexes are less likely to chat with neighbors.[3] Size of building or complex has minimal effect on exchanging things, though. The number of units is, however, a factor in explaining noise constraints. The impact of number of units on overall neighborhood satisfaction appears to be somewhat greater than that of floor level.

Presence of Community Facilities. This intervening variable seems to have the greatest effect upon chatting with neighbors and being bothered by noise. Overall, the indirect path coefficients indicate that the presence of community facilities generally lowers the quality of neighborhood life rather than enhancing it. This is contrary to the proposal by Hayden (1980) and others that community facilities enhance the lives of female inhabitants. However, studies of community facilities other than play space would need to be examined before treating our finding as more than tentative. Moreover, such studies should also take into account the actual design of the facility, not merely its presence.

Preference for Another Dwelling Type. Preference for another dwelling has a slight (but not statistically significant) suppressor effect on the relationship between apartment dwelling and the frequency with which residents chat with neighbors. That is, mothers living in nonpreferred housing seem to do more chatting with neighbors. Perhaps they talk to their neighbors about their unhappiness. The remainder of the indirect effects are in the expected direction — reducing the quality of women's residential experiences. Preference for another type of dwelling reduces the relation between dwelling type and exchanging things with neighbors, worrying about disturbing the neighbors, and overall satisfaction.

Overall Indirect Effect. As can be seen from the last column in Table 2, the intervening variables together reduce the relationship between dwelling type and quality of neighborhood life to nonsignificant and, for the most part, minuscule relationships.

It is of interest to explore the impact maternal employment might have in these relationships. Separate analyses of the intervening mechanisms for those in the labor force and those who are not were undertaken. No systematic difference was revealed.

There is a possibility that mechanisms other than the ones we considered could account for some of the negative effects of apartment living. These include neighborhood heterogeneity and whether residents own or rent their homes. We were able to examine the effect of neighborhood heterogeneity with two questions: "Would you say that most of the people in (name of neighborhood) are about the same age, somewhat different in age, or very different in age?" There was little difference in the responses given by single-family and apartment dwellers so that homogeneity could be discounted as a factor.

106

Homeownership occurred so infrequently among the apartment dwellers in the sample that we were unable to test its effect.

CONCLUSION

It is clear from our analysis that apartments, but not other types of multiple dwellings, adversely affect some aspects of the quality of women's residential experience. It is also evident that each of the intervening mechanisms accounts for one or more of the modest adverse effects of apartment living. Women who lived on higher floors communicated less with their neighbors, but people on the lower floors were more troubled by noise. Women in larger complexes seemed to communicate less with neighbors and to have more noise problems. Community facilities (at least in the form of play areas) created bothersome noise without facilitating neighborhood interaction. Finally, preference for another type of residence seems to affect all aspects of the quality of neighborhood life. In short, floor level, number of units, community facilities, and dwelling preference appear to account for nearly all of the above effects.

Results from this study suggest that while high-density housing may increase women's access to jobs, childcare, and other opportunities, those who reside in apartments may encounter certain costs. Interactions with neighbors are depressed, noise becomes a problem, and many women would prefer to live in some other type of dwelling. While the costs are modest, they impinge on important behavioral roles such as neighboring and childcare.

It should be noted that while our study pinpoints the features of apartments that contribute to a lower quality of neighborhood life, we are not able to identify the mechanism at work in great detail. For example, we have no way of knowing whether the mothers in our study who resided on the higher floors had more difficulty supervising their children which in turn lowered their satisfaction with the neighborhood. When the evidence from other studies is combined with our results, such a mechanism is plausible. But further research is needed to detail the precise mechanism at work.

The present study also has implications for planning and design. Specifically, the results indicate to planners, architects, and builders:

(1) that within multiparty structures, effective soundproofing must be a high priority item toward livability;
(2) that low-rise buildings are more likely than tall ones to promote high levels of neighboring;
(3) that smaller structures or projects are more likely to promote neighboring and satisfaction.

The fourth intervening variable, housing type preference, does not translate into a policy suggestion. Americans are not likely to be persuaded or otherwise induced to abandon their traditional preference for their own house and yard.

NOTES

1. Adverse effects of floor level such as these have been observed by others (c.f., Gillis, 1977; Mitchell, 1971).

2. This finding is consistent with the research of Cohen et al., (1973) who find that juvenile residents on the lower floors of high rise buildings show auditory impairment and lower reading achievement. They attribute this to noise from nearby expressways rather than sounds coming from neighbors.

3. The effect of the number of units on depressing neighborhood interaction has also been noted by Newman (1972).

REFERENCES

Alwin, D., and R. Hauser
1975   "The decomposition of effects in path analysis." American Sociological Review 40:37-47.
Andrews, F., J. Morgan, J. Sonquist, and L. Klem
1976   Multiple Classification Analysis. Ann Arbor, Michigan. The University of Michigan Institute for Social Research.
Booth, A.
Forth-   "Quality of children's family interaction in
coming   relation to residential type and household crowding. In J. Wohlwill and W. van Vliet (eds.), Habitats for Children: The Impacts of Density. Hillsdale, New York: Erlbaum.
Cohen, S., D. Glass, and J. Singer
1973   "Apartment noise, auditory discrimination, and reading ability in children." Journal of Experimental Social Psychology 9:407-22.
Edwards, J., A. Booth, and P. Edwards.
1982   "Housing type, stress and family relations." Social Forces 61:241-57.
Fava, S.
1980   "Women's place in the new suburbia." Pp. 129-49 in G. Wekerle, R. Peterson, and D. Morley (eds.), New Space for Women. Boulder, Colorado: Westerview Press.
Gillis, A. R.
1977   "High-rise housing and psychological strain." Journal of Health and Social Behavior 18:418-31.
Hapgood, K., and J. Goetzels
1974   Planning; Women and Change. Washington, D.C.: American Society of Planning Officials.
Hayden, D.
1980   "What would a non-sexist city be like? Speculations on housing, urban design, and human work." Signs: Journal of Women in Culture and Society 5 (3, supplement) S170-87.
Jeth, N.
1976   "Kitchen planning and design." Unpublished paper.

Lopata, H. Z.
1980   "The Chicago Woman: A Study of Patterns of Mobility and Transportation." Signs: Journal of Women in Culture and Society 5 (3, Supplement) S161-69.
Michelson, W.
1977   Environmental Choice, Human Behavior, and Residential Satisfaction. New York: Oxford University Press.
Milgram, S.
1970   "The experience of living in cities." Science 167:1461-68.
Mitchell, R.
1971   "Some implications of high density housing." American Sociological Review 36:18-29.
Newman, O.
1972   Defensible Space. New York: Macmillan.
Palm, R., and A. Pred
1974   "A Time-Geographic Perspective on Problems of Inequality for Women." Working Paper no. 236, Institute of Urban and Regional Development, University of California, Berkeley.
Saegert, S., and G. Winkel
1980   "The home: A critical problem for changing sex roles." Pp. 41-63 in G. Wekerle, R. Peterson and D. Morley (eds.), New Space for Women. Boulder Colorado: Westview Press.
Simmel, G.
1950   "The metropolis in mental life." In R. Wolff (eds), Sociology of Georg Simmel. Glencoe, IL: Free Press.
U. S. Bureau of the Census
1982   Statistical Abstract of the United States: 1982-83. Washington, D.C.
van Vliet, W.
1983   "Families in apartment buildings: Sad stores for children?" Environment and Behavior 15:211-34.

Reprinted with permission from **Sociological Focus,** vol. 18, no. 2, pp. 97-107, 1985.

PART IV
PLANNING AND
DEVELOPMENT

9 Women plan London

BEVERLEY TAYLOR

One of the most contentious pieces of legislation proposed by the Thatcher government in 1984 was the abolition of the Greater London Council (GLC) under its controversial political leader, Ken Livingstone. If Mrs. Thatcher does succeed in wiping out this and other metropolitan councils in Britain, a number of progressive initiatives which have brightened an otherwise gloomy political scene will be lost. Among these will be the Women's Committees of some local councils and, with them, their financial and political support of women's organizations and issues.

Thanks to the efforts of feminists working within the Labour Party, many of the left-wing borough councils in London have recently set up these committees, which have been instrumental in making women's needs visible in a local government system dominated by male councillors, male officers and male ways of organizing and thinking.

The GLC Women's Committee was one of the first to emerge, in 1982, to be followed in a number of boroughs in London and elsewhere. It remains one of the largest, both in budget and staff; over 70 women now work in the Women's Committee Support Unit at the GLC. The Unit makes grants to women's groups and organizations throughout London for projects involving women's centres, infant daycare, toy libraries, safe transportation and health campaigns; it is involved in the promotion of equality for all women, including black and ethnic minorities, lesbians, women with disabilities, older women, girls; it is an information and campaigning resource, and it works with other GLC committees and departments -- housing, transport, planning, arts and recreation, and employment, to ensure that women's needs are recognized in all aspects of the Council's work.

Thanks to the GLC Women's Committee, the revised Greater London Development Plan (GLDP) -- the strategic plan for London -- includes a chapter on "Women in

109

London." For the first time in this country, women's issues have been explicitly recognized in a land use plan.

The chapter describes those concerns of women living in the capital that relate to strategic planning: employment and training, housing, mobility and access to services, recreation and child care. It outlines the objectives of the Plan with respect to women's needs, and suggests policies to address these issues.

THE WOMEN AND PLANNING WORKING GROUP

A key factor in introducing the chapter into the Plan was the innovative organizing undertaken by the Women's Committee. In an attempt to bridge the wide gap between the autonomous women's movement and the local state, women were co-opted into the Committee from open meetings, and Working Groups were set up to focus on particular issues, such as black women, women with disabilities, transport, employment, child care. One of these was the Women and Planning Working Group which brought together many women involved in different aspects of planning in London, through both community action and local government. The obvious focus for the group, which formed in August 1982, was the fact that the Planning Committee of the GLC was going ahead with revisions to the outdated GLDP.

Many of the professional planners within the GLC were skeptical at first about the relevance of women's issues to a strategic plan, claiming that they were not directly related to land use or that they were more relevant to local plans. But women were and are aware that the issues which concern them the most -- paid employment, child care, housing, transport and security -- all have major implications for the way in which land in our cities is used. As the GLC Plan now states: "Women in London live in a city designed by men for men and have had little opportunity to influence or shape the urban environment. Planning policies, in regulating the use of land in the public interest and recognising that women form the majority of this public, can go a long way towards changing this."

THE ISSUES

Women make up 52 per cent of London's population but are at a considerable disadvantage due to the unequal distribution of wealth, their poor access to resources and opportunities, their limited mobility and caring responsibilities.

Over 65 per cent of women in London are in paid work, yet their salaries are low and they continue to be segregated into a limited number of industries and occupations. Their jobs have been affected but cuts in public expenditure, the decline in manufacturing, and the introduction of new technology. Caring responsibilities and restricted mobility make many women reliant on jobs they can find close to home, jobs which tend to be badly paid, casual positions in non-unionized firms. Work-at-home is on the increase and there is a lack of training opportunities.

Women continue to bear most of the responsibility for the care of dependents -- not only children but also the sick and elderly and people with disabilities. This is largely unseen and unpaid work which greatly limits opportunities for paid work or other activities outside the home.

110

Women's access to housing is also extremely limited. Housing policies continue to focus on the needs of the nuclear family, and design of both public and private housing plays a major role in the reinforcement of the sexual division of labour and the isolation of women in the home. Many women need safe accommodation in order to escape domestic violence; poorer, often black, households fare the worst in the housing stakes.

Mobility is also restricted by low income, by women's care work, by inadequate public transport and fear of attack or harassment. Women depend on public services, but in many cases these are in a state of decline or are becoming centralized, making access inconvenient. In addition there is a lack both of child care facilities and of public places where women can meet.

A SEPARATE CHAPTER?

One of the major discussions in preparing the Plan was whether the issues outlined above should be in a separate "women's chapter." Some planners argued that it would be better to incorporate the issues of concern to women in other chapters of the Plan. Although the Working Group agreed that chapters on such topics as employment, housing, shopping and transport should also reflect women's needs, they felt that a separate chapter was vital to provide space for stating things on women's own terms rather than having to fit them into conventional planning topics. During the major public participation exercise which took place during the early months of 1984, the idea of a women's chapter was an effective way of attracting women into the participatory process and showing them how planning relates to their lives.

Public participation is a statutory requirement for the preparation of British "structure" or strategic plans but the GLC went beyond the minimum requirements and consulted many community groups and other interested organizations before the first draft of the Plan was finalized.

Major conferences were held on "The Future of London," where the Working Group circulated position papers; the participation of other Women's Committee Working Groups was also promoted. Specific steps were taken to encourage women to take part in the public consultation on the Draft Plan. A "Women Plan London" leaflet and free-post questionnaire were widely distributed, of which more than 600 were returned; an open meeting was attended by over 250 women. The excellent response convinced both planners and politicians that the issues raised in the proposed chapter had widespread support among women in London.

POLICIES

The response was invaluable for the final drafting of the "Women in London" chapter. Women felt that it should be strengthened by including more policies which the Boroughs would have to implement in their Local Plans. So the first of the Policies in the final Plan reads:

Policy Wom 1

...London Borough Councils must promote and improve opportunities for women in their areas by identifying the social and economic needs and problems of local women and formulate appropriate local plan policies to meet those needs.

Women particularly wanted more emphasis on the role of caring for dependents and on personal security, so two further policies were added:

Policy Wom 3

Local plans must frame appropriate policies for the provision of a full range of childcare facilities and facilities for other dependents which fully reflect local needs.

Policy Wom 4

London Borough Councils must take into account the personal security needs of women and the importance of creating an urban environment which is safe and secure for women to use at all times in drawing up local plans and when considering new developments in their areas.

The inclusion of a women's chapter is not the only innovative feature in the Plan, which also contains a chapter on Race Equality and Ethnic Minorities. The inclusion of the two chapters in the Draft Plan drew public attention to the planning needs of other groups in the population. As a result of public pressure the final Plan also contains chapters on people with disabilities and elderly people. The pressure to have a "women's" chapter has therefore also created an approach which recognizes that land use policies and decisions have an important impact on the distribution of opportunities and resources to different groups of the population. These chapters are now grouped under a section of the Plan entitled "Equality in London."

A WASTE OF TIME?

At the final stage of the plan-making process, the document is submitted to the Secretary of State for the Environment. A public enquiry is then held which may result in some modifications before the Plan is approved as a binding document. The Thatcher government has been doing its best to stop the revision of the GLDP, and the Local Government (Interim Provisions) Act was passed last year which absolved the Secretary of State from any responsibility to consider proposals submitted to him for the alteration of the GLDP or any other strategic metropolitan plans. Despite this, the Plan was submitted to the government by the GLC in September 1984.

Some skeptics argue that all the hard work involved in the revision of the GLDP has been a waste of time, since the new edition will never become a statutory document.

But the final outcome is not all that important because great gains have been made through the process itself. Valuable networks and contacts have been established and a group of women has learned a great deal about the issues they need to focus on and how to work together effectively. Women and planning issues have been raised at public consultation meetings and in publicity material. The very existence of the women's chapter in a "glossy" document like the Greater London Development Plan has given women's issues a great deal of credibility in planning circles. A precedent has been set for other authorities to follow and the GLC is now using the Plan when commenting on the local plans being prepared by the London boroughs.

Most important perhaps, the ideas set out in the chapter can provide women in London with a tool with which to campaign for changes in local plans and development taking place in their areas. However, local campaigns are likely to be effective only in certain boroughs; without a coordinated London planning strategy as put forward in the GLDP, these changes are likely to result in greater inequalities of opportunity in different parts of London. The abolition of the GLC would be a big step backward in planning for equality.

Reprinted with permission from **Women and Environments**, vol. 7, no. 2, pp. 4-6, 1985 (Subscriptions: $13/yr. outside N. America: $18. From: Women and Environments, Centre for Urban and Community Studies, 455 Spadina Ave., Toronto, Ontario M5S 2 G8, Canada).

10 Women and the man-made environment: The Dutch experience

JAN PENROSE

The earliest impetus for women's involvement in Dutch planning came from diverse women's organizations which lobbied for the formation of Women's Advisory Committees for Housing in the 1950s. Their efforts were successful in that such committees were actually established in municipalities but there were qualifiers: the positions were voluntary and members were appointed by the mayor and aldermen. This meant that women's input remained largely subjugated to the decisions of men. At this time, women's sphere of activity was effectively limited to the municipal level and to encouraging planners to incorporate the practical insights of women into the design and layout of housing.

It was not until 1975 that advances in the women's movement as a whole led to the establishment of an infrastructure which encouraged female involvement at all levels of planning. At this time, the national government formally recognized the widespread neglect of women's interests in Dutch society by setting up a Women's Emancipation Advisory Commission to assist in the creation and implementation of a coherent policy on women's emancipation. Two years later, the government appointed the first Undersecretary of State for Emancipation and established an Interdepartmental Coordination Committee responsible for ensuring that all ministries are involved in the preparation and promotion of women's emancipation policies. In addition, each ministry has its own emancipation committee which must integrate the broad objectives of women's emancipation policy into the department's specific field of activity. This means that the Ministry of Housing, Physical Planning and Environment, among others, must conduct its activities in accordance with the objectives of women's emancipation, which are currently: 1) redistribution of paid and unpaid work; 2) economic independence for women; and 3) combatting sexual violence.

By coordinating the activities of a whole range of women's interest groups and by providing them with the respectability of governmental support, the general emancipation policy has raised the profile of women's issues and stimulated the formation of additional organizations in specific fields. In physical planning and housing, such progress is evidenced by changes in the objectives of Women's Advisory Committees for Housing. Where their advice to planners initially focused on the pragmatic concerns of the housewife, their current input reflects the changing position of women in society. Their traditional interest in the design and layout of housing has expanded to include the environment of the home in a much broader sense. In 1983, these municipally-based committees were complemented by a National Foundation of Women, Building and Housing which sought to combine and coordinate incentives and to stimulate women's involvement in all areas of building and housing.

At the same time, a number of women working in physical planning and housing set up their own working party within the Netherlands Institute for Physical Planning and Housing. This professional organization has provided women who work in physical planning and housing with a forum for discussing their role in humanizing the man-made environment, for presenting concerted analyses of developments in their fields from the perspective of the female user, and for promoting new ideas about the layout of the home and its environment. The very existence of this kind of group is indicative of women's growing involvement at decision-making levels. However, the fact that it is perceived as necessary suggests that formal channels have not been effective enough in implementing the objectives of women's emancipation policy.

This latter suggestion is borne out by practical experience. Since the 1970s, advances within the women's movement have helped to structure and, thereby, strengthen support for women's interests in the fields of planning and housing, but women's actual involvement in these fields has remained overwhelmingly responsive or ameliorative rather than initiatory. Two examples should illustrate the tendency for planning in the Netherlands to circumvent women's interests and to minimize their professional influence. At the same time, these examples show how a strong emancipation policy has lent structure to efforts to alter the existing man-made environment.

The first example is Bijlmermeer, a massive high-rise housing project of the 1960s located on the outskirts of Amsterdam. At the time of its inception, planning policies were based on the strict division of land use and Bijlmermeer was specifically designed to fulfill an urgent need for housing. In retrospect it seems to have been designed with the intention of keeping women in their place. The lack of local employment opportunities, a paucity of day-care facilities and a public transportation system which catered to the needs of people who worked full-time in Amsterdam, reinforced the traditional male/female distribution of paid and unpaid work. This set-up effectively precluded greater economic independence for women. In addition, the physical layout of this residential area, while aesthetically interesting from a distance, was dangerous to walk through. The net result was a further reinforcement of women's isolation.

By the time an emancipation policy was introduced, Bijlmermeer had acquired a deeply entrenched reputation as an unattractive place to live. Although the units themselves were well designed, the surrounding environment was viewed as dangerous and undesirable and the area came to be dominated by those who were already marginalized in Dutch society, particularly immigrants and the unemployed. Women's committees were not involved in the initial planning of Bijlmermeer but local women's groups have since played an active role in efforts to reverse the cyclical degradation of their neighbourhood.

These efforts began with improvements in safety. Public open spaces were better maintained and brush was cleared away from the sides of walking and cycling paths. An enormous, central parking garage -- the scene of much violence -- was partially destroyed. To reduce problems of orientation, building entrances were clearly demarcated with colour and all obstructions were removed. Accessibility was further enhanced by the addition of exterior elevators which created alternate entrances and eliminated long walks through enclosed public galleries. Finally, intercom systems and locks were installed in entrances to improve security in the buildings themselves.

The creation of a safer environment has helped to ease women's isolation in Bijlmermeer but the problems of female restriction to unpaid domestic labour and, consequently, economic dependence have been more difficult to address. Although local improvements in day-care and public transportation have granted women greater freedom, the cost -- in both time and money -- of travelling to work, continues to discourage female participation in paid employment; these disincentives are even more prohibitive for women seeking part-time jobs.

Although there are currently no employment opportunities within the residential area, ongoing changes suggest a brighter future for the women of Bijlmermeer. In the first place, their neighbourhood lies close to a large industrial area which continues to attract new businesses. Second, the central area of Bijlmermeer is in the process of being built up with offices and a large shopping centre. The prospects for employment which these developments present suggest that women will gradually acquire access not just to jobs, but jobs that cover a full range of skill requirements and, hence, prestige. Where easy access is important to those trying to combine domestic and paid work, the qualitative aspect is important in righting the traditional imbalance between male and female employment.

Experiences associated with Bijlmermeer clearly indicate the difficulty of adapting man-made environments to the changing needs of women. The case of Almere, a new town 20 kilometers to the east of Amsterdam, offered the unusual possibility of incorporating women's interests into all phases of planning. Here was a chance for women to play an initiatory role, but while the land was empty and new it was destined to comply with policies that were old and established, and man-made. Despite remarkable advances in emancipation, women's organizations did not participate in the planning of Almere.

Although women's organizations could be ignored, planners were compelled to incorporate the goals of Dutch emancipation policy into their plans for Almere. This, combined with changes in the basic objectives of planning in the Netherlands, meant that Almere avoided some of the problems which had characterized Bijlmermeer. However, it also meant that women's role in planning the built environment remained largely reactive.

The most dramatic difference between Almere and earlier planning projects is an urban concept which advocates the mixing of land uses and which actively promotes easy accessibility to a wide range of facilities and services. By locating small industrial estates among residential areas and by integrating commercial units with houses (in a one to seventy ratio), planners have attempted to address the two main economic goals of emancipation policy: to provide local employment opportunities, both in industry and in neighbourhood-based shops and services, and to facilitate female participation in the paid labour force, thereby permitting greater economic independence. This organization of space also reduces the time and complexity of performing necessary domestic functions. Although this does not guarantee a redistribution of paid and unpaid labour, it does make such a redistribution possible by altering some of the spatial constructs which have traditionally reinforced the status quo.

The mixing of urban functions has also helped to fulfill the third objective of emancipation policy by eliminating some situations which are conducive to sexual violence. Most obviously, it has reduced the tendency for certain areas to be deserted at predictable times of the day. Additional efforts to make the environment safe for women include the location of dwellings on the ground floor of building blocks, the absence of tall bushes between sidewalks and roads or cycling paths, and the location of bus stops such that 75 percent of all homes in Almere are within 400 meters of a stop.

While the planning of Almere reflects a growing awareness of women's needs, significant problems remain. The fact that 65 percent of the population is employed outside of Almere perpetuates time/distance constraints that subtly reinforce traditional divisions of labour; it is usually men who do high prestige work in Amsterdam, and it is women who are the intended beneficiaries of planning that facilitates the combination of local employment with domestic duties. The subtle perpetuation of long-standing spatial constraints is also evident in the fact that over 80 percent of Almere's houses are designed for traditional nuclear families even though less than half of 11 Dutch households have retained this form. This situation demonstrates that the needs of the growing number of women who have modified their traditional roles as wives and mothers continue to be ignored. It also illustrates the continued prominence of male perceptions of how society, and the space in which it functions, should be organized.

Reprinted with permission from **Women and Environments**, vol. 9, no. 1, pp. 12-14, 1987 (Subscriptions: $13/yr. outside N. America: $18. From: Women and Environments, Centre for Urban and Community Studies, 455 Spadina Ave., Toronto, Ontario M5S 2G8, Canada).

11 Women and local economic development

VICTORIA WINCKLER

Recent industrial reorganisation has resulted in many local authorities adopting local economic initiatives. However, on the whole these have not recognised a major element within reorganisation, namely the changing sexual composition of employment. This paper argues that, in focusing on land development policies without explicitly recognising women's employment needs, women's labour market disadvantages can be perpetuated. In order to include women's employment within local economic initiatives they need to move towards a more innovatory approach, centred on employment rather than land. The paper concludes by looking at several ways in which this can be done.

The massive reorganisation of the economy and employment which has taken place nationally and internationally in recent years has also restructured the local economies of many areas of Britain. The problems they now face, coupled with a retrenchment in central government regional policy, have meant that almost all local authorities now adopt some form of local economic intervention.[1]

Economic reorganisation has at the same time involved changes in the gender composition of local employment, so that women are coming to play an increasingly important role in the local formal economy. It is, however, a role which is both distinctive to that of men and, perhaps more importantly, disadvantaged relative to men.

Although the extent of intervention in the local economy and the forms that it takes are varied indeed,[2] few agencies or authorities have explicitly recognised either the new significance of women's employment or the problems women face both in and out of the labour market. This is because local economic development is traditionally concerned with development per se, using measures which are based on land and property rather than on employment and people. Often the lack of explicit attention to women's employment needs means that it is the needs of men workers which are catered for. As a result, much economic development work is at best insensitive to women's needs and, at worst, reinforces inequalities between the sexes. In so doing, it can also jeopardise its own legitimacy and success.

The paper starts by outlining recent changes in women's employment in Britain, and then goes on to examine how 'mainstream' local economic development policies have not recognised women's particular employment situation, drawing on examples from Wales where the sexual composition of employment has changed very rapidly and where there has also been a long history of economic development work by a variety of agencies. The final section demonstrates how both land-based and people-based measures can be made more sensitive to women's employment, drawing in particular on the work of those local authorities which have begun to take gender bias seriously.

119

Women and employment in Britain

The ways in which economic restructuring has changed the structure of local labour markets in Britain in general, and in their sexual composition in particular, are without doubt very complex and are the subject of much recent and continuing research.[3] What is clear from this, nevertheless, is that industries and services have reorganised in ways which take account of existing gender differences, both at home and at work. The aggregate effect of this over the last twenty years has been the widespread entry of women into waged work, whilst male employment has declined.

Specifically, industrial reorganisation has been built around the domestic division of labour, that is the separation of the tasks of caring for dependants and of domestic labour, and their allocation to women, from participation in the formal economy in order to maintain the household, allocated to men. This division of labour colours women's experiences of employment and their place within it. As women come into the labour market, they do so under different conditions from men.[4] Young women are not expected to remain in employment for long, and women's responsibilities for dependants—children and elderly relatives—is a major constraint on the kinds of paid work available to them. The vast majority of women still take a break from paid work for child-rearing, and the presence of children, especially the age of the youngest child, has been found to be the key predictor of women's economic activity.[5]

When women eventually return to the labour market, they find themselves with few recognised or marketable skills, little recent experience of work and with the range of job opportunities open to them constrained by their domestic commitments. The nature of a job, the hours women are able to work, and the location of jobs they can take are limited by their place in the domestic division of labour. For example, a recent survey, the 1980 *Women and Employment Survey*, found that women returning to work after childbirth frequently did so to a lower grade job, especially if they worked part-time.[6] Women returning to work have done so, therefore, as a captive workforce, and one on which employers have increasingly drawn to fill jobs. This has been most marked in the labour-intensive service sector, where women, along with ethnic minorities, have been used as a cheap, flexible and often part-time labour force. It is estimated that women have taken nine out of ten new service sector jobs in recent years, with roughly half of these being part-time.[7] Some manufacturing industries have also drawn on women workers in this way, sometimes, along with some services, moving to the peripheral regions of Britain in order to do so.[8]

However, the division of labour between the sexes is not just confined to the domestic sphere. There are substantial sexual divisions within employment, and these too are an important means of creating and reproducing sexual inequality. The stereotyping of some jobs as 'men's' and others as 'women's', often instigated by employers with trade union and workers' agreement, is central to this.[9] This is reinforced by differences in the conditions of employment in 'men's' and 'women's' work, particularly pay, whilst discrimination against women in recruitment and promotion, both overt and indirect and though illegal still endemic, along with unequal access to training, make it difficult for women to break out of traditional female activities. Young women are less likely to get technical and scientific qualifications, and women are also less likely to be released for training by their employer in working time.[10]

The effects of all these processes are evident both nationally and locally in the increased importance of women's employment coupled with its distinctive location within the economy. In March 1985 women comprised 44 per cent of the British workforce, compared with 36 per cent twenty years previously.[11] In some parts of Britain this figure is higher, not so much because of the expansion of women's employment as the collapse of men's. In Wales, for instance, there is the interesting paradox that, such has been the decline of men's employment since 1980, with the loss of jobs in male-dominated coal, steel and heavy engineering, women are predicted to be the majority of the workforce in Wales by 1990; yet women in Wales are *less* likely to be economically active than women in any other region of Britain.[12] Nevertheless, for Welsh women, as for all British women, waged work is now the norm rather than the exception. The majority of all women of working age were economically active (65 per cent), and for women aged 16–19 and 40–49 over 75 per cent are economically active.[13] Even in the age group where women are least likely to have paid work, the child-bearing and rearing years of 25–29, over half, 54 per cent, are economically active. A very high proportion of women return to work after a break for child-bearing, sometimes returning in between births, and women are also returning to work sooner after childbirth than previously. Women can now expect to be in employment for approximately two-thirds of their working lives.[14]

Women's earnings are essential to many households. Far from earning 'pin-money', a recent survey found that the loss of women's earnings would cause considerable hardship in 60 per cent of households surveyed.[15] Women's earnings can play an important role in the wider local economy also, keeping many households above the poverty line. In Wales it has been estimated that 'second incomes' play a major role in alleviating the region's poverty.[16] Moreover, a growing number of households do not have a male 'breadwinner', either because he is unemployed or in the increasing number of single-person and single-parent households. In 1979 there were nearly three-quarters of a million female-headed single-parent households in Britain.[17] And finally, if a woman wants to work then surely she is entitled to do so in the same way as the vast majority of men, regardless of whether or not her income is considered to be essential to the household. Paid work is thus an integral part of women's lives, of women's households, and of the local economy.

However, women occupy a distinctive place within that economy. Firstly, it is one of concentration and segregation within particular industries and occupations. Over three-quarters of all working women work in the service sector, compared with less than half of all working men. Even within services, women are concentrated into retailing, public services and the various consumer services, with these providing almost two-thirds of *all* women's jobs. This concentration can be even greater within local economies. In Wales 38 per cent of women are in education, health and national and local government, compared with 31 per cent in the south east of England.[18] Similarly, whilst manufacturing only accounts for 17 per cent of all women's jobs, half of these are in electronics and electrical engineering, textiles, clothing and footwear, and the food, drink and tobacco industries, compared with a quarter of men's manufacturing employment.[19]

Women are also confined within industries to the bottom of the occupational hierarchy. For example, 73 per cent of clerks and typists are women, compared with only 21 per cent of office administrators and managers.[20] It is still exceptionally difficult for women to break out of these areas—despite the occasional headline about the first woman to penetrate another male preserve:

half of all women work in areas in which they are greatly over-represented (at 70 per cent or more of the workforce), with this concentration of women into 'women's work' *increasing* this century.[21]

Secondly, women's pay and conditions of employment are typically inferior to those of men. Both women's hourly earnings and total earnings are well below men's, with total female full-time earnings being only 64 per cent of male earnings.[22] Women workers are less likely to have the same conditions of employment as other workers, such as holiday entitlement and sick pay, and are also less likely to have trade union protection.[23]

Thirdly, in order to combine waged work with their domestic responsibilities, 46 per cent of all women work part-time, that is less than thirty hours a week, with many more working on a casual basis. Amongst women in the peak child-rearing years of 25–29, this proportion rises to 77 per cent.[24] The problem with part-time working is not the hours worked in themselves, but the pay and conditions which accompany them. Part-time workers experience the lowest pay, the poorest conditions, and the least protection of almost any other group of workers.[25]

Fourthly, although there are many more women in waged work than previously, women also face increasing unemployment. Women's unemployment is especially problematic because it is readily hidden, both in statistics and in policy-making. The under-representation of women in a wide range of employment statistics has already been documented,[26] but there are special difficulties in using unemploy-ment statistics for women. Currently, to appear in the British unemployment statistics, an individual must not only register with the local unemployment office and declare that he or she is both willing to work and is available for work, but, since November 1982, must also be in receipt of benefit. This definition of unemployment excludes some women who are nevertheless actively seeking work. Many women, particularly with children, are discouraged from registering as unemployed if they are not entitled to any benefit, since they perceive no advantages in so doing. Even those women who do actually register as unemployed do not appear in the unemployment statistics if they live with an earning male partner and so do not get benefit. There is the further hurdle also in that women with children who wish to register as unemployed have to demonstrate their availability for work by showing that they have adequate child care arrangements.[27]

All this amounts to a substantial under-representation of women in official unemployment statistics. The 1980 *Women and Employment Survey* found that only 54 per cent of women who were unemployed (using the survey's definition) were registered as such.[28] This means that studies of the local economy which rely on official estimates of unemployment understate·the extent of female unemploy-ment. For example, in December 1983 there were 7183 females registered as unemployed in the Cardiff travel to work area compared with 20 892 males.[29] But if these registered females represent only half of all women who are actually looking for a job and would take one, then the figures for male and female unemployment are much closer.

In addition, women's unemployment is hidden by their domestic role, with unregistered unemployed women often being seen as, and indeed seeing themselves as, primarily 'housewives', yet who would be prepared to take a job if one was available.[30] Again, the *Women and Employment Survey* found that of the 35 per cent of women classified as economically inactive, 20 per cent were looking for work, and a further 44 per cent were planning to return to work in the next five years.[31] In other words, nearly two-thirds of those supposedly out of the labour market were, using a wider definition, found to be part of it. Female unemployment is therefore a considerable problem, and one which tends to be underestimated.

The economic reorganisation of the economy in the last two decades has resulted in an expansion in female employment, based upon the sexual division of labour between home and work and within work itself. Women's place in the local economy is a distinctive one, one in which in almost all respects women are disadvantaged. Initiatives aimed at developing the local economy have not however recognised either the extent and significance of women's employment or the specific problems which women face.

Women and conventional employment planning

Mainstream economic development policies and measures have on the whole not served women well. By overlooking women's place in the local economy they have tended implicitly to prioritise men's employment needs above women's, and in failing to recognise existing gender inequalities they have contributed to their maintenance and reinforcement.

Women's employment is overlooked because mainstream local economic development is orientated precisely towards *development* rather than employment as such. Economic development has relied heavily on the use of land- and property-related measures as a means of attracting firms and encouraging expansion, with this taking a wide range of forms, from registers of land availability to the provision of advance factories. The focus is therefore on land and property rather than on people and jobs. For example, most authorities and agencies record their 'success' in terms of, say, factory units let, and not as either the number or type of jobs created. Indeed there has been some controversy over the number of jobs generated by the Welsh Development Agency's activities,[32] though the number of units let is quite clear. In focusing solely on physical development, the social and economic are written out of policy, yet it is those social and economic processes which, as we have seen, generate inequality.

It is important to stress here that policies which do not differentiate between men and women in either their analyses or implementation are not necessarily policies which do not discriminate against women. Given the inequalities which exist in the domestic division of labour and in employment, then policies based on non-differentiation between the sexes can simply reproduce and reinforce those inequalities. To treat men and women as if they are the same, when they have quite different labour market experiences, is not to treat them equally. But this is exactly what has happened in many local strategies. The emphasis on certain measures which ostensibly treat men and women equally, but to which they have differential access, has tended to create a, doubtless inadvertent, bias against women.

The priority given to land development in economic planning means that, firstly, women's place in the labour market is not recognised and their needs are not catered for. It is rare indeed for statements on local economic policy to incorporate the fact that there are two sexes in the workforce, let alone to look at the different labour market situation of each sex. The special problems faced by women in employment, from problems of child care, access to jobs and training,

123

to female unemployment, low pay and poor conditions are not usually stated, whilst part-time work, despite its growing importance in local employment, is also usually overlooked. This failure to recognise sexual divisions in employment is the starting point of women's marginalisation in local economic planning.

Secondly, land development measures, advance factories, the registers of premises and so on, are all centred upon the promotion and development of manufacturing industries. This has been noted in national surveys of local economic development,[33] as well as in the work of specific agencies. For example, the land register issued by Mid Glamorgan County Council, South Wales, as at August 1985 consisted of 87 separate vacant sites and premises, every one of them for manufacturing. The Welsh Development Agency has stated that its main area of concern is manufacturing,[34] and only five per cent of its investment goes into services.[35] Whilst the aim of developing a strong manufacturing base, with skilled, well-paid jobs, is laudable in itself, those skilled manual, full-time jobs in manufacturing are, specifically, men's jobs, with the vast majority of women working outside manufacturing and those in manufacturing being in unskilled jobs.[36]

The areas of the local economy in which women are predominant are strikingly absent from policy. The public sector services, which alone account for over a third of female employment, are rarely mentioned, and neither are other major areas of women's employment such as retailing, office work or the miscellaneous 'consumer' services. Yet these areas, although booming in the past, are now also under threat and require as much planning intervention and support as manufacturing. Although the precise effects of new technology are still disputed, there can be little doubt that in many traditional areas of female employment new technology is likely to cause job loss.[37] Computers in offices, retailing and distribution can greatly increase output with a static or even declining workforce.[38] Similarly, the public services which have been a major source of jobs for women, are also static or declining in employment.[39] The offsetting boom in computer-related employment is still being eagerly awaited in many localities. An increasing number of agencies and authorities are, however, turning to services as a source of potential economic development, as the pool of footloose manufacturing firms dries up and competition increases.[40] The Welsh Development Agency, for example, has recently announced its shift towards service development, especially business developments,[41] whilst South Glamorgan County Council, in South Wales, is also promoting an 'office park' on the outskirts of Cardiff.[42] But crucially, these business and producer services are one area of the service sector in which male employees outnumber women, at 51 per cent compared with less than half in all other services except transport.[43] Despite these shifts, the bulk of local economic development work remains orientated towards manufacturing through its policy measures, and as such, represents a prioritisation of men's employment needs above women's.

Secondly, the emphasis on property-based forms of local economic development can, by excluding gender divisions from their scope, end up reinforcing traditional labour market segregation and disadvantage. The employment effects of property development are assumed to 'trickle through' from industrial developments or financial aid to the local labour market,[44] but the precise ways in which this takes place are not included within the planning remit. Yet it is at this point, in the translation as it were of economic activity into employment effects, that jobs are constructed as 'women's jobs' or 'men's jobs'. This includes the anticipation of the availability and characteristics of women workers through, for example, designing the hours of work (part-time or full-time, shift times coinciding with school hours) and job titles; and local traditions and sexual stereotypes of work, such as union practices, and alternative sources of work. For example, Inmos, the silicon chip factory in South Wales, designed its shift system in such a way as to attract and retain a female workforce. Hence, existing sexual inequalities are reproduced within the jobs generated by local economic strategies. The irony here is that it may in fact be women, rather than men, who get these jobs, as has been the case in many of the manufacturing firms attracted to South Wales, but they are getting them on the basis of their 'super-exploitation', with the pay and conditions to match.

In addition, the actual form of much land and property development work appears to reinforce the domestic division of labour and hence women's vulnerability in the labour market. The location of many industrial sites on the periphery of towns, separate from residential development, increases the segregation of home and work. Frequently without access to private transport and needing to be close to domestic facilities such as shops, launderettes and schools, women are unable to travel to jobs on new industrial estates whilst, at the same time, working men are further removed from the domestic sphere and inhibited from taking a part in domestic tasks. For example, many of the Welsh Development Agency's advance factories have been located along the M4 in South Wales, difficult to reach from the Valleys communities where some of the most severe employment problems are felt, and especially so for women.[45] The lack of facilities on such estates simply increases the difficulties for women who do work there, and again makes it harder for men to participate. So here, too, by not recognising the domestic division of labour, economic development work has implicitly planned for jobs for men, based on the masculine experience of waged work, rather than women and women's employment needs. Insofar as economic development has created jobs for women this has largely been by default, with it being women's vulnerability which has been exploited, and hence existing inequalities reproduced.

Third, the few times in 'mainstream' economic development when the labour force itself may be considered are in promotion work and in the provision of information and advice to potential employers. Here there are many avenues for the reproduction of gender divisions, although detailed evidence of this is necessarily hard to obtain. Nevertheless, some authorities can use the vulnerability of the female labour force as an attraction to firms, as has been advised by at least one body.[46] Similarly, advice to new enterprises may exclude service activities, in which most women have their skills and expertise. The British Steel Corporation's industrial development off-shoot, which works in steel closure areas, is oriented towards helping redundant workers use their skills to establish new industries, yet it is not widely recognised that a substantial number of women have lost their jobs from steel also. In the so-called southern coastal corridor of Wales, whilst 11 800 men's jobs were lost in metals 1976–81, over 1000 women's jobs disappeared also.[47] There can be similar problems in devising schemes to help the long-term unemployed, usually the registered unemployed and therefore usually men. Stereotypes occur equally in development work advertising. The Welsh Development Agency, whose activities have undoubtedly provided jobs for many women, studiously ignores this in its promotional advertisements, from which it would be hard to guess that women are almost half of Wales' workforce.

The limited direct intervention which does take place in the labour market again appears to prioritise men's needs above women's. Few local authorities promote training as part of their economic development work, and if they do there are rarely measures to encourage women to acquire non-traditional skills. The other measure commonly used, 'key-worker' housing, is centred on the notion of a male breadwinner, bringing his wife and family to the area, and does little for working women.

Finally, the implicit 'planning for men's jobs' in much local economic development challenges the legitimacy of planning itself. If women see that their interests are not served by the planning process, and that local economic initiatives are biased towards male needs and thereby reinforce traditional gender divisions, then they are unlikely to have any belief in the value of planning. Only by planning for both sexes, in a way which is not based on stereotypes of men's and women's roles, can there be popular support for local economic planning. The legitimacy of local economic initiatives is also threatened by its own failure if women's employment is overlooked. If the aim, implicit or explicit, of an initiative is male, or undifferentiated job creation, and as almost any job creating project will employ women as well as men, then the initiatives will inevitably 'fail' in their own terms. Unemployment is unlikely to fall, since many women taking jobs will be unregistered, and hence the initiatives will be seen to have been unsuccessful. In order to maintain legitimacy and to become more successful, I believe that local economic strategies need to recognise the importance of women's employment and begin to tackle the issues of gender divisions, both in the workplace and in the home.

Taking account of women's employment

Some local authorities have recently addressed themselves to the specific problems faced by women, and have begun to develop measures aimed at catering for women's job needs as well as those of men, and some of these, plus some other suggestions will be briefly discussed here.[48] The point of these policies is not to expand female employment at the expense of jobs for men, but to ensure that economic development includes women's *as well as* men's employment needs. To do so requires measures which are sensitive to gender divisions, and which in many cases are gender specific. These can benefit both sexes. By opening up job opportunities in a meaningful way, as opposed to formal, legislative equality of opportunity, the employment prospects of women and men can be enhanced.

Although these measures may appear to be simply 'job redistributive' instead of 'job creative', they nevertheless need to be incorporated into the range of economic development measures used by local authorities. If the concern of local economic development is genuinely to improve the structure of the local economy and reduce unemployment, then this concern must extend not only to the number of jobs saved or created, but to the quality of the jobs and who fills them, since these too are essential elements in the overall 'health' of the local economy. Further, the incorporation of an awareness of gender divisions can increase the sensitivity of employment planning, for example by improving economic forecasting. The employment consequences of, say, an office development, could be more accurately assessed if divisions within the workforce were considered. In addition, a consideration of how women's employment needs can be met raises questions about the wider organisation of work and the economy, and in

126

particular of the relationship between production and reproduction, between home and work. This in itself can reveal 'new' areas of possible job creation. Hence the processes of job redistribution can also provide the basis for job creation. Finally, it hardly needs pointing out that economic development is not a technical, rationalistic process but one which is inherently political. Increasing numbers of local authorities have taken the political decision not to promote forms of economic development which are, amongst other things, biased against women and which reinforce gender inequality.

What of the measures themselves? Most policies promoting women's employment are 'people'-oriented, but nevertheless it is possible to identify other kinds of measures. Perhaps first and foremost must be the recognition that women's employment is both important and requires local intervention. Women's unemployment and the problems they face within employment need to be recognised. Areas which are traditionally 'women's work' need to be considered within the economic strategy. All too often a review of local employment fails to include the key sectors for women of public services and retail employment, and job loss and job quality there are ignored. Some local authorities have recognised the significance of their own employment and have begun to look at ways of improving women's job prospects within them, from implementing and monitoring equal opportunity measures, internal training, job-sharing, and workplace nurseries, to expanding employment and resisting reductions in staff and privatisation.[49] Outside, some agencies and authorities have expanded their remit to include service sector employment, though sometimes in desperation rather than as part of a positive reorientation of policy. Afan District in South Wales, for example, which lost over 8000 jobs in four years in the steel rundown at Port Talbot and other works, now welcomes any job creating enterprise, including services. Other services, such as entertainments and leisure employment, retailing and health and educational services, are also important employers and need analysis. The Greater London Council (GLC) has been something of a pioneer here. Whilst other enterprise agencies have included relatively little on services, with West Midlands County Council including just two out of fourteen 'sector studies' on services,[50] the GLC has produced documents on, amongst other services, the contract cleaning industry, office work and on childcare as a form of work.[51]

Part-time work also needs to be included as a serious employment option for both sexes. Steps could be taken to improve the quality of existing part-time work, for example by ensuring that the wages and conditions of part-timers conform to statutory requirements and by encouraging unionisation of part-timers, as well as by extending part-time working to higher paid occupations and sectors, for example through promoting job-sharing schemes, again with local authorities having an important role to play. Similarly, local authorities can concern themselves more fully with the conditions of work, such as low pay, home working and health and safety. The West Midlands County Council has funded a regional low pay unit, and a health and safety at work unit, and several local authorities now have home working campaigns.[52]

Within property-based measures it is possible to increase the sensitivity to women's needs. The location or retention of existing industrial sites close to residential areas and the provision of adequate public transport facilities can be key means of improving women's access to a range of jobs opportunities. Taff-Ely District, in South Wales, has recently adopted measures for industrial development close to residential areas, to ease access to jobs in an area with exceptionally low levels of car ownership, including women's access to work. The refurbishment of existing industrial premises and toleration of 'non-conforming' industrial land-uses close to residential areas can be helpful. The provision on sites themselves of essential household services, such as shops and a launderette, could ease men's and women's domestic tasks, whilst shared nurseries on industrial estates could also facilitate women's employment. Some employers could be encouraged to provide these, for example one civil service office in South Wales which employs over 3000 women on a relatively remote site has a bank, a small grocery and a general shop. The civil service has also provided nurseries at five sites, although these have run into some difficulties.[53] Nevertheless, these certainly warrant consideration by local authorities and agencies, either to encourage employers to provide facilities or to provide them themselves.

Secondly, local employment initiatives could consider ways of preventing sex discrimination and promoting equality of opportunity within the workplace, through intervening in the process of job design and recruitment. Local authorities' own employment has already been mentioned here—several have examined their recruitment and promotion policies for evidence of direct or indirect discrimination, and these have been eliminated.[54] Further efforts, for example in training and conditions of employment, can also be made, usually at relatively little cost. Such equality policies are more difficult to encourage in non- public sector employers, but nevertheless some local authorities have sought to impose conditions on firms receiving financial help, or on firms from which the authority purchases, known as 'contract compliance'. The GLC had within it a unit to deal specifically with these aspects.[55] Women workers can be made more aware of their rights as workers, for example of their rights to maternity leave, minimum wages, and redundancy terms, through local authority campaigns, or by briefing trade unions and encouraging them to negotiate on behalf of women workers.[56]

Training can play a crucial role in breaking down the barriers to women's employment, both by encouraging young women to train in essential, non-traditional skills thus avoiding their becoming confined to female 'ghettoes' themselves, and by helping older women, particularly those without marketable skills and those returning to work, with 'second chance' training. Not only can training, especially in specialist skills which are in demand, improve women's access to better quality jobs, but it can also encourage subsequent job creation, as skilled workers may establish their own businesses or cooperatives. There are now several training workshops in Britain, jointly funded by local authorities and the European Social Fund, which offer women-only training in non-traditional areas such as computing, electronics and carpentry. One, South Glamorgan Women's Workshop, provides a workplace nursery and this has proved invaluable in enabling women to attend the course.

Improving childcare facilities is central to the improvement of women's employment position, and it is this which also questions the established organisation of the economy. Nurseries, holiday play-groups and after-school care are all services which are essential to women's employment opportunities, and which are considerably under-resourced at present. Local authorities need to recognise the importance of this need and try to improve their own provision as well as encourage others to do so. In meeting the demand for better childcare facilities new jobs can be created. For example, the GLC managed to create jobs in 140 childcare projects whilst at the same time providing care for many children.[57]

The implication of this is wider, however. Tasks which are currently carried out privately, by individuals, unpaid in their homes, can also be carried out in the formal economy, as paid work. This is because the separation of paid from unpaid tasks, of the production of services from the reproduction of household members, is not fixed. Jobs can move in and out of the formal economy as the way in which they are carried out changes.[58] A good example here is washing, which has varied in its organisation from being a paid service carried out by individuals (such as the washer-woman), to a commercially organised service (such as laundries) to its unpaid, private, mechanised form today. There are thus needs to be met, tasks to be done, which can be carried out either paid or unpaid.

These tasks can be a basis for creating jobs as well as easing women's domestic work. Recently, the GLC has considered ways of creating jobs from 'domestic production', looking not just at services, such as childcare, laundries and canteens, but also at necessary domestic goods or 'domestic technology'.[59] In the same way, community needs may be an important source of jobs, from local transport and shops on outlying estates, to housing or environmental improvement schemes. Similarly, the West Midlands County Council established a 'Unit for the Development of Alternative Products'. Clearly these new areas of paid work do not offer the entire solution to the economic crisis of many areas, but nevertheless they can be an important contribution to both local employment and local needs.

There are then several ways in which it is possible for planning intervention to consider women's employment needs. This section has outlined a few, some of which have been implemented by local authorities. There are doubtless many more which remain to be developed, for the essence of local economic strategies is in the end their *local* nature, their ability to be sensitive to local circumstances, including women's employment, and to be sensitive in a way in which conventional land-based initiatives can not be. In so doing, they will generate planning which is not just more effective but which does not perpetuate women's disadvantaged position in society. Some of the measures considered in this paper rely on the use of limited resources, but more traditional employment creation measures (such as factory and infrastructure provision, grant aid and promotional work) are also expensive. The initiatives which have been outlined here do, however, offer the long-term prospect of a more equitable creation and distribution of employment.

NOTES AND REFERENCES

1 Boddy, M., *Local Government and Industrial Development* (School for Advanced Urban Studies Occasional Paper 7), Bristol. University of Bristol, 1982.

2 Boddy, M. and Barrett, S., *Local Government and the Industrial Development Process* (Working Paper 6, School for Advanced Urban Studies). Bristol, University of Bristol, 1980.

3 For example Massey, D., *Spatial Divisions of Labour*, London, Macmillan, 1984; Cooke, P.,

'Labour Market Discontinuity and Spatial Development', *Progress in Human Geography*, 7, 1983, pp. 534–565. Also see the recent Economic and Social Research Council initiative, 'The Changing Urban and Regional System', ESRC *Newsletter*, No. 55, p. 77, 1985.

4 Beechey, V., 'Women and Production: A Critical Analysis of Some Sociological Theories of Women's Work' in Kuhn, A. and Wolpe, A.-M. (eds.), *Feminism and Materialism*, London, Routledge and Kegan Paul, 1978.

5 Martin, J. and Roberts, C., *Women and Employment. A Lifetime Perspective* (DE/OPCS Survey), London, HMSO, 1984. The main findings are summarised in Martin, J. and Roberts, C., 'Women's Employment in the 80s', Department of Employment *Gazette*, May 1984.

6 Ibid.

7 Department of Employment *Gazette*.

8 Massey, D. and Meegan, R., 'The Geography of Industrial Reorganisation. The Spatial Effects of the Restructuring of the Electrical Engineering Sector under the Industrial Reorganisation Corporation', *Progress in Planning*, 10. 1979, pp. 155–237; Fothergill, S. and Gudgin, G., *Unequal Growth*, London, Heinemann, 1982.

9 Cockburn, C., *Brothers: Male Dominance and Technological Change*, London, Pluto Press, 1983. demonstrates the importance of heavy physical labour to masculine identity in the printing industry.

10 Equal Opportunities Commission, *Ninth Annual Report*, Manchester, EOC, 1984.

11 Department of Employment *Gazette*, July 1985.

12 See Williams, G. A., 'Women Workers in Wales', *Welsh History Review*, 11, 1983, pp. 530–548; *The Guardian*, 27 January and 5 February 1983; see Winckler, V., 'Women, Work and the Recession in Wales', *Cambria*, 10, 1983, pp. 61–69 for a critique.

13 Martin and Roberts, op. cit.

14 Over 90 per cent of women return to work after child-bearing, with the average length of time absent from paid employment being four years for women having a first child 1975–79. Martin and Roberts, op. cit.

15 Ibid.

16 Wilding, P., 'Income and Wealth in Wales' in Rees, G. and Rees, T. L. (eds.), *Poverty and Social Inequality in Wales*, London, Croom Helm, 1980.

17 Department of Employment *Gazette*, December 1982.

18 Department of Employment, unpublished figures.

19 Department of Employment *Gazette*, March 1980.

20 Hakim, C., 'Sexual Divisions within the Labour Force: Occupational Segregation', Department of Employment *Gazette*, November 1980.

21 Ibid.

22 Department of Employment *Gazette*, October 1982.

23 Martin, J. and Roberts, C., op. cit.

24 Ibid.

25 Hurstfield, J., *Part Time Trap*, London, Low Pay Unit, 1978.

26 Equal Opportunities Commission, 'Women and Government Statistics', EOC *Research Bulletin*, 4, Autumn 1980.

27 The test of availability for work was introduced following the recommendations of Sir Derek Rayner, *The Payment of Benefits to Unemployed People*, London, HMSO, 1981.

28 Martin and Roberts, op. cit.

29 *Welsh Economic Trends*, No. 9, 1984, Appendix, V.

30 Walby, S., *Women and Unemployment* (Lancaster Regionalism Group Working Paper 5), Lancaster, University of Lancaster, 1981.

31 Roberts and Martin, op. cit.

32 See Cooke, P., 'Post-Industrial Wales?' in Damesick, P. and Woods, P. (eds.), *Regional Problems, Problem Regions and Public Policy in the UK*, Oxford, Oxford University Press, forthcoming.

33 Boddy, M., op. cit.; Joint Unit for Research on the Urban Environment, *A Review of Local Economic Initiatives*, Birmingham, JURUE (University of Aston), 1981.

34 Welsh Development Agency, *The Strategy of the Welsh Development Agency for the Provision of Finance and Advice to Industry in Wales*, Treforest, n.d.

35 Welsh Development Agency, *The First Five Years*, Treforest, 1981.

36 Equal Opportunities Commission, 1984, op. cit.

37 See West, J., 'New Technology and Women's Office Work' in West, J. (ed.), *Work, Women and the Labour Market*, London, Routledge and Kegan Paul, 1982.

38 For example, see Huws, U., *Your Job in the Eighties*, London, Pluto Press, 1982.

39 For example, the civil service has lost 14 per cent of its jobs in the period 1979–1984.

40 Boddy, M., op. cit.

41 Welsh Development Agency, *Corporate Plan of the Welsh Development Agency*, Cardiff, 1984.

42 South Glamorgan County Council, *First Review of the Structure Plan: Draft Policies*, Cardiff, June 1984.

43 Department of Employment *Gazette*, October 1982.

44 Boddy, M., 'Local Economic and Employment Strategies' in Boddy, M. and Fudge, C. (eds.), *Local Socialism?*, London, Macmillan, 1984.

45 On the location of Welsh Development Agency sites, see Cooke, P., 'Discretionary Intervention and the Welsh Development Agency', *Area*, 12, 1982, pp. 269–77; on women and new

town industrial development, see Lewis, J., and Foord, J., 'New Towns and New Gender Relations in Old Industrial Regions: Women's Employment in Peterlee and East Kilbride', *Built Environment*, 10 (1) 1984, pp. 42–52.

46 Joint Unit for Research on the Urban Environment, op. cit.

47 Cooke, P., forthcoming, op. cit.

48 Most of the initiatives referred to here have been developed by the Greater London Council Enterprise Board, and also the West Midlands County Council and Enterprise Board. The future of these initiatives following the abolition of the metropolitan counties is as yet unclear. However, these are by no means the only local authorities to have looked at women's employment needs, nor are they the only models of intervention.

49 Greater London Council, *Equality Update*, London, GLC, 1983; Greater London Enterprise Board, *Organising for Equality*, London, GLC, n.d.

50 West Midlands County Council, *Action in the Local Economy*, Birmingham, West Midlands County Council Economic Development Committee, 1984.

51 Greater London Council, *The Contract Clean Up* (Economic Policy Group Strategy Document 9), London, GLC, 1983; *Behind the High Street* (*Shops and Warehouses*) (Economic Policy Group Strategy Document 11), London, GLC, 1983.

52 West Midlands County Council, op. cit.; Pond, C., *Low Pay: What Can Local Authorities Do?* (Low Pay Unit Pamphlet 27), London, Low Pay Unit, n.d.

53 Joint Review Group on Employment Opportunities for Women in the Civil Service, *Equal Opportunities for Women in the Civil Service*, London, HMSO, 1982.

54 Greater London Council, *Equality Update*, London, GLC, 1983.

55 Greater London Enterprise Board, *Saving Jobs ... Shaping the Future*, London, GLEB, 1984; West Midlands County Council, op. cit.

56 See Gough, J., 'Local Economic Planning and Class Consciousness', paper presented to IBG *Conference on Geographical Aspects of Social Stratification*, London, September 1984.

57 Greater London Council, *Child Care—Meeting Needs and Making Jobs* (Economic Policy Group Strategy Document 14), London, GLC, 1983.

58 Gershuny, J., *After Industrial Society, The New Self-Service Economy*, London, Macmillan, 1978.

59 Greater London Council, Industry and Employment Committee, Report No. IEC 953, *Domestic Production*, London, GLC, 1983.

ACKNOWLEDGEMENTS

I would like to thank the anonymous referees of this paper and Roger Allen, South Glamorgan County Council, for their helpful comments on earlier drafts of this paper. I would also like to thank the various local authorities and agencies for providing me with literature and information.

Reprinted with permission from **Town Planning Review**, vol. 57, no. 3, pp. 303-318, 1986.

Postscript.

This article arose out of a concern that conventional approaches to economic development were failing to take into account the particular characteristics of women's employment. Since it was written (in early 1985) there have been a number of developments worth noting which further emphasize the need for women's employment to be incorporated into policy.

First, the most recent figures available on women's employment indicate that the need for policy intervention is even more pressing than before. At the national level, women's employment has continued to expand so that by 1986 women formed almost 45% of the British workforce. However, that expansion has been almost entirely in part-time work, and in work which is frequently low paid and with poor conditions. Clearly, to omit explicit reference to women in local economic development is to ignore a substantial part of the workforce and to concur with women's concentration in the most disadvantaged sections of the labour market.

However, the picture at the regional level is rather different. Women have actually *lost* jobs in the last five years in several areas (North West England, Wales and Scotland), with the rate of loss in Wales at 9% between 1979 and 1986 approaching that for male employment. Clearly, economic decline is as much a problem for women as for men in these regions. Yet, despite high levels of activity amongst numerous development agencies to regenerate these regional economies, none has acknowledged in its policies the particular problems faced by women. Ironically, much of women's job loss in these regions has come from the rundown of manufacturing and the fall in employment in public services - precisely those developments which were previously argued to obviate the need for planning intervention for women.

Second, there have been some important policy developments. Most notably, the abolition of the metropolitan counties and Greater London Council on 31 March 1986 also brought an end to some genuine attempts to reformulate economic development policy in the light of women's employment needs. Although many of the statutory authorities taking over the functions of the former councils have also adopted similar policies, they clearly do not have the same impact because they are fragmented. Meanwhile, there remain other authorities, especially outside the metropolitan areas, which still do not recognize nor incorporate women's employemnt into their development policies. The availability of funding from the European Social Fund for women as a priority group has encouraged some authorities to introduce
some special measures for women and has also helped to legitimize provision for women as an area of local authority activity. Few, however, have reorientated general policy explicitly to include women in local economic development, let alone reconsidered the basis of their work.

Finally, the section of the article which set out some of the policy options open to development agencies aimed to demonstrate with current examples that it is possible to

132

take account of women's working patterns and employment needs, rather than to prescribe action. Hence, although there have undoubedly been several new initiatives on women's employment since the article was written, they add to rather than undermine the argument. Indeed, at a time when the gap between the 'prosperous' south and 'poor' north of Britain is widening, the need for local initiatives which reflect the specific characteristics, problems and potential of a locality is even more important. Policies clearly cannot be copied unproblematically from one locality to another. What is essential, however, and regrettably needs reiterating, is that those local needs and opportunities include women's as well as men's requirements. For, in the long-term, this is the only way in which local economic development policies as a whole can be success-ful.

Acknowledgements

Thanks are also due to Gareth Rees, Teresa Rees and Richard Davies.

PART V
UNSHELTERED WOMEN

12 The plight of homeless women

MADELEINE R. STONER

The plight of the homeless population in the United States has recently drawn public attention. This article focuses on the growing number of women among the homeless, their special needs, and the harsher conditions of life for homeless women than for men. It suggests a comprehensive three-tiered service system to address the needs of the homeless population in general, and homeless women specifically, and recommends several courses for political and social action that address systemic causes of homelessness.

Last winter Rebecca Smith, age sixty-one, died in New York City. She froze to death in the home she had constructed for herself inside a cardboard box. She preferred it, she said, to any other home. Rebecca Smith had spent much of her life in a state psychiatric hospital under treatment for schizophrenia. Life in the box was preferable. In a sense, many people watched her die: her neighbors, the police, the Red Cross, and finally a city-dispatched social worker and psychiatrist. In a larger sense, the nation watched too, because her death made the front page of the *Washington Post*.[1]

The senseless tragedy of Rebecca Smith's death immediately prompted nationwide concern for the plight of the homeless. Those who have worked with the homeless find this new acknowledgment of the thousands of homeless people in our midst rather strange. They also find somewhat remarkable the morbid curiosity demonstrated about them and the quickness with which they are branded a bunch of smelly sociopaths, chronic "crazies," to be dealt with someplace, but not here. Yet people and organizations are beginning to pay thoughtful attention to the problems of the homeless, and programs and services are emerging to meet the needs of this long-neglected population. Concerned groups are organizing to provide an increasingly vocal advocacy network for coping with the needs of the homeless. Despite this activity, however, existing public and private welfare policies preclude adequate service delivery for the homeless population.

The intent of this article is to describe the homeless population and the special needs of women within it. In carrying out this intent, the article first reviews apparent causes of homelessness and the types of programs that currently exist for women. It then suggests a design for a comprehensive service system for homeless women and concludes with a proposal for political and social action that will be essential if the systemic causes of homelessness are to be eliminated.

The rapidly increasing number of homeless people in America poses a new challenge to cities all over the nation. New York City has had to divert major resources to cope with an expanding street population because a court decree requires the city to provide public shelter for homeless men.[2] Throughout the country the capacity of agencies to make a place for everybody is being severely tested. Columbus, Ohio, a city badly hit by the declining economy, was forced to open the first public shelter accommodating 150 people a night.[3] The Traveler's Aid Society in affluent Houston has housed as many as 1,000 economically disabled people a month. This is nearly 40 percent more than the previous year.[4] In Denver, one church opened a shelter and within a week 400 people had applied.[5] In 1981 the Community Services Society of New York estimated that 36,000 people in that city were without homes.[6] More recently, Los Angeles County Department of Mental Health officials estimated that a minimum of 30,000 people are living on its streets.[7]

While these numbers are alarming, they also are misleading because there are so many methodological barriers to obtaining a sound census of the homeless. What is important is that public and private agencies, researchers, and the media are reporting readily visible evidence that the number of homeless people is rising and that radical changes in their circumstances and composition have taken place over the past fifteen years. These changes call into question the propriety of relief measures that traditionally have been applied to the contemporary homeless population.

Workers with the homeless report that more women, elderly, and young people—particularly black women and members of other minority groups—have slipped into a population once dominated by older alcoholic white men.[8] Any profile that attempts to develop an aggregate notion of the type of person in today's homeless population obscures the most distinctive features of this group: its variety and its heterogeneity. Surveys of these people are unreliable as they include

136

only those who have been in public or private shelters. Yet, these clearly serve only a small proportion of street people.

Clarification of the picture of who the homeless are is possible by considering why people find themselves homeless. Summary evidence from those who have studied the homeless population indicates that the antecedents of homelessness are: (1) lack of housing, (2) unemployment and poverty, (3) deinstitutionalization, and (4) domestic violence and abuse.[9]

Research conducted by the Vera Institute of Justice on user characteristics of homeless people in a women's shelter demonstrated that there is a direct link between such factors as evictions and lockouts and the consequence of homelessness.[10] As economic pressures for the reclamation of land for renovation and upgrading mount, evictions will continue to increase. The City of New York's Human Resources Administration has reported that a fourth of the recent applicants to its men's shelters are there due to job loss.[11]

Census data on poverty reveal that from 1980 to 1981 an additional 2.2 million people entered the official poverty index as unemployment figures increased.[12] According to the Census Bureau figures, the burden of this poverty falls disproportionately on families headed by women, on children, on young adults, and on ethnic minority groups.[13] The "feminization of poverty" has particular significance in the growing and shifting homeless population. Many women have no place to turn but to the streets. Significantly related to both income and homelessness is another fact, namely, that public assistance is denied to people who have no address.[14] People lose their benefits when they become homeless and, in turn, the means of finding another home.

There is considerable documentation to indicate the presence of large numbers of severely disturbed individuals in streets and shelters, many with histories of psychiatric hospitalization. Ill-planned deinstitutionalization, such as that leading to the death of Rebecca Smith, often is cited as the most prominent cause of homelessness. Whether or not this is so, recent studies have attested to the growing number of psychiatrically disabled among the homeless poor. An informal census conducted in the Los Angeles skid row district indicated that 90 percent of the women there were mentally ill and had histories of psychiatric hospitalization.[15]

Many homeless women and adolescent females report that they left their homes after repeated incidents of abuse by their spouses, rape, incest, and desertion. Despite the strengths of the Domestic Violence Prevention Act, cutbacks in expenditures for welfare programs include severe slashes in provisions for battered and abused women and displaced homemakers.[16]

137

Living and Coping Patterns of Homeless Women

Although there is a substantial body of literature concerning male vagrants and transients, until recently very little existed concerning unaffiliated women who are not alcoholic. Bahr and Garrett[17] conducted studies comparing dislocation factors among men and women in urban shelters and explained the differences by sex in the etiology of homelessness and the family backgrounds of this population. They also examined the drinking habits of men and women admitted to emergency shelters in New York City. Judith Strasser[18] provided a sensitive descriptive profile of the shopping bag lady population, exploring personal appearance, hygiene, daily routines, health conditions, and their use of services. Ambulatory schizophrenic women were described in a report by the New Orleans Traveler's Aid Society.[19] Most recently the media have exposed the box people—the Rebecca Smiths who have come to inhabit city streets or live underground in subway stations.

Because the little that has been written about homeless women has focused on the skid row environment and alcoholism, research is needed that does not treat women as derelicts but as homeless people with specific women's problems and needs. This is necessary because the apparent systematic avoidance of dealing with homeless women in research and literature suggests that women receive harsher judgment and less adequate services than men even at this marginal level of society. As women and their families continue to enter the ranks of the homeless—as victims of the economy, of landlords, of a depleted mental health system, and of spouses—society can no longer neglect them.

What may be a benchmark study of this problem was conducted by the Manhattan Bowery Corporation in 1979.[20] The strength of this report, which was not widely circulated, lies in the fact that it dispels many of the myths about shopping bag ladies. Several of its findings are particularly important: (1) Little is known about the homeless population, except that we are sure its numbers are growing. (2) The three municipal shelters for women in New York City are unable to meet the growing demands of the homeless population. It is the only city in the United States providing public shelter for women. (3) Homeless women are singularly vulnerable to crime, the elements, and other hazards of the streets. (4) Some characteristics, viewed as bizarre (e.g., foul odors), are conscious defense mechanisms. (5) Mental disability per se is not a pervasive reason for women's alleged refusal to use available services. (6) The primary causes of their disaffiliation are to be found in the socioeconomic circumstances of poor, middle-aged, and elderly women—in particular, their isolation. Homeless women do not choose their circumstances. They are victims of forces over which they have lost control.

One of the first studies that looked beyond the alcoholic woman was conducted by Baumohl and Miller in Berkeley, California, in 1974.[21] They observed that there was a substantial presence of women among the homeless in that city, larger than had been found in comparable studies of the homeless. Their report pointed out several differences between men and women of the street. The women are younger, less educated, away from home for shorter periods of time, and they more frequently obtain income from legitimate sources. Despite the fact that more women than men receive either public assistance or money from home in order to survive, many are forced to panhandle, deal drugs, shoplift, or become prostitutes. This homeless style of life, hazardous for anyone, holds acute dangers for women, rape being high among them. The study reported that most women trade sexual favors for food, shelter, and other necessities, and it described frustrated desires for conventional monogomous relationships and intense conflicts following coercive sexual encounters.

A 1982 study of vagrant and transient women in Columbia, South Carolina, reported that the study sample was predominantly Caucasian, forty years of age or younger, natives of South Carolina, and none having more than a high school education. The majority were not employed, and most had incomes of less than $3,000 per year.[22] An important distinction between this study and previously cited ones is that it encompassed a broader environment than skid row and did not specifically focus on alcoholism. In relation to problems perceived by the study sample, the majority were dissatisfied with their present lives and identified as their most serious problems lack of money, nowhere to live, unemployment, separation from family, lack of friends, and illness. The majority who were sick sought professional care in health clinics. Most respondents hoped to be employed and have a place to live within one year.

This study also produced findings that significantly differed from previous descriptions of disaffiliation. One was that although the study sample complained of loneliness and isolation, there was a greater sense of affiliation than in earlier studies. Another finding pertained to the use of services: the majority of the sample received meals from a women's shelter and had sought help from social service agencies, but a sizable minority had not sought such help. Most services used by the study sample were general or lay community oriented rather than specifically designed to meet the needs of women and, in particular, homeless women.[23] This suggests that homeless women may only turn to shelters when other social services are unavailable.

In a survey of 100 first-time applicants in 1979,[24] the Vera Institute of Justice has produced the most detailed study of user characteristics of the New York City Women's Shelter. The demographic data closely parallel the men's shelter population and disclose that: (1) half of the women were under forty, with 16 percent sixty years and older; (2) 40 percent were white, and 44 percent were black; and (3) 61 percent had lived in the city for at least one year.

The most useful data from the Vera Institute Study for application to the design of services and preventive measures are those citing reasons for selecting shelter. Of those women who gave information on prior residence, 13 percent had come directly from hospitals. Nearly half had lived in single rooms in hotels immediately prior to coming to the shelter. Over a fourth of the first-time applicants cited as their reason for seeking shelter illegal lockouts or evictions, or ejection from a household (by family or friend).

The question of who the homeless women are cannot be completely answered without considering how they are portrayed. Earlier research, reinforced by popular notions, supported views of homeless women as derelict eccentrics who choose their life-style. The persistent denial of women's existence on skid row only served to consolidate long-held beliefs that homeless women are even more derelict and eccentric than homeless men, and thus the most socially undesirable of all marginal people. Equating the term derelict with homelessness has contributed to a belief that this is a "less needy" population. Because women have been less visibly homeless and less troublesome or feared than men, society and social agencies have regarded them as even "less needy" than homeless men. As a consequence, these unacknowledged women have tended to fall between the threads of the safety net, into the streets.

A personal testament to this notion has come from Jill Halverson, director of the Downtown Women's Center in Los Angeles, who reports that she always perceived skid row as being only for men. During her ten years first as a public welfare caseworker and then as a caseworker in alcoholic rehabilitation programs, she saw women sleeping in parking lots, in X-rated movie houses, and in roach-infested cheap hotel rooms. She discovered that women were on skid row, but that all of the agencies on Los Angeles' skid row were geared to serve men, not women.[25]

Images portrayed in the popular press appear to be changing. The tendency to blame the victim and the notions of dereliction and eccentricity are fading. At a conference in Orange County, California, in August 1982, conferees attested to the fact that homelessness is not confined to large cities. It is a national problem that reaches the smallest communities as well. Estimates that there are 4,000 homeless women in Orange County bear this out.[26] As Orange County and other communities across the nation are witnessing the increasing numbers of homeless single women and homeless women with children, there is an increasing awareness that these women are the by-products of the

140

"feminization of poverty," often the result of family breakdowns through divorce, desertion, and abuse that have led to mortgage foreclosures or evictions for nonpayment of rent.

Implications for Social Work Practice

The growing population of homeless women holds immediate and far-reaching implications for social work practice and for the design of effective social services. With the exception of a loosely organized system of emergency shelters, little exists among traditional and alternative service agencies to meet the special needs of this population. The prospect of starting from the beginning to tackle this social problem is especially daunting in an atmosphere of declining resources, but to do so is imperative. We need a system that goes beyond emergency shelter to provide food, services, and a range of living facilities to meet the varied but basic needs of the wide spectrum of women who are now homeless. And to meet this urgent need it is necessary that preventive activities include political and economic elements. However, the formulation of any systematic and comprehensive plan must take into account the strengths and weaknesses of the programs for homeless women that currently exist and assess their potential as effective answers to this serious problem.

The current programs for homeless women appear to have four characteristics: (1) they are predominantly under private auspices, (2) they are proportionately fewer than those available for homeless men, (3) there are fewer professional social workers or other professionally trained people directly involved in staffing women's shelters, and (4) existing shelters for women tend to operate with lower standards of care than those for men.

Until very recently, there were 800 beds in Los Angeles' skid row for homeless men, but only two for women. Now there are thirty-five beds for women.[27] Similar patterns prevail throughout the nation, suggesting a woeful failure to serve the population of women in need of shelter. It is likely that life for many women outside the shelters is worse, but it may also be possible that the prevailing substandard conditions in many women's shelters makes life on the street more attractive. Rebecca Smith believed this.

New York City now has four public shelters for women. Four years ago, it had one.[28] New York City is notable for operating public shelters because of the court decree requiring the city to provide meals, clothing, and beds; social and medical services are limited. The admissions procedures are more stringent then those for men in public shelters.

At intake a delousing shower is required, just as it is in shelters for men, along with an inventory of all belongings and evidence of psychiatric clearance from Bellevue Hospital. Gynecological exams are required by two of the shelters.

Whatever their bed capacity, shelters are overcrowded, and they accommodate more women than there are beds by filling hallways, chairs, and even using table tops. Facilities are adequate according to certification standards, but these standards are low. In one such shelter, Bushwick Annex, investigators found substantial fire code and food handling violations, inadequate toilet facilities, overcrowding, and inadequate staffing and security. These shelters tend to be located in fringe areas of the city, surrounded by dangerous and isolated neighborhoods where the women seeking the shelter are constantly harassed. Two of the shelters provide meals, but not on their premises. The women are transported by bus to another shelter for breakfast; they remain in the second shelter until they are bused back at night to sleep.[29]

New York City is an exception: most cities are not legally required to provide shelter. More typically, cities operate programs like Sundown in Los Angeles County. Sundown provides a list of hotels that will put people up for the night or a weekend. The program sometimes provides food, but essentially arranges one night's support for which transients do not qualify. Sundown staff report a growing demand. Approximately 1,300 people called the program asking for food and shelter in 1981. During the first few months of 1982, the calls averaged 1,400 a month and are expected to increase.[30]

Throughout the nation, the main source of refuge for homeless women consists of private nonprofit shelters. Public shelters that operate outside of New York, as in Washington, D.C., are restricted to men. On the whole, the private shelters are sponsored by organizations such as the Volunteers of America, churches and missions, and groups of concerned individuals. The Traveler's Aid Society, Salvation Army, and the Young Women's Christian Association also provide services, but these tend to be confined to the provision of food, drop-in centers, and travel arrangements home.[31]

There are two types of private shelters—the smaller, more casually run operation, and the longer-established institutions deeply rooted in mission work. Shelter provisions in the missions are characterized by intake and admissions procedures similar to those of public shelters. Waiting lists are common and rates are not cheap. Monies are taken out of Supplemental Security Income checks, and psychiatric care is often required of residents. Conditions vary among the missions but closely resemble those of the public shelters.

The more casual programs that prevail in the private sector attract full occupancy, primarily because they are smaller and offer a more

142

humane and dignified quality of care according to most shelter residents. Operating costs are met by donations, voluntary labor, and contributions of clothes, furniture, and food. Social workers, psychologists, and psychiatrists are involved only peripherally on a consulting or emergency basis in most of these programs. Generally, these shelters are informal and stress the dignity and privacy of residents, many of whom are known only by first names. Many of the volunteer staff are residents of the shelters. A Catholic church in Boston's Pine Street has turned its basement over to a group of volunteers who operate a shelter there and have moved from their homes to live in the shelter. Some of these people have donated the proceeds from the sales of their homes to operate the shelter.[32] Social life is encouraged in these shelters, and it is known that strong bonds often develop among shelter residents, particularly in the less formal facilities. Because of their religious auspices, religious relics are seen everywhere. Religious services are held, but attendance is generally not required. Many of the shelters will accept no public funding, even when offered, because of their distaste for regulations and bureaucracy.[33]

Physical conditions in these private shelters vary. Some provide only mattresses on the floor, but the emphasis on human dignity and patience appears to compensate for less than adequate standards. An added advantage of many of these shelters is their connection to other services, such as religion-affiliated hospitals. They also operate as a network in some cities so that homeless women can be found by their families. There is reason to believe that women tend to prefer these smaller, casual shelters to the public shelters because of their nonjudgmental ambience as well as their less restrictive policies and practices.

The Christian Housing Facility in Orange County, California, provides a unique service for families. It offers temporary shelter, food, and counseling. Priority of services goes to families or victims of family violence. In 1981 this facility had 1,536 residents, a 300 percent increase from the previous year. The main facility is a remodeled house, but motels are used in emergency cases. This shelter views its function as that of helping people return to permanent housing. Residents are required to submit to counseling and search for jobs. Once they are hired, residents pay 10 percent of their salary to the house. According to its 1980 annual report, 504 persons, 103 of these children, left with a home, a job, and an income after an average twenty-day stay.[34]

Christian Housing is an example of a shelter designed to help people in transition. Its model of service differs from that of the mission and informal church settings in that it works with those people who are most capable of independent functioning rather than the "down and out."

Most night shelters provide little in the way of day services, and so, even with a meal and a bed, street life remains a reality for most of the homeless people who turn to such facilities. Drop-in shelters providing other services are beginning to emerge.

The Downtown Women's Center, opened by Jill Halverson in Los Angeles' skid row four years ago, is a prototype of drop-in centers. It is a former sheet metal shop that is now a bright and cheerful daytime drop-in center for as many as fifty homeless women a day. At the center the women can shower, eat a hot meal, and nap on one of four daybeds. A sense of community is fostered. A senior consulting psychiatrist from the community services division of Los Angeles County's Department of Mental Health who has studied and cares about the plight of homeless women visits the center regularly. He provides a range of services for the women, from individual therapy to group sessions and informal rap groups. The type of care given at the center departs from most traditional notions of what constitutes good psychiatric care, and there is a sense that no rules apply to therapy with homeless women except that they will respond positively when they have a sense that they are in a supportive environment where staff are patient, caring, and respectful. The director of the center possesses no professional training or qualifications and will not accept public funding. She does, however, accept offers of help from private individuals and groups.

In New York City, the Antonio G. Olivieri Center for Homeless Women opened in February 1981 as a daytime drop-in center for homeless men and women. However, male applicants so far outnumbered female applicants that the services were redirected to women only.[35] This center offers meals, showers, delousing, assistance with income entitlements, and access to medical and social services. Women are not required to give their names, nor are they obliged to take part in any activities. The center is open twenty-four hours daily, every day, and offers a form of shelter without beds. Women sleep on chairs, the floor, and desk tops. Tolerant and caring staff make this overcrowded, understaffed, and chaotic center a secure environment for women. Because of the high demand on the center, it has established a time limit of two weeks of continuous care, after which women are assured of seven days' lodging in the public shelter. They may then return to the Olivieri Center for another two weeks.

In addition to night shelters and drop-in centers, outreach services are expanding to deal with homeless people. The Manhattan Bowery Project sends out mobile vans with workers to locate homeless people and offer them food, shelter, and clothing.[36] Responses to such outreach programs vary. Center workers made every possible attempt to bring Rebecca Smith into care, but she refused.

As the number of homeless women continues to increase and the reasons for their plight extend beyond mental illness and alcoholism, women are turning to shelters that in the past they might have turned

144

away from, or not sought at all. Some women who are homeless because of mental illness or alcoholism have tended to avoid shelters and escape from the rigors of mental hospitals and detoxification centers. This was Rebecca Smith's case history. The new homeless women who are increasingly in this plight for reasons related to unemployment, poverty, eviction, and abuse appear to be more accepting of social services and shelters.

What is clear from this survey of shelters and services for homeless women is the fact that public shelters operate under restrictive and demeaning policies and practicies. Women prefer the private shelters and, among these, choose to be in a small and informal setting, no matter its conditions, rather than the more institutional missions with characteristics of public shelters. The overcrowding in all shelters dispels the myth that women choose life in the streets. Most women want shelter, but given the scarcity of private shelters and the harsh conditions of public and mission facilities, it is understandable why many homeless women continue to find themselves without any place to sleep at night.

A Comprehensive Service System for Homeless People

The evidence from drop-in centers, churches, missions, public shelters, and outreach efforts demonstrates the need for additional and better-quality shelter. Most programs presently operating are, at best, temporary and do not begin to approach the full dimensions of the problem.

Rational planning to meet the needs of homeless people in general, and homeless women in particular, must take into account the heterogeneity of the population and provide a range of housing and services. Some advocates for the homeless have proposed a three-tiered approach to the development of housing and services: (1) emergency shelter and crisis intervention, (2) transitional or community shelters, and (3) long-term residence.[37] Each would incorporate a cluster of elements, identified briefly below.

The *basic emergency shelter*, the first tier of shelter, should be made as accessible and undemanding as standards of hygiene and security allow. Clean bedding, wholesome food, adequate security and supervision, and social services should be available. Existing facilities such as school buildings, churches, armories, and converted houses could be adapted for such purposes. Each shelter should be community based as opposed to being in physically or geographically isolated locations.

145

Transitional housing would recognize that there are homeless people who, given the opportunity and supports, could eventually live independently. This type of shelter would make more demands on residents in terms of assuming self-responsibility and would provide longer-term social services and vocational rehabilitation. Staff would actively attempt to secure appropriate entitlements as well as necessary clinical care. Transitional housing settings could provide an address enabling residents to receive public assistance.

Long-term residence in effect would provide homes and offer services and aids necessary in the everyday lives of residents. The broad scope of such a program, incorporating aspects of low-income housing and a full complement of service personnel, does not make it a realistic prospect in today's political climate. Nonprofit sponsorship of such programming is more feasible than public funding and support.[38]

An outstanding example of such a three-tiered approach is the Skid Row Development Corporation in Los Angeles. Formed in 1978, the corporation is funded through private (the Los Angeles Central City Association) and public sources (the Los Angeles Community Redevelopment Agency), but its goal is to be independent from city and county funding. Starting with a first-year operating budget of $95,000, after two years it generated an operating budget of $300,000, and the figure is growing.[39]

The primary service objective of the corporation is to provide an alternative housing resource to emergency shelter on skid row by recycling apartments in south central Los Angeles. The corporation has designed transitional housing for indigent women and men. Its Women's Transitional Housing Program calls for a separate building apart from its men's facility. Plans are under way for the completion of long-term housing, and the corporation has planned a series of projects to relocate and rehabilitate apartment buildings slated for demolition in various parts of the city and county. Those who do well in transitional housing will be priority tenants, and the remaining units will be rented to individuals and families needing affordable housing.[40]

Ballington Plaza opened in July this year under the auspices of the Skid Row Development Corporation and is practical proof that long-term housing for the homeless population can be developed and filled where there is the interest and will to do so. This 270-unit housing complex located in Los Angeles' skid row is intended for low-income men and women who are elderly or handicapped and neither drug- nor alcohol-dependent. It offers the first real alternative to sleeping in the streets, transient hotels, or run-down missions. Rents range from $95 to $155 per month. It has full security, cooking facilities, and is an attractive three-story yellow stucco building with bay windows and a large central courtyard with grass, benches, and a parklike setting. This is a prime example of a suitable facility: it is the first in the nation

146

to provide permanent housing for the homeless population. Most programs continue to be confined to the provision of temporary shelter, and many have time limits on the length of stay.

Recommendations for Policy Changes and Social Action

The underlying causes of homelessness show every sign of persisting, and the dimensions of the problem are increasing. Structural unemployment, inadequate and insufficient community-based psychiatric care, housing scarcity, domestic violence and abuse, and the recent cutbacks in income maintenance programs and social services are intensifying it. Given a confused and confusing political climate unsympathetic to the needs of the more vulnerable people in the country, it is difficult to guage the prospects for a more enlightened public policy toward the homeless population in general and for bringing greater balance to providing for homeless men and women. There are hopeful signs, however, that the public is beginning to understand that the roots of mass homelessness lie in the pathology of society, not of individuals. There is increased public sympathy for the homeless and for their need for more adequate shelters. This is evidenced by the rapid rise of advocates for homeless people. Coalitions on behalf of the homeless are springing up throughout the nation: in Boston, Denver, Portland, Seattle, Los Angeles, New York, and Philadelphia. A National Coalition for the Homeless has begun to provide an active lobby and information resource for homeless people and their advocates.[41] The leverage that these advocacy groups can muster at local and national levels in the courts, legislatures, and social agencies is critical in improving the lot of the homeless as well as reducing their numbers.

An important event, already mentioned, occurred in New York in 1981 when the Consent Decree settling the *Callahan* v. *Carey* case was signed and forced New York City to open more shelters for men and, indirectly, women. A subsequent court action was initiated when, on February 24, 1982, a class action suit, *Eldredge* v. *Koch*, was filed in New York State Supreme Court on behalf of homeless women in an effort to upgrade and expand shelters. The suit contends that the conditions in the public facilities effectively deter many homeless women from applying for shelter.[42] Resorting to the courts is a powerful tool that other cities and states have not utilized enough with respect to homeless women. Even though public shelters do not adequately deal

147

with the needs of the homeless population, with the courts' help, these may nevertheless be a powerful beginning to securing entitlement shelter.

Many of the existing coalitions are actively attempting to educate the public about the homeless population and to dispel the many negative stereotypes, attitudes, and myths about them. This is an important strategy, and there have been discernible changes in public views of the homeless. In addition to securing improved shelter, changing attitudes, and legal action, advocates of the homeless must direct their energies toward changing policies in several areas mentioned below:

1. Every effort must be made to ensure a quantitatively and qualitatively adequate supply of emergency shelter and to apply equal standards to shelters for women and men. New York Governor Mario Cuomo's budget of $50 million to build or remodel 6,000 units of housing for the homeless is an example for other states.

2. Shelters should be accessible to the target population, and their admissions procedures should be simple. Shelters should be community based, in contrast to policies operating in some cities that support physically isolated shelters.[43]

3. Community efforts to develop transitional and permanent housing and vocational rehabilitation modeled on the Skid Row Development Corporation in Los Angeles should be undertaken and supported.

4. The diminishing rate of single-room occupancy hotels, despite their problems, should be reviewed. Cities and counties should drop tax incentives for conversion of these hotels. Despite their adverse conditions, single-room occupancy beds are at a premium, and many people consider themselves fortunate to obtain and keep them. Departments of welfare should, however, implement programs that would guarantee that monthly checks go directly to beneficiaries, rather than the hotel owners.

5. Departments of mental health and mental retardation should expand their outreach programs so that their links with homeless people can precede—and possibly preclude—police intervention. Increasing the number of mobile vans, drop-in centers, and crisis-intervention provisions would be steps in this direction. Outreach efforts also need to provide clinical certifications necessary to obtain Supplemental Security Income and Disability benefits, for which some homeless men and women can only qualify once they obtain a residence. Staff of the Skid Row Project sponsored by the Los Angeles County Department of Mental Health have conducted training sessions for agencies that serve the homeless to inform their workers about the details and requirements for obtaining such benefits. Preliminary reports indicate that there was a 90 percent increase in the number of homeless people receiving such benefits in 1982 since these sessions took place.

148

6. Cities and states, along with private agencies, should be encouraged to build or convert facilities so that there are adequate supplies of transitional and permanent affordable housing.

7. Support for legislation to prevent further erosion of the single-room housing stock and illegal evictions or lockouts is needed. The Gottfried-Calandra anti-lockout and illegal eviction bill would allow city police in New York to intervene on the tenant's behalf when they are illegally locked out or dispossessed from their homes.[44] This bill can serve as a model for other cities.

8. Mental health agencies and health settings can redirect some of their programs to meet the needs of homeless women in spite of reduced operating budgets. This would include revised practices and increased support services related to deinstitutionalization. Recent policies that direct mental health services toward chronic mental illness provide the legal framework for developing these services.

9. The public assistance allowance should be raised to account for inflation. Unless this happens, homeless people who become ready to assume independent households will not be able to afford the necessary rents and the tide of building abandonment will continue.

There is evidence that public curiosity, sympathy, and genuine concern for the plight of homeless men and women are increasing. Examples of well-run supportive services for this population are also on the rise in communities throughout the country. But the comprehensive programming based on the three-tiered approach that offers a range of housing and linkages to services and a sense of community is seldom seen.

As the ranks of the homeless increase, and the numbers of women within those ranks rises, concerted and planned action must be taken to develop policies and programs that will prevent another Rebecca Smith from dying in her cardboard home.

Notes

1. *Washington Post* (February 4, 1982).
2. Callahan et al. v. Carey et al., Index No. 42582/79, Supreme Court of the State of New York.
3. These data were reported at a conference sponsored by the National Conference on Social Welfare (The Homeless: An Action Strategy, Boston, April 28–29, 1982).
4. Ibid.
5. Ibid.
6. Ellen Baxter and Kim Hopper, "Private Lives/Public Spaces: Homeless Adults on the Streets of New York City," mimeographed (New York: Community Service Society of New York, February 1981).

7. Rodger Farr, "The Skid Row Project," mimeographed (Los Angeles: Los Angeles County Department of Mental Health, June 1982).

8. *Los Angeles Times* (July 11, 1982).

9. Baxter and Hopper, pp. 30–48.

10. Vera Institute of Justice, "First Time Users of Women's Shelter Services: A Preliminary Analysis," mimeographed (New York: Vera Institute of Justice, 1981).

11. Jennifer R. Wolch, "Spatial Consequences of Social Policy: The Role of Service Facility Location in Urban Development Patterns," in *Causes and Effects of Inequality in Urban Services*, ed. R. Rich (Lexington, Mass.: Lexington Books, 1981).

12. U.S. Bureau of the Census, "U.S. Poverty Rate, 1966–1981."

13. Ibid.

14. Los Angeles County, Department of Public Social Services General Relief Regulations, Regulations 40–131, Determination of Eligibility. Section 3.31 requires the following identifying information: proof of identity, social security number, proof of residence, statement of intent to continue living in Los Angeles, and proof of U.S. citizenship. Regulation 40-119.2 states that general relief applicants are to be referred to the district office where they first appeared to request aid. Interim relief can be given if the applicant possesses an affidavit from a salaried employee of a board-and-care facility, alcoholism recovery home or detoxification center, or a recognized community agency within Los Angeles County. These regulations are prototypical of general relief regulations throughout the United States and serve as deterrents to homeless people who seek public assistance.

15. These data were first reported by Rodger Farr and Kevin Flynn, who directed the Skid Row Project of the Los Angeles County Department of Mental Health in June 1982.

16. Anne Minahan, "Social Workers and Oppressed People," *Social Work* 26 (May 1981): 183–84.

17. Gerald R. Garrett and Howard M. Bahr, "Women on Skid Row," *Quarterly Journal of the Studies of Alcohol* 34 (December 1973): 1228–43, and "The Family Backgrounds of Skid Row Women," *Signs* 2 (Winter 1976): 369–81.

18. Judith A. Strasser, "Urban Transient Women," *American Journal of Nursing* 78 (December 1978): 2076–79.

19. New Orleans Traveler's Aid Society, *Flight Chronic Clients* (New Orleans, 1980).

20. K. Schwam, "Shopping Bag Ladies: Homeless Women" (report to the Fund for the City of New York, Manhattan Bowery Corporation, April 1, 1979).

21. Jim Baumohl and Henry Miller, "Down and Out in Berkeley" (report prepared for the City of Berkeley, University of California Community Affairs Committee, May 1974).

22. John T. Gandy and Leonard Tartaglia, "Vagrant and Transient Women: A Social Welfare Issue," mimeographed (report prepared for the National Conference on Social Welfare, Columbia, South Carolina, May 1982), pp. 6–8.

23. Ibid., pp. 13–16.

24. Vera Institute of Justice (n. 10 above).

25. This was reported in personal interviews with J. Halverson during the spring and summer of 1982.

26. This estimate was reported at a conference on homeless women in Orange County, California, August 1982.

27. Rodger Farr, "The Skid Row Project" (n. 7 above), and "Concerned Agencies of Metropolitan Los Angeles Directory of Services for the Homeless," mimeographed (Los Angeles, December 1982).

28. Kim Hopper, Ellen Baxter, Stuart Cox, and Laurence Klein, "One Year Later: The Homeless Poor in New York City, 1982," mimeographed (New York: Community Service Society Institute for Social Service Research, 1982).

29. Ibid.

30. *Los Angeles Times* (July 11, 1982).

31. This information is based on interviews with staff of the agencies, investigation of annual reports, and program descriptions on file with the United Way of America.

32. These data were reported at the conference in Boston, April 28–29, 1982 (see n. 3 above).

33. Reported at the Boston conference (see n. 3 above). The Downtown Women's Center is another example of such refusal to accept public funds.

34. Christian Temporary Housing Facility, *1980 Annual Report* (Orange, Calif.: Christian Temporary Housing Facility, 1980).

35. Hopper et al. (n. 28 above).

36. Reported at the Boston conference (see n. 3 above) by Marsha Martin, director of the Manhattan Bowery Project.

37. D. Sakano, "Homeless New Yorkers: The Forgotten among Us" (testimony given at the New York State Assembly hearings, November 19, 1981).

38. Hopper et al. (n. 28 above).

39. Skid Row Development Corporation, *Annual Report, 1979–1980* (Los Angeles: Skid Row Development Corporation, 1981).

40. Ibid.

41. The National Coalition for the Homeless is based at the Community Service Society of New York.

42. Eldredge et al. v. Koch et al., in pretrial discovery process at the time of this writing, Supreme Court of the State of New York.

43. *New York Times* (February 11, 1983).

44. New York Senate, Illegal Eviction Law, 1982, Introduction 3538-B, Amendment to Multiple Dwelling Law of New York, Proposed Amendment Section 302-D.

13 Unreasonable access: Sexual harassment comes home

ANNETTE FUENTES and MADELYN MILLER

By law, landlords and their agents are entitled to reasonable access to the apartments they rent. But this six-month investigation by City Limits has uncovered a serious nationwide problem of patently illegal and health-threatening incidents of sexual harassment by landlords, superintendents and others with access to women's homes that is anything but reasonable.

Quantifying the magnitude of sexual harassment is difficult. Silence born of fear and powerlessness stifles reports from victims. All those surveyed were unanimous in the belief that the incidence of harassment is enormous and not incidentally tied to the growing housing shortage. Three years after her unforgettable incident, Jodie Gould polled 45 women tenants in her building. One-third had experienced unwanted touching, kissing and fondling from the super. Gould, a publicist for Avon Books in Manhattan, is now on a mission to publicize the issue of sexual harassment so that other women in other buildings can begin to fight it. And on a national level, precedent-setting legal actions indicate that sexual harassment in housing is moving from being a dark and shameful secret to becoming a focus of fair housing advocacy.

> November 1983: A federal court in Toledo, Ohio found landlord
> Norman Lewallen guilty of violating the federal Fair Housing Act for
> evicting Tammy Shellhammer and her husband after she refused to
> perform sexual acts with him. It is the first case to include sexual
> harassment in the definition of sexual discrimination in housing.

153

November 1984: A Milwaukee landlord was found guilty of housing discrimination for demanding sex of a woman tenant in exchange for rent and to avoid eviction. Plaintiff in the Chomicki case, as it is known, was awarded $19,000.

March 1986: An administrative law judge in New York City ruled that sexual harassment was a legitimate complaint under the city's Administrative code and ordered a hearing in the case of a woman whose landlord physically abused her and requested sexual favors. In constructing the case, the Commission on Human Rights used the Shellhammer decision to establish the link between sexual harassment and fair housing -- the first such example in the state.

DEFINING TERMS

Sexual harassment of women as it relates to housing takes many different forms. It can be the unwanted physical or verbal advances of the landlord, superintendent or even the realtor who is showing a vacant apartment. Innuendo, gestures and the suggestion that repairs, normally required services or even the granting of an apartment will be expedited if a woman complies with the requests of building owners or personnel are also harassment.

And when a woman rejects those advances, refuses to cave in, retaliation may also take a sexual, even violent, nature and lead to denial of services or eviction. The common denominator in all sexual harassment, though, is the abuse of power and authority by men who can affect a woman's housing situation and hence, the well-being of her and often her children.

Power abuse is also a central concept in another discriminatory practice women face: sexual harassment at the workplace. That direct correlation between two forms of harassment was the foundation on which the Shellhammer case was built. Attorney Tom McCarter, a fair housing specialist in Toledo, based the Shellhammer's complaint on cases developed under Title VII, the equal employment opportunity statute of the Civil Rights Act of 1968.

The federal judge who ruled on the Shellhammer case was guided in his definition of sexual harassment in housing by a 1982 employment case, Henson vs. City of Dundee. In that case, the court described two forms of harassment: creation of an "offensive environment," and extracting or seeking to extract "sexual consideration in exchange for job benefits." Applying such criteria to housing, the judge determined that sexual harassment would consist of either creating an offensive environment with a pattern of harassment, or conditioning tenancy upon sexual consideration. After Tammy Shellhammer refused the sexual overtures of Lewallen, he evicted her and her husband Thomas -- clearly an example of tenancy conditioned upon sexual consideration, as the court decided.

Parallels between sexual harassment at work and in housing are clear, says K. C. (Karen) Wagner, director of Working Women's Institute in Manhattan. Located at Cornell's Institute for Industrial and Labor Relations, Working Women's Institute has for

154

almost a decade provided education on workplace harassment of women workers. Two years ago, Wagner began getting calls from women complaining of problems with their landlords or supers.

"They would always start off by saying, 'I know you focus on the workplace, but it's happening at my home,'" says Wagner. "People were calling us as a resource and for the first time, we really got evidence that it was an issue."

Workplace harassment was also an amorphous, unnamed problem that countless women faced alone until the women's movement of the early 1970's made it a civil rights issue. Speak-outs at which victims of such employment abuse publicly decried what they had privately suffered in silence encouraged others to do likewise. Similarly, it is hoped that women subjected to sexual harassment in a housing context will increase litigations and other forms of resistance once the ice is broken.

"I think when women realize that there are viable alternatives, that other people have come forward, that they don't have to endure this, then we will see increased reporting," states Carla Wertheim. As director of program services for the Metropolitan Milwaukee Fair Housing Council, she was instrumental in bringing the Chomicki case to trial. Lots of media coverage and public support for the issue in Milwaukee caused reports to the Council of Harassment to mushroom -- a call a week in 1984-85, says Wertheim. Calls still come perhaps once a month, but "they don't leave their names. Women are afraid of their landlords and of being blacklisted from housing. There is still lots of reticence because sexual harassment is still a very sensitive issue."

Terribly underreported is how Dr. Lois Veronen characterizes sexual harassment in housing. She is an associate professor at the University of South Carolina's Crime Victim Research and Treatment Center and thinks that psychologically, this crime closely parallels rape. "It's the same context. Women blame themselves for certain aspects of their behavior. Many women who've been victims of sexual harassment are reluctant to define themselves as victims."

"Sexual harassment is really going around and no woman is going to admit it's happening because she's too ashamed," asserts Lenora Casso, a resident at the Women In Need homeless shelter last winter. "Common practice" is how she described harassment from realtors and landlords and agreed with Dr. Veronen. "These feelings are like in rape. All you want to do is suppress and forget about it. And that's how they feel when they're laying with those landlords and supers."

HOME SWEET HOME

Comparisons between sexual harassment at work and in housing go only so far. There's a point beyond which such linkages fail because the home is supposed to be one's haven in a cruel and heartless world. When the boss says lay down or be laid off, at least a woman can run home, to safety. When the landlord stalks her in that one refuge, where can she run?

"At home is more devastating. It's the place to go and be secure with your family," states Shanna Smith, director of Toledo's Fair Housing Center. The driving force behind the Shellhammer case, Smith recalls that in Lewallen's building, one woman hid under her bed every time he came on the premises.

"If women have no refuge, no place where they feel safe, if the home doesn't help in terms of restoration," states Dr. Veronen, "there is incredible psychological and physical damage." Women who've been assaulted in their homes have heightened anxiety, fear and generalized feeling of dysfunction, she says. Being ever vigilant, not knowing when the culprit will drop by, is absolutely exhausting and creates incredible damage.

For homeless women seeking housing, harassment is yet one more ignominy, proof once again of their third class status. The path out of the shelter, it seems, is paved with invitations to prostitution. According to Susan Diaz at Women in Need, it is taken for granted that you will face this treatment. "I had an experience in the Bronx. I had been to a couple of buildings where the landlords were there and they had apartments available. They get to the point where they say, 'all right, I'll give you the apartment if you'll be my girlfriend now and then.' Here you are frustrated, you want to get the hell out from where you're at, and the only way you're going to get out is to use our bodies."

The landlord convicted in the Chomicki case preferred to rent to single household heads, all women. He kept one apartment vacant for sexual encounters-in-lieu-of-rent. He carried a gun and walked the halls with a dog. Perverse patrols to make the women feel good and unsafe in the privacy of their homes.

Most of the women had bare-bones incomes and when Dolores L. asked for a month extension, he agreed but added his usual carnal caveat. He called one night to say he was coming over to collect payment. She managed to avoid sex with him but not an attempted eviction and a month of harassment, with him prowling the building. Dolores filed with the Fair Housing Council and stopped sleeping at night. She testified against him in great fear for her life but her courage paid off when he was found guilty.

MURPHY'S LAW

In New York as in Toledo or anywhere else, the targets of sexual harassment by housing owners and personnel are usually those men perceive as easy prey for a variety of reasons. For one, just being a woman can be enough to invoke trouble. "Women are seen as victims and vulnerable," says Harvey Fisher, Deputy Director of Fair Housing at the city's Commission on Human Rights. At the West Central Queens Neighborhood Stabilization Program, Ted Finklestein says five time more women than men come to complain about all types of landlord troubles. While he has few specific reports of sexual harassment, "a lot of women are afraid when the super comes in for repairs. The ever-present threat of rape is there."

Single women with no men either living with them or visibly present around their apartments are especially vulnerable. The macho credo that forbids a man to trespass the bounds of another man's relationship also dictates that an unattached woman is fair game. "I'm surprised we haven't had more of an increase in reporting," says Fisher. "We know more and more single women are renting alone or with roommates. It seems to me the super can take advantage more easily."

But being a woman without a man does not complete the profile of candidates for sexual harassment. The missing factor is money. "Usually it is women with no man in the house, who are poor, captive of the economics of their plight and forced to live in substandard housing," states Tom McCarter.

"Low income women are much more vulnerable here," says Shanna Smith.

156

"They are easy targets for landlords." Investigating the Shellhammer case, Smith found 27 women in Norman Lewallen's building who'd been sexually harassed by him. All were on welfare. The choices for them boiled down to having sex with the landlord or risking eviction; one woman who did refuse his demands found her belongings piled on the street. High unemployment boxes women into a corner, with few housing options, Smith says. "I find them taking more abuse from landlords because there is so little alternative."

Women struggling to support children on public assistance or no-frills earnings bear greater pressure to keep a roof over their collective head. "With the increase in homelessness, the fear of it is a dynamic that gets played out, creating different risks and consequences," says K. C. Wagner.

"The landlords, they seem to know who to prey on," Lenora Casso states. "The supers. They know who to pick, who's vulnerable. You might not have ever sold your body in your life but it comes to the fact that you got to house your kids then you might take that step and sleep with that landlord just to keep yourself from a shelter. Guilt doesn't matter when you've got three kids and you're living in the Martinique."

For poor women, homeless women, women with little reason to believe they can buck the system and every reason to feel helpless, the risks of speaking out against harassment may seem too great.

Gloria Pagan decided it was too risky not to speak out so May 2 she swallowed her fear and headed to the Queens Neighborhood Stabilization office. "My nerves are wrecked. I can't sleep. It's all piling up on me," she explains. Since rejecting several sexual advances by her landlord, her life has been miserable.

"At first he was fine, like a very good friend," Pagan, 38, recalls. She and her three children lived in their Long Island City apartment for seven years. The landlord and his wife moved into the dwelling across from theirs two years ago and seemed to get along well in the close-knit community Pagan and the other tenants had going. But she "never gave him reason to think I was interested in him."

Nevertheless, during a backyard barbecue in July, 1985, he followed her into the building and cornered her in the hallway, pawing her until she broke away. He approached her and another woman tenant later dressed only in underwear and started to expose himself but they shouted and walked away.

Since then, he has called the cops twice on her and her children; he went to her neighbors in March asking if they had complaints against her in a bid to evict her; he holds her rent checks and continually harasses guests to Pagan's home. But worst is his constant surveillance. "Every time I open the door, he's there by the peephole. My niece caught him with his ear on the door." On May 7, she got a letter from his lawyer threatening to terminate her lease at the month's end unless she complied with a list of demands. Number one is giving him a key to her home.

Pagan is on public assistance and the $279 rent she pays is about all she can. "Where am I going to go? I can't afford to just pick up and move." Besides she says, "This is my home, my neighborhood. I know everybody." At least one other woman in the building that she knows of was sexually harassed by him, also Puerto Rican and on welfare. Pagan's neighbor encourages her to fight because he's been harassing everybody. At this point it is a matter of survival. "I'm afraid he might push me to the limit, attack me or my 16-year-old daughter." She filed harassment charges with the state housing division and waits for her day in court.

Sexual harassment is also another weapon in the arsenal of landlords who wage war on tenants in order to empty a building. Invading armies have always sexually abused the women of their enemy nations. And for Terese Scofield, living at 285 St. Johns Pl. in Brooklyn was to live under siege in 1984. Goons and drug dealers were fixtures in the graffiti littered lobby. The owners were Jonathan Eichner and Louis Hrusovsky, one of the Village Voice's ten worst landlords. They were developing the buildings on either side of 285 as luxury co-ops.

Scofield, now an organizer with ACORN, took a fifth floor apartment April 11, 1984 with a friend and joined the tenants association fight to save the building for its low income residents.

On July 23, G., a friend of Scofield's staying in her apartment was brutally raped by an intruder who called her "Terese" and said things about emptying the building. "This block is ours, you're not going to change things," Scofield remembers her friend repeating. G. was taken to Kings County Hospital and the police arrived on the scene but they never pursued the case. "I couldn't believe the cops didn't voucher all the evidence," says Scofield. A blanket, books the rapist touched and a comb he'd used sat in a bag in her closet for five months. Scofield filed a complaint with the Civilian Review Board but that, too, went nowhere. Her friend is still, two years later, unable and unwilling to discuss the incident.

LEGAL FOOTHOLD

Three cases of sexual harassment by landlords and supers have been filed with the New York City Commission on Human Rights to date. One was settled last year (see sidebar); two others will go to hearing this summer. The federal decision in Shellhammer vs. Lewallen will figure prominently in the proceedings.

"In pleading and the trial, they will cite Shellhammer and employment cases," says Harvey Fisher, "it becomes a legal foothold." "They" refers to Bill Herbert and Cathryn Clemens, staff attorneys for the Commission. Herbert got a green light in April from an administrative law judge who found sexual harassment by a landlord was a form of sex discrimination under the city's Administrative Code. Now a hearing date must be set.

The city's Code prohibits various forms of discrimination within the city and is administered by the Commission on Human Rights. It is substantially equivalent to federal civil rights legislation but federal courts pack a stronger remedial punch than the Commission, imposing harsher penalties. Federal court decisions also can become the basis for future litigations. That's why the federal decision in Shellhammer is a vital precedent setter.

"The whole point in Fair Housing is the right to the quiet, peaceful enjoyment of your house," explains Shanna Smith. "Sexual discrimination also means harassment." She didn't know the problem existed until calls came in from Lewallen's tenants in 1983. Limited funding and staff have slowed the Toledo Fair Housing Center in pursuing the issue. But with time, energy and three good lawyers, she intends "to broaden this aspect of the law," adding, "it already has taken on national significance." Human rights commissions across the country are now calling Toledo for advice on handling sexual harassment in housing complaints.

One angle that makes this new fair housing issue more difficult to tackle than other recognized forms of discrimination is the gathering of proof. In racial discrimination cases, black and white testers are sent out to seek the same apartment. Can just any woman go out to test for sexual harassment and if no advances are made, does that rule out harassment or only that the harasser has specific preferences in women? Fisher recalls the dilemma in his office over checking a sexual harassment complaint against a landlord. "We contemplated wiring someone or sending out a co-worker. It raises the issue of who does a sexist view as attractive. The upshot was we decided it was too dangerous."

The Shellhammer case posed similar difficulties for the Toledo Fair Housing Center. "We were hesitant to expose volunteers to this," says Shanna Smith, "so another person and I decided to do the testing." At landlord Lewallen's building, Smith and her colleague got all the proof they wanted and more. "He offered to make arrangements for the other woman. He got specific with me, said if I slept with him I'd never have to pay rent. I got it on tape." The vice squad was brought in, too, by the implication of prostitution.

Legal actions to challenge discriminatory harassment are important steps in redressing a clear and present danger to women's civil rights. There needs to be much more done, though, to support those exposed to sexual abuses at home or in pursuit of a home to talk about it. Only when huge numbers of women began entering the workforce, the problem of sexual harassment gained critical mass. And only when working women came out of isolation to discuss it did the problem gain momentum for change. Unions incorporated sexual harassment into the strategy for organizing women workers, especially clericals.

As more women are living outside the traditional male-headed family, the need for protection from harassment becomes imperative. Using the workplace model in combating harassment "women must organize tenant associations. Especially with women living alone and as heads of households," concludes Karen Wagner. "Women must break the silence, seek support and counseling. Take what we know about workplace harassment -- the fear, stress, anxiety -- and apply it to housing. Advocates must be alerted to it."

Her encounter with the super was the catalyst for Jodie Gould forming a tenants association at her Upper West Side building. The association's main demand is that landlord Jacob Haberman remove the superintendent. "When he's in a position of authority in the building, such behavior cannot be tolerated," Gould says.

Since drawing together other women tenants to discuss building wide problems, Gould sees a more aggressive attitude that can be channeled to change. "We all thought it was an isolated situation we could handle by ourselves. Once you find out other women are experiencing it, it makes you powerful." Armed with a new strength in unity and knowledge of their fair housing rights, women can begin to turn the tables on sexual harassers wherever they live.

Reprinted by permission from **City Limits**, June/July 1986, pp. 1, 16-22.

14 Emergency housing for women in Canada

DONNA DUVALL

$\mathbf{W}$omen who are in need of temporary accommodation usually come from one of the following groups:

> --those who have suddenly become homeless due to eviction, fire, marital breakdown, etc.
> --those who are in a domestic situation in which they are being physically and/or mentally abused
> --those who are psychiatrically disabled
> --those who have been in conflict with the law (female offenders).

Before examining the type of help available and the different types of shelters for women in Canada, it is important to understand the general position of Canadian women as housing consumers.

WOMEN AS HOUSING CONSUMERS

In reviewing the major Canadian housing policy documents produced from 1970 to 1982, McClain and Doyle (1983) concluded:

Adequate recognition was not given to women as housing consumers, nor do we have nationally sponsored statistical research which emphasizes sex differences as available in measurement of access to and affordability of housing. Thus, the base from which we judge the housing condition in Canada, and the projections

161

of future need and consumer demand have left a significant and growing part of the population out of the equation.

The first major research taking into consideration women as housing consumers was carried out by the Canada Mortgage and Housing Corporation and the United States Department of Housing and Urban Development in 1982. One of their findings was that the most disadvantaged household type in both countries is the single parent, female headed household. Thirty-eight percent of these households in Canada and 61 percent of those in the United States were in core housing need.

Oakley and Oakley (no date) suggest that the failure to acknowledge and address the specific housing requirements of women is not due to oversight but rather the result of institutionalized bias based on a patriarchal social system. McClain and Doyle (1983) described women as the "forgotten housing consumers."

Institutionalized sex discrimination in Canada also results in women earning less than men. In 1980, Canadian women working full time, full year earned an average of 64 percent of what their male counterparts earned which means that there are comparatively many more poor households headed by women than by men. In 1982, only 9.7 percent of male headed households were below the poverty line compared to 41.9 percent of female headed households. At the same time, the number of households headed by women has increased dramatically in the past 20 years: from 13 percent in 1961, it rose to 16.5 percent in 1971 and to 25.5 percent in 1981.

As a result of their disadvantaged economic position women tend to find it difficult to obtain housing on the private market. One consequence of this is that female headed households end up being the major consumers of public housing -- and there are long waiting lists for public housing. Furthermore, women with children often face landlord discrimination even if they can find affordable housing in the private sector.

WOMEN NEEDING EMERGENCY ACCOMMODATION

HOMELESS WOMEN

Although it is generally accepted that there are growing numbers of homeless women and men in Canada, accurate figures are not available. An indication of the size of the problem is provided by a study of the Metropolitan Toronto Community Services Department in 1982 which found that 3,400 persons in Metropolitan Toronto were known to be homeless. It was pointed out these figures are likely to be too low for a population of almost three million in the Toronto Metropolitan Area as they do not include anyone who was not a client of the agencies surveyed or who was not in a hostel at the time of the survey.

The hostels surveyed by the study were operating at overcapacity, with 1,556 residents compared with 1,529 available beds. There was particular concern about the hostel designed for youth -- 261 percent capacity -- and the hostel serving families -- 103 percent capacity -- since this means that a quarter of the hostel residents were caught up in a cycle of moving from one hostel to another.

According to hostel staff, the main causes of their clients' homelessness were lack of affordable housing, lack of money, unemployment and domestic conflict. The largest increase in clients came from youth, postpsychiatric patients and individuals who

162

were unemployed but willing to work.

More specifically, the study identified the increasing problem of homelessness as being due to the following causes interacting with each other:

--a decline in affordable rental stock (especially rooming houses) in centally located areas
--low vacancy rates in the rental market;
--high levels of unemployment (the unemployment rate for Canada in January 1984 was 11.5 percent for women and 13.0 percent for (men); and
--provincial policies of deinstitutionalization of psychiatric patients.

Hostels, in Toronto as elsewhere -- originally intended to provide emergency accommodation to people temporarily without shelter due to family breakdown, eviction, etc., as well as to people with a transient lifestyle -- are now becoming a permanent form of shelter because of the lack of affordable alternatives. Many of the hostel users were previously accommodated in rooms and apartments in inner city neighborhoods, a supply which has declined as a result of redevelopment.

Another source of information on the number of homeless is the housing registry maintained by the Social Services Department of the Regional Municipality of Ottawa-Carleton. This registry provides information on available housing in the private market.

The vacancy rate for private sector rental accommodation in Ottawa dropped in the summer of 1982 and has remained low: the current rate as of April 1984 was 0.3 percent. As the supply of rental units decreased, rents increased. As a result, a sizable number of tenants were unable to find affordable rental units in spite of the fact that the province of Ontario has rent control legislation. Even there, however, not all rental accommodation is covered by this legislation and landlords are constantly finding new ways of getting around rent controls.

As the rental market became tighter the housing registry acquired a new role of providing emergency housing. Barton (1983) reported that from February to June 1982 there was an average of 842 calls a month regarding emergency housing. Of the approximately 125 to 150 people per month who applied for housing, on average, appropriate housing was found for only 12 of them. The rest had to remain with friends or relatives or be accommodated in motel rooms. In 1983, the region spent 930,000 dollars (Canadian) on emergency housing. Of this amount, 360,000 dollars went to motel bills.

According to Barton, the majority of people seeking emergency accommodation through the housing registry are young, single mothers with children, many of whom have recently been separated.

Persons who have to be accommodated in motels face a number of problems due to not having a fixed address. Some schools have a policy of not accepting children who do not have a fixed address. In addition if the family is not already receiving social assistance they cannot apply for it as long as they do not have a fixed address.

One of the ways in which the needs of the homeless in Canada are being met is through church-run programs which provide temporary accommodation. These services have tended to operate as winter emergency programs from the beginning of November until the end of April. The cost of operating these programs is usually borne by one or more levels of government. However, the facilities and staff, usually all volunteers, are provided by the churches.

A further indication of the growing number of homeless is provided by the fact that in 1983 the province of Ontario spent seven million dollars on church run programs for the homeless. For 1984, forty-five million dollars have been set aside for existing, expanding and new programs for the homeless.

As the need for emergency shelters has increased more imagination is being shown in finding buildings which can be used for temporary accommodation of the homeless. In Ottawa, vacant schools, churches and a recently vacated police station have been turned into emergency shelters. The owners of a 50 room hotel which has just closed have offered it as temporary shelter for the next eight months until scheduled renovations to it begin.

BATTERED WOMEN

There are no reliable figures on the incidence of family violence in Canada. MacLeod (1980) estimated that one in ten Canadian women is battered by her husband or common-law spouse. Her figures were based on an analysis of divorce records and infor-mation provided by shelters for abused women. MacLeod's figures translate to 500,000 Canadian women being battered in their home. MacLeod also reported that wife battering often occurs during pregnancy and that 50 percent of batterers had themselves been beaten as children.

According to Smith and Chalmes (1984) there are no Canadian studies of the extent to which women involved in violent marriages or relationships seek help from intervention services outside their homes. Estimates from US studies vary from approxi-mately 25 percent (Gelles 1978) to 43 percent (Schulman 1979) of abused women who do not seek assistance of any sort. Part of the reason for abused women not seeking assistance may be the shortage of emergency shelters for them to turn to.

Allan (1983) reports that the first transition house evolved from a neighborhood drop-in center for women and children in a suburb of London, England in 1971. Within a year similar shelters had begun in Australia, Denmark, Germany, France, the United States and Canada. All of the shelters were organized by women in the community who became aware of the fact that other women were living in violent situations and needed help.

The first transition houses for battered women in Canada were opened in the provinces of British Columbia and Alberta in 1972. As of July 1984 there were 165 emergency shelters for women across Canada. These shelters provide a temporary home for battered women and their children and provide them with information about legal and social services.

A report prepared by the Canadian Advisory Council on the Status of Women (1983), described some of the problems faced by shelters for battered women:

They are run by women working long hours for low pay, and they rely heavily on volunteer help. Even with this dedicated work, some shelters finally fold for lack of funds. Their numbers are pitifully few in relation to the need for them...Rural and northern women, already the most geographically isolated, have the least access to these houses. Those houses that do exist cannot accommodate all of the women who come to them for help.

Most transition houses rely on a combination of provincial and local welfare money, short term grants from the various federal government departments and charitable donations. The welfare eligibility criteria exclude many women. Because the shelters need the welfare per diem payments to survive they are forced to accept primarily women who are eligible for welfare.

It has been estimated that approximately 18,000 women stay in transition houses annually -- in Canada -- and that these women bring 21,500 children with them to transition houses each year. Due to the funding problems faced by transition houses, there are very few provisions for children.

The increasing numbers of homeless women have created shelter problems for battered women. Barton (1983) noted that women with housing problems are being forced to seek accommodation at shelters which previously had been used only by battered women and women are being forced to stay longer than necessary at transition houses because of their inability to find affordable housing for themselves and their children.

One positive development has been the establishment, in January 1982, of a Canadian National Clearinghouse on Family Violence, which provides information and consultation to individuals and groups concerned with domestic violence and gathers information on wife battering as well as child abuse, incest and elder abuse.

In addition to "transition houses" devoted exclusively to the needs of battered women several other ways of providing emergency accommodation have been proposed:

> --There are currently 12 Family Resource Centers (FRC) in the sparsely populated northern part of the province of Ontario. The FRC serve the need for temporary accommodation of a number of groups including battered women, pregnant teenagers and people with no money -- usually women with children.
> --Through the use of "safe homes" in the province of Ontario, which has announced plans for 200 such homes across the province. They are based on the "lock parent" model which currently exists for children -- one home on each lock, identified by a prominent sign in a front window, where children can go in case of an emergency such as being threatened by a stranger.

Safe homes for battered women would be linked to existing services for battered women such as transition houses and crisis telephone services. The names of safe home operators would be given to battered women through these services. Safe home operators would be paid a modest annual retainer fee plus a per diem when the bed which is reserved for battered women is used. There would be a full time counsellor for every ten to 20 safe home operators. Safe homes could also take the form of small apartments which are rented for this purpose.

The city of Toronto, which has a large number of immigrant families, has been trying to find ways of meeting the need for emergency accommodation of immigrant women, who are being battered. Three proposals have been put forward.

--The first proposal, which came from two churches, proposes setting up two transition houses, one in the midst of the Greek, Yugoslavian and Albanian immigrant community, and one in the Italian and Portuguese immigrant area with staff who speak their languages since immigrant women tend to be socially and culturally cut off from shelters for battered women. Each of these centers would have a paid counsellor and be linked to store front counselling services in the communities.

--A variation of the above which consists of a store front counselling service and a network of safe homes for battered women operated by members of the ethnic community to which they belong.

--A third proposal, which was rejected, was for a large shelter which would service immigrant women from all ethnic communities.

THE PSYCHIATRICALLY DISABLED

The psychiatrically disabled have tended to find accommodation in boarding or rooming houses. Rooming houses usually provide a room for sleeping and shared kitchen and bathroom facilities.

There are three types of boarding homes:

--The first type consists of commercial unlicensed boarding homes which provide room and board.

--The second type is also unlicensed, but the operators receive a per diem which is cost shared by the federal, provincial and municipal governments. In the province of Ontario, homes in this category are known as "Domiciliary Hostels." There is pressure to have homes of this type licensed.

--The third type provides 24 hour supervision as well as room and board. Some but not all of these homes are licensed. In Ontario this type of home, called "Homes for Special Care," is licensed by the provincial Ministry of Health, and their operators are paid a per diem. Only persons discharged from a psychiatric hospital can stay at these homes.

Halfway houses and group homes also provide accommodation for the psychiatrically disabled. These homes tend to have restrictions on the length of time that individuals can stay. They are usually operated by nonprofit groups and accommodate at the most 20 people.

In Ottawa in 1981 the YM-YWCA Housing Service placed 130 psychiatrically disabled people in rooming houses. The Homes for Special Care and Domiciliary Hostels accommodated approximately 329 psychiatrically disabled persons. The two halfway houses and three group homes can accommodate a total of 31 women. However, 2,515 female in-patients who had been identified as having some type of psychiatric disability were discharged from the hospitals in the Ottawa region from April 1, 1980 to March 31, 1981.

Numerous groups have questioned the advisability and practicality of relying primarily on the boarding home/rooming house market to meet the housing needs of the psychiatrically disabled (Parker and Rosborough 1982). In most major Canadian cities affluent middle class families are purchasing rooming houses in city cores and converting. them to single family dwellings. Sociologists refer to this process s "gentrification." Parker and Rosborough found that Ottawa had experienced a 50 percent decrease in its rooming house stock in the last five years due to this phenomenon. Residents of the remaining rooming houses are regularly evicted and find it very difficult to find afford-able alternative housing.

An opinion survey, conducted for the Canadian Mental Health Association on the adequacy of existing services for the psychiatrically disabled, identified specific problems which included:

...the scarcity of halfway houses providing short-term, high-support accommo-dation; the needs of the young, eighteen to twenty-five year old group; and the long waiting lists for existing housing alternatives. In addition, when respondents were asked to rank services in order of priority for future development, accommodation received top priority" (Parker and Rosborough 1982).

The three directors of the group homes for women in Ottawa interviewed by Barton (1983) pointed out that because of the shortage of suitable affordable accommodation the group homes end up allowing women who are ready to move out to remain there. At the same time all three group homes had an occupancy rate of over 96 percent and were forced to turn away many psychiatrically disabled women who required accommodation.

FEMALE OFFENDERS

A number of Canadian cities have community residences for adult female offenders. The purpose of such houses is to provide a supportable environment for these women while they restructure their lives and look for accommodation, employment, etc. Some of these units are operated by the Elizabeth Fry Society, an autonomous organiza-tion dedicated to providing services for and changing the conditions for women in conflict with the criminal justice system in 17 Canadian cities. Residences for adult male offenders are operated by the John Howard Society and St. Leonard's.

Residences tend to be small (under 20 residents) and filled to capacity. In Ottawa there are two residences -- Fergusson House with a capacity of ten and MacPhail House which can accommodate nine women. The occupancy rate in the former for 1982 was 98 percent -- 24 women had to be turned away; for the latter in 1982, it was 88 percent -- 167 women could not be accommodated.

EMERGENCY SHELTER

MODELS

A detailed description of typical cases will provide more insight into the modes of action, problems and policies related to emergency accommodation.

The Hamilton Inasmuch House, the oldest family shelter in Canada, opened in 1965 in response to a Social Planning Council report recommending a temporary shelter for women. It is part of the Women's and Family Ministries Division of the Mission Services of Hamilton. The Mission is a registered nonprofit Christian organization and provides care to victims of domestic violence, teenage girls in crisis and women with or without children needing temporary shelter. The House has 21 beds (11 bedrooms), a children's toy room and a fenced yard with play equipment.

Recognizing the need to provide longer term accommodation for abused women in some cases, the Mission purchased the house next to Inasmuch and joined the two facilities by a connecting link. After an assessment period at Inasmuch House, selected women and their children are permitted to reside at this "Next Door" for a prolonged period while court cases are being settled, while husbands are being counselled or until they feel it is safe for them and their children to return home. The capacity of Next Door is eight adults.

Women in Transition, initiated through a grant from the now defunct Canadian government Local Initiatives Program (LIP), was opened in Toronto in 1974. It is an innovative social service which was specifically set up to house women and children who have been forced to suddenly leave their home and who must confront marital breakdown and single-support parenthood against the backdrop of immediate homelessness. It also services the following groups: single-support mothers; mother and children who suddenly become homeless due to fire, eviction, etc.; mothers who have been released from total-care institutions (hospitals, psychiatric units, prisons, etc.) and are about to be reunited with their children; mothers and their children who have been abroad for some years and wish to return to Canada; mothers moving from another province (Cools 1980).

In general, only women with children are admitted. For women with marital problems -- nearly always physical abuse -- the maximum length of stay is four to six weeks. For women with housing problems every effort is made to limit the stay to two weeks. The maximum number of residents that can be accommodated is 18. Immigrant women make up one in three residents of the house. There are seven staff members, and, as Cools notes, like most emergency shelters, limited funds prohibit the payment of the kinds of salaries professionally trained personnel can demand.

Constance Hamilton Co-op, a 31 unit town house complex in Toronto, was the first housing cooperative in Canada created by women for women. It is named after the city of Toronto's first woman councillor. Start-up funds came from the municipality; however, the main funding was in the form of a two million dollar mortgage insured by the federal government through Canada Mortgage and Housing Corporation.

The co-op was designed for the needs of women in general and for women with children in particular. All units have large combined kitchen and dining areas so that mothers can cook while their children play within view. A six bedroom unit for women who need crisis housing is incorporated into Constance Hamilton Co-op. Women are allowed to stay for six months to a year. A part time counsellor, who does not live in the project, is available, and a house committee helps women from the crisis center partici-pate in co-op affairs and integrate with the rest of the community. Men may live in the project but may not become members, a decision made to ensure that women retain control of the co-op and its management (Goliger 1983).

The lack of day-care facilities in the area is one of the biggest problems faced by the co-op residents. Without such facilities, it is exceedingly difficult for women with young children to become economically self-sufficient.

An innovative design helped to overcome the problem of meeting-room space,

168

which Canada Mortgage and Housing Corporation's funding formula does not allow for. The ground floor laundry was therefore designed so that it has a picture window overlooking the park, space to hold a meeting and children's play space. Furthermore, a series of "storage rooms" which could be used for a food cooperative, workshop or an exercise room were incorporated into the basement (Simon 1982).

Monroe House in Vancouver -- the first second-stage transition house in Canada -- emerged from a recommendation at a conference on Family Violence in Vancouver in 1977. This recommendation was based on the fact that transition houses are not able to give women enough time for such things as sorting out their legal problems, recovering from their physical injuries and beginning job retraining.

Operated since 1979 by the Vancouver YMCA with funding from the province of British Columbia, Monroe House is a large old house with six self-contained one bedroom apartments and a staff office, consisting of two co-managers and one on-call person who is available in case of vacation and sickness. The co-managers identified the basis for referral to Monroe House as:

Only battered women with children are accepted; no difference is made between physical and psychological battering; she cannot be potentially abusive to herself or to her children; and she must not be at that time chemically or alcoholically dependent (Lancaster and Quinby 1983).

From 1979 to 1982, Monroe House accommodated 67 women and 114 children. Eight of these were native Indian women, 19 were from various ethnic backgrounds -- Greek, Italian, East Indian and Portuguese -- and 40 whose first language was English.

CONCLUSION

The needs of homeless, battered and psychiatrically disabled women and female offenders for temporary shelters have been recognized by the various levels of government in Canada. However, the number of emergency shelters of all types is inadequate to meet the demand: they are operating at capacity and are forced to turn away women in need of emergency accommodation.

More emergency shelters would definitely accommodate some of the women who are currently being turned away. However, there are several other factors which are complicating the problem: the high unemployment rate; the wage gap between women and men; the conversion of rooming houses into single family homes or luxury townhouses; and the low vacancy rate for private sector rental accommodation in many Canadian cities.

The first two factors relate to the economic situation of women. The last two relate to the supply of affordable rental accommodation. Emergency shelters will continue to be swamped by requests from single mothers, recently separated women, etc., who are unable to afford private sector rental accommodation and can only join many other families on the long waiting lists for public housing until the economic status of women improves. Furthermore, shelters will continue to be flooded with requests for accommodation from women who cannot find affordable accommodation, and shelters will have to allow women to stay longer than they need because of the lack of reasonably priced accommodation to which women in emergency shelters can move, until the problem of the supply of affordable rental accommodation is properly addressed.

The author is with the Research and Policy Branch of the Canadian Human Rights Commission, Ottawa, Ontario, Canada. She has published several articles on women's housing problems. The views expressed here are entirely those of the author.

REFERENCES

Allen, C. (1983), "Refuse from the storm -- Transitional housing for battered women," *Habitat,* vol. 26, no. 1, pp. 2-4.

Barton, D. (1983), *Housing in Ottawa -- Carleton: A Women's Issue* (Ottawa, Elisabeth Fry Society).

Cools, A. (1980), "Emergency shelter: The development of an innovative women's environment," in *New Space for Women,* G. R. Werkele, R. Peterson and D. Morley (eds.) (Boulder, Colorado, Westview Press).

Canadian Advisory Council on the Status of Women (1983), *As_Things Stand -- Ten Years of Recommendations* (Ottawa, Canadian Advisory Council on the Status of Women).

Canadian Mortgage and Housing Corporation (1981), *Housing Affordability Problems and Housing Needs in Canada and the United States: A Comparative Study* (Ottawa, CMHC).

Gelles, R. J. (1978), "Abused wives: why do they stay?' in *Violence in Canada,* M. A. Beyer Gammon (ed.) (Agincourt Ontario, Methuen Publications).

Goliger, G. (1983), "Constance Hamilton Co-op -- Housing by women for women," *Habitat,* vol. 26, no. 1, pp. 22-26.

Lancaster, J. and A. Quinby (1983), "Vancouver's Monroe House -- A second stage transition house," *Canadian Women's Studies,* vol. 4, no. 4, pp. 56-57.

MacLeod, L. (1980), *Wife Battering in Canada: The Vicious Circle,* prepared for the Canadian Advisory Council on the Status of Women (Ottawa, Canadian Government Publishing Centre).

McClain, J. and C. Doyle (1983), *Women as Housing Consumers* (Ottawa, Canadian Council on Social Development).

Metropolitan Toronto Community Services Department (1983), *No Place to Go -- A Study of Homeless in Metropolitan Toronto: Characteristics, Trends and Potential Solutions* (Toronto, Metropolitan Toronto Planning Department).

Oakley, A. and R. Oakley (n/d) "Sexism in official statistics," in *Demystifying_Social Statistics* (London, Pluto Press).

Parker, A. L. and L. Rosborough (1982), *A Matter of Urgency: The Psychiatrically Disabled in the Ottawa-Carleton Community* (Ottawa, Canadian Mental Health Association).

Schulman, M. (1979), "A survey of spousal violence against women in Kentucky," in *Battered Women,* D. M. Moore (ed.) (Beverly Hills, California, Safe).

Simon, J. (1982), "Co-operative housing for women," *Landscape Architectural Review* (Nov.), pp. 5-7.

Smith, P. and D. L. Chambers (1984), "Does sheltering help abused women?" presented to the Annual Meeting of the Canadian Sociological and Anthropological Association in Guelph, Ontario from June 6-9, 1984.

Reprinted by permission from **Ekistics** 310, Jan./Feb. 1985, pp. 56-61.

PART VI
WOMEN IN THE
THIRD WORLD

15 Women's housing needs in the Arab cultural context of Tunisia

SUSAN E. WALTZ

The social phenomena of modernization and urbanization have brought mixed blessings to Tunisian urban women in lower economic strata. Without question, amenities assured by mass production, urban markets and increased social services have eased some of life's burdens, but newer ones are steadily assuming their place. One modern problem lies in the area of housing.

The difficulty with supply or access to housing, common in Third World countries, is not the most troublesome problem. Housing market rigidities do exist in Tunisia, but they do not uniquely or primarily affect women. Their problem is rather one of limited and/or poorly allocated space.

The observation appears simple; rising urban density throughout the world has made problems of reduced domestic space nearly universal. Yet the problem does not affect everyone indiscriminately. Men and children may sense some deprivation, but in societies where women normally work at home and are responsible for domestic affairs, those same women are the primary victims. Tunisian women in lower economic strata easily fall into this category, but the rather unique social context of their lives -- shared to varying degrees across the Maghreb and the Levant -- has rendered the problem especially acute.

SEXUAL SEGREGATION

Conservative critics and Western admirers alike acknowledge that the Tunisian government has carried female emancipation further than any other state in Islam. In 1956, President Bourguiba introduced a Code of personal status abolishing polygamy, requiring the bride's consent as a prerequisite to marriage and allowing wives to initiate divorce. A 1981 amendment guarantees alimony, including housing and child support, for divorced women.

It is tempting to infer from the Code that the sexually segregated social system that prevails in Islam is being gradually dismantled in Tunisia, and many observers have yielded to that temptation. Signs of such change, however, are only minimal, and social indications of the desirability of such change are not necessarily more abundant. The reforms provided by the Code are widely heralded, and the growing number of women entering the workforce every year do testify to social support for women's right to participate in economic activities outside the home. On another plane, the growing visibility of amorous young couples in secluded areas of Tunis' few parks hints at the loosening of a traditionally strict moral code. Nonetheless, in the eyes of the average Tunisian, society remains sexually segregated. Social taboos still prevent a respectable woman from stopping at a cafe, and similar taboos make it unacceptable for a man to approach a house where he is not known. In the city, women's social life revolves around women, almost exclusively inside their homes. Men, by contrast, socialize outside the home -- while strolling, sitting in a cafe, in a sports stadium or at work.

Today, both Westerners and the Tunisian elite hold the practice of sexual segregation in disdain. Yet in times past, when the dominant mode of living was the extended family, the claustrophobic effects of seclusion were mitigated in several ways. First, the presence of other women assured a social life. To be sure, close proximity was often the source of antagonism between in-laws, though the practice of endogamy helped minimize these problems. Regardless, total isolation was not frequent. Perhaps more importantly, the dwellings were necessarily spacious. A woman might be spatially confined by social custom, but the area in which she lived was not limited to 75 square meters, and a large courtyard assured access to air and light.

Those mitigating factors have now all but disappeared for poor urban women. Even in the more socially conservative lower income brackets, the nuclear family has replaced the extended grouping. Further, the size of lots intended for low cost housing has been cut severely in efforts to create affordable housing in high demand, expensive urban areas. Planners do, nonetheless, allow for community facilities, such as wide streets, schools, cafes and shops, recognizing their inherent social value. Yet with the inevitable trade-off between these amenities and residential lot space, the practice of social segregation requires women to bear disproportionately the price of community improvements. It is their private space that is being sacrificed bit by bit each time.

THE HOUSING NEEDS OF URBAN WOMEN

A closer look at the life of the urban poor, seen through the testimonies of Tunisian women, will amplify and elaborate these concerns. In 1982, some 35 women in three different communities in the capital city of Tunis were interviewed about their needs and problems in the area of housing as part of a comparative inquiry into women's housing needs. About half of the women were married and financially supported by their husbands and/or children; the others were single heads of households, either widowed, divorced or maintaining their families while their husbands were abroad as guest workers.

All belonged to households whose incomes were easily lower than the national median; most fell into the lowest quintile.

The Communities

The community of Mellassine figures prominently among Tunis' several well established squatter settlements and is now the target of upgrading efforts. Comprised of some 12,000 self-constructed dwellings built over the past 50 years at the edge of a salt marsh, Mellassine suffers from insanitary conditions and a reputation for delinquency, transience and poverty. Twelve women were interviewed here, half of them married and living conjugally and the other half heading their families alone. The nature of this settlement is such that we were able to sample renters as well as owners of the stone and baked earth dwellings.

The planned community of Ibn Khaldoun offers a wide mix of units, from basic core housing to comparatively elaborate three-bedroom dwellings. The six women interviewed here were owners, though strictly speaking, in most of the cases the deed was registered in the husband's name alone. Dwelling units visited were of the simplest model, originally comprised of a single room, a courtyard, a latrine and a kitchen space. In every instance, however, these basic structures had been improved by the addition of a second room. Most of the families contacted here had come to Ibn Khaldoun from Djebel Lahmar, a squatter settlement that underwent radical upgrading in the late seventies.

In the Tunis Medina at the heart of the city three oukalas were visited. An oukala by strictest definition is a dwelling once intended for a single extended family that has been transformed into numerous smaller, relatively inexpensive rental units for several families unrelated by parentage. Today oukalas house more than half of the population of Tunis' crowded inner city (fig. 1). The average oukala has ten rooms, and ranges in size from those housing two or three families in one or two room units to grand old urban residences now harboring twelve to 15 families. The structures themselves are often quite complex, with a room or two near the entry or with a second story, but the basic model remains that is traditionally found in North African urban dwellings: several rooms arranged around a central courtyard. Any given family occupies only one or two of these rooms, and the common courtyard is shared by all occupants. In each of the three oukalas visited -- one simple structure with two families; one smaller two-story structure with nine families; and one relatively spacious old mansion now housing six separate families, some of them quite sizable -- all the available and interested women occupants were interviewed en masse.

The Residents

In each of the communities respondents were asked to tell about their overall living conditions and their surroundings. There were the inevitable complaints about inefficient, inadequate or altogether missing community infrastructure, about the cost attached to many services, problems with water and sewage, and, in the Medina, about the difficulties of living in a souk or market place. But a set of complaints about neighbors was equally frequent, except in the Medina. Over two thirds of those interviewed in Ibn Khaldoun and Mellassine openly expressed social alienation, whether in sad observations that everyone keeps to himself or in admission of fear or mistrust of neighbors. By contrast, in the Medina, many spoke enthusiastically of their fellow tenants; in one oukala even with the claim that they sorely missed each other when one was away.

Fig. 1 Tunis Medina   Source: Rivkin

Fig. 2 Interior Courtyard of *dar arbi* Source: Waltz

175

Except in Ibn Khaldoun, where most residents had already been relocated once, most of the women were anxious to move, but that desire was clearly related to hopes for improved housing. A kitchen was essential; then a bathroom and an area for laundry. And several rooms, all arranged around a courtyard. Typical of the residents of Tunis' high density, inadequately serviced areas, most of the women had moved to Tunis from a rural area, though some in childhood. They may have come from traditional mud huts (gourbis) or small houses, but undoubtedly their ideas about housing were derived from the traditional dar arbi (fig. 2) a spacious walled compound comprised of several vaulted rooms surrounding a courtyard where work is often done communally, quite typical throughout Tunisia. Ideally, the dar arbi is large enough to accommodate two or three nuclear units within an extended family.

For most immigrants, it was probably in Tunis that they first encountered any radically different model. It was not surprising, then, when asked directly whether the dar arbi was better than European style housing, the women expressed a strong and almost unanimous preference for the traditional model.

There is, however, some danger in accepting this opinion at face value. In 1973, the Tunisian Association for the Preservation of the Medina interviewed some 30 families of at least modest income who had applied for housing in the hafsia area of the Medina that was then in the design stage. They found that the common desire was for a house with functionally-specific rooms and no patio -- in short, the antithesis of the dar arbi. It is not clear whether the subjects were of Tunisian or rural origin, but the question may be irrelevant. Those who have monitored the situation for some time feel that as pressures to improve social status mount, so rises the demand for housing in high rise apartments and independent villas. Within the social strata of limited income, there is perhaps some desire to emulate the bourgeois of urban origin, because the notion of an "ideal" house incorporates not just one's own origins, but also one's aspirations. And aspirations to improve social standing can cause problems with housing -- leading people to ask for or install themselves in housing units which are functionally unsuitable (fig. 3). Thus one notes with amusement the apartment dweller at the "Feast of Aid" trying to butcher his freshly slaughtered sheep in a tiny kitchen on the fourth floor of an apartment building, and less humorously, lonely women in cold concrete buildings, isolated from both family and potential friends.

WOMEN'S LIVES

Reconciling consumers' contradictory demands is undoubtedly one of the major challenges facing planners today. No solution, though, can be offered without an adequate and conscious understanding of social patterns as they have been and as they are evolving. Adapting housing to people requires empathy for the consumer. In low income urban Tunis where most residents are not of urban origin, planners must take into account the function of domestic space in both urban and rural settings.

Whether she lives in an extended family compound or in a smaller unit, the rural woman is responsible for at least all family management that is restricted to the home -- cleaning, cooking, laundering and caring for children; men often do whatever marketing is done. In even the humblest dwelling a special corner is designated as kitchen, and the ever present courtyard serves routinely as laundry room, children's play area, a place to prepare tea over the coal-burning brazier, and space for preparing flour for

176

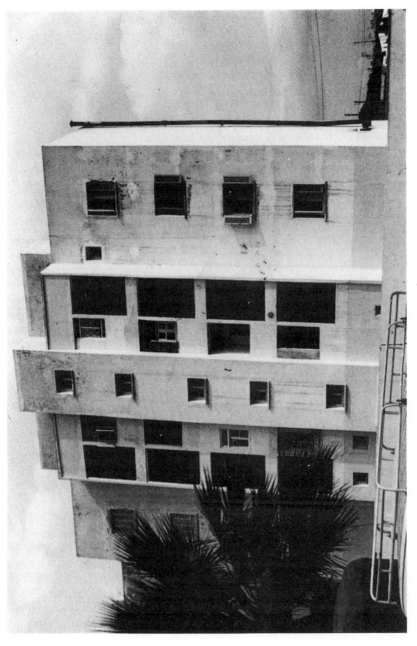

Fig. 3 Apartment building in the vicinity of Mellasine   Source: Rivkin

couscous or wool for weaving.

By many of their chores women are bound to their homes, but others also take them outside the home quite frequently and for long periods of time. Women are normally responsible for drawing water from village wells or springs, and they gather kindling for the oven; many also work in the fields.

Unquestionably, many of the tasks performed by women are onerous and tedious; what makes them bearable is that they are shared tasks. The rationale for communal work may be complex and involve social taboos, but the fact remains that one never finds one woman alone gathering kindling, just as one never finds a woman alone at the well. And while women living within the compound of an extended family may do their household chores separately, the social interaction between women is incessant. Outside the home, social taboos assure a woman's social life; inside, it is facilitated by a spacious courtyard, where she may share in work, casual exchanges or formal social occasions with neighbors and relatives. For the rural woman, the home is hers and is her haven -- but it is not the only place she knows. Though social life may be sexually segregated, there is generally plenty of it.

Traditionally, the urbanite's life is radically different from that of her rural sister. The city dweller's basic chores remain the same -- cooking, cleaning, laundering and caring for children. But gathering firewood is no longer necessary, and even before the widespread residential installation of running water, many homes were equipped with their own wells. In the cities women do shop more frequently than in rural areas, but even so, overall, the city woman who respects established social taboos leads a life fare more restricted and secluded than does her rural sister, and consequently the attributes of the dwelling assume added importance. It is true that more and more urban women are joining the workforce, but as yet employed women form a decided minority -- about 20 percent of all adult women -- and employment figures distributed across age groups indicate that withdrawal from the work force is common during childbearing years. The mitigating effects of work beyond the home, thus, cannot be counted on exclusively to break the seclusion of the home.

In the past, as noted, seclusion was not so problematic. Today, however, the practice of sexual segregation for a woman confined to cramped, European-type quarters translates into restricted social relations, but restricted light and air as well. For the transplanted ruralite, that deprivation is even more important.

WOMEN'S SPACE: RECOMMENDATIONS

The most salient problem to emerge from this study was that of limited space. Women in all but one of the dwellings raised the issue, usually more than once. Whether the immediate concern was the size of the rooms or their number, the unifying theme was space. The problem is acute in the cramped quarters of Mellassine and the Medina, but it is no less so for the residents of Ibn Khaldoun's relatively spacious units. There, economics have dictated the necessity of taking in lodgers; thus an area intended for a single nuclear family is quickly destined for two. The space problem consequently applies to renters and owners alike.

Urban planners and architects who have heard this plea before, tend to dismiss it as impractical because urban land is at such a premium and urban lots can no longer be spacious. To date, the single compromise seems to be more rooms -- generally, two plus a kitchen -- in the core units being built, but this compromise is at the expense of the courtyard -- and traditional design. Without question, the intense pressures on available urban space are real, and if anything, will increase. Equally real, however, are the social costs attached to the space problem to which women with a single voice are calling attention. In a context of widespread social change, it would be impossible to isolate the adverse effects of inappropriate housing, but surely this problem is making some contribution to the seriously rising incidence of neuroses, psychological depression and suicide among women.

Despite widespread pessimism about a successful resolution of space problems, there are several possible solutions which merit exploration.

The first potential solution affects the design of low cost units underwritten by the public sector. The first inexpensive units under construction in 1982, though architecturally esthetic, make far less than full use of lot space. For a rising middle class expressing a preference for European-type housing and intending to build vertically, the allocation of space is not problematic. However, for Tunisians for whom the dar arbi remains the ideal dwelling, the garden space outside the walls of the home is wasted. For these individuals, probably comprising the majority of Tunis' poorer half, compound walls should maximize inner space.

At the same time, residents need the maximum freedom to allocate space within the compound. In several conversations about the utility of the courtyard, women indicated that both the function and the utility of the courtyard changed over time as the family unit itself changed, as did indeed the need for multiple and sizable rooms. It might, of course, be added that with social transitions occurring at widely disparate rates, the function of domestic space can be expected to vary widely even across families demographically very similar. When told about the idea of low priced, very simple and virtually unfinished structures, the women were quite enthusiastic. "The essential thing is the property and the basic structures; the rest can follow," was a typical reply. That the rest will indeed follow is borne out by the experience in Ibn Khaldoun. The original intention was to visit six women living in the most basic units, but it was learned that at that time, seven years since the project's inception, it would be difficult to find unim-proved units. In fact, all six of the residents visited had added at least a second room to the original structure.

A second potential solution, more experimental in nature, owes its conception to the oukalas of the Medina, where a large courtyard is normally shared by several women. These common courtyards are sometimes a source of conflict because they are constantly invaded by men and because privacy for individual families is not assured. But experi-ences in one oukala, a fine old architectural structure now in serious disrepair, offer promise that with some important modification the oukala model could address both spatial and social problems that modernization has brought to women in Tunisia.

Six families, one with eight children, live in an aging edifice in an area of the Medina where many venerable and gracious dwellings still stand in various states of repair. Two features in the oukala were immediately remarkable: the common courtyard was quite neat and clean, as though it were private space; and high ceilings gave a welcome illusion of space, enhanced by decorative tiles, carved plaster and Andalusian painting typical of Tunis' older luxury dwellings. From the women we learned that the care of the communal courtyard, about 100 square meters large, was not problematic: each woman cleaned the area used for family laundry and other chores, and for more routine cleaning of the stairs and courtyard they had devised a rotation.

In the course of interviewing, a third, less tangible, feature became apparent: the social atmosphere in the oukala was quite pleasant; the women were lively and engaging as they had not been elsewhere. And they were proud of their homes. Undoubtedly personalities played some role in this -- but undoubtedly, too, the physical environment made its contribution. This relative harmony between neighbors was intriguing, because everywhere else the most common complaint about the community had been the neighbors, expressed in fear, dislike, distrust and regional stereotypes. The contrast between this oukala's harmony and sentiments more commonly expressed in the other two communities takes on added significance when compared to antithetical observations in a Moroccan shantytown. In the Moroccan settlement, almost half of those interviewed cited friendly relationships with neighbors -- not relative -- as the primary positive aspect of the neighborhood. In that community, though, women enjoyed a communal space which they had created by suspending clotheslines across the narrow streets that traversed main shopping streets, socially designated as the area for men. In Tunisia, the bitter irony is that the very social practices which encourage suspicion of neighbors -- viewed as a protection for the family -- are also threatening to undermine the family by encasing the newly urban woman, deprived of the neighborly and family relations she would have known in a rural milieu, in a social cocoon.

A shared communal area could be one viable means of expanding women's space, but for it to be useful and for it to have social benefits as well, certain principles need to be observed:

> --First, it would necessarily be adjacent to the dwelling, though it should expand rather than substitute for the private courtyard -- which might, however, be reduced in size;
> --Secondly, in the interest of assuring spontaneity and informality -- the substance of routine social exchange -- it should not be associated with some already existing structure, such as a party cell or a family planning center;
> --Finally, the area should be shared by only a few women and should remain firmly closed to men.

One physical arrangement that suggests itself is a series of modest units, each with its own small courtyard, built around a communal courtyard, subdivided if the number of units were substantial (fig. 4). From a rear entrance the units could have access to the courtyard, designated by structure as an extension of inner space, and therefore women's space; a front door would open onto a public pathway or street. Reducing street width in one direction would minimize the land costs of the communal courtyard -- essentially taking space socially reserved for men and reallocating it to women.

This most radical solution might well prove most effective in combating both the immediate space problem and the modern problems of social isolation. Obviously, though, it is an innovative solution and would require experimentation.

A third, less drastic, means of addressing space constraints would entail only indirect enlargement of the areas reserved for women. Thus, for example, stimulation of the female labor market might provide relief for some individuals to the extent that the workplace could provide access to air, light and social activities. The ramifications of such a policy are extensive, of course, and require their own treatment.

More strictly in the housing domain, playgrounds, envisioned but rarely built in almost every planned community, could alleviate the space problem. Regardless of their employment situation, Tunisians are convinced of the utility of childcare facilities, which

180

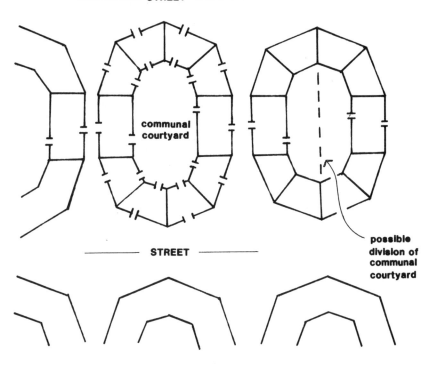

STREET

communal
courtyard

STREET

possible
division of
communal
courtyard

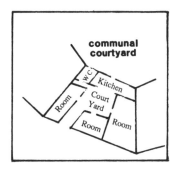

communal
courtyard

W.C.

Kitchen

Room

Court
Yard

Room

Room

Fig. 4

**Sketch of housing complex with
core units around communal yard.**

181

if nothing else they see as establishing an important foundation for success in school. Freeing mothers from children at least part of the time makes employment possible, first of all, but even if employment is not sought, periodic absence of children still increases the personal space available to the mother. Physically structured but informal play areas might also expand space for women, while at the same time providing a place where their small children can play safely.

Finally, facilitating access to other public spaces traditionally used by women -- most notably the public baths -- might in some measure alleviate space constraints. Public baths are known as a place for social encounters and escape from daily routine, but with rising prices, they have become prohibitively expensive to many families. While any of these policies to facilitate women's access to the exterior world might ameliorate in some small degree the claustrophobic perceptions of urban women, they should not be expected to redress the basic problem. These solutions might be easier to effect because they involve less physical infrastructure, but they tend to skirt the real issues and thus by themselves offer only partial solutions.

CONCLUSION

As the pressures on housing capacity and urban space which have evolved over the last few decades continue to grow, the problem singled out in this study will also mount. Although the observations reported here were based almost exclusively on experiences in Tunisia, it is expected that other societies with similar pressures and similar social patterns will experience them, too. Less centralized states might avoid some of the problems through supervised autoconstruction, but even so, site planning for urban services and infrastructure will remain an essential component of housing policy. To minimize social costs, it is essential that some generally applicable solution to the problem of reduced inner space be included routinely as an integral part of that site planning. Whether the solution be one of those proposed here or some other is at this point of relatively little importance. What is important now is for planners to recognize the existence of the problem and to realize that it is not without solution. The common cry of consumers, who happen to be women, deserves immediate attention.

NOTES

1. Funding for the study was provided by the Office of Housing, U.S. Agency for International Development. The author is with the Department of International Relations at Florida International University, U.S.A. She specializes in psychological response to social change, geographically focused on North Africa and she has been a Consultant to the U.S. Agency for International Development's Office of Housing on projects in Morocco, Tunisia and Mauritania.

2. Information gathered from a small, nonrandom sample cannot be called representative. Verbatim transcription of responses helped to guard against illusory correlations, that psychological mechanism whereby we hear what we expect to hear, and one obvious drawback to the case study approach. Even so, readers are cautioned that the comments reported here can only be regarded as suggestive.

3. These women could not, in any case, have been expected to express any hostility, interviewed as they were in a group. By the same token, though, many expressions of friendship and cooperation were encountered that went well beyond what the situation required.

4. M. Chabbi, "Aspirations' et structure de l'espace residentiel," in Systeme Urbain et developpement au Maghreb, A. Zghal et al. (eds.) (Tunis, CERES Productions, 1976).

5. Ibid.

6. While some village women may not be able to articulate, or may not even realize, the importance of the social contacts their outdoor chores afford them, evidence of their importance is offered by women living in isolated areas anxious to establish large families for the express reason of combating loneliness and isolation.

7. National Union of Tunisian Women, El Mar'a, no. 32-33 (September-December, 1980).

8. A. Baffoun, "L'Acces des Tunisiennes au salariat," in Femmes et Multinationales, A. Michel et al. (eds.) (Paris, 1981), p. 240.

9. S. Waltz, "A Socio-Economic Study of Ben M'Sik, Casablanca," prepared for the Office of Housing, Agency for International Development, 1978.

10. Cf. Baffoun, op. cit., p. 238.

Reprinted by permission from **Ekistics** 310, pp. 23-34.

16 Women and habitat: Nairobi 1985

DIANA LEE SMITH

The needs of female-headed households - which predominate among poor families - were a central issue addressed at the Forum 85 Women and Habitat workshop, held alongside the UN End-of-Decade Conference in Nairobi last July.

The needs of households run by women must be considered in planning, design, legislation, and in recognition of the need for child care facilities. The needs also include provision for subsistence food production, relieving women's responsibility for water and energy supplies, inclusion of women in construction, and removal of barriers to women's earning opportunities.

Ingrid Munro, who became UN Director of ISYH (International Year of Shelter for the Homeless) last September, opened the workshop with a call for help from Non-Governmental Organizations (NGOs) in identifying habitat issues concerning women. One-quarter of the world's population occupy inadequate, unhealthy or disaster-prone shelter, and 30 percent of the world's households are female-headed. Problems include disease, malnutrition, lack of employment and income, and excessive demands on their time. Women in these desperate environments work up to 20 hours daily, juggling jobs, child care and domestic duties.

Munro urged NGOs in developing and developed countries to pressure governments and aid agencies on women and habitat issues. Developing country governments should formulate programs and pressure donors to support credit and assistance for women, cheaper building materials that women can handle, women's access to land and housing, participation in decision-making, support for services women need, and removal of legal sanctions on women's work in the home and the informal sector. The burdens of childcare on women and young girls has to be addressed. She called on journalists, researchers, political parties and representatives, and on women's groups, to play their roles actively on these issues.

HOUSING AND INFRASTRUCTURE: WOMEN'S NEEDS AND GOALS TO THE YEAR 2000

The basic issues are common to all women, but particular strategies vary according to culture and technology development. Specific problems addressed by this group include:

Food: Rural women and subsistence producers have to compete against large scale cash cropping; they need agricultural inputs including credit. Urban women need planned space for food gardening; employed women need access to communal food facilities.

Water: Rural women in developing countries must travel long distances for water, and poor urban women must cope with scarce and costly supplies.

Energy: rural women, once again, must travel long distances for firewood, while both rural and poor urban women depend on decreasing supplies.

Access to workplace: Rural women suffer lack of transport and must often carry heavy loads. Suggested strategies include ox-carts, goat carts, improved yokes and back packs.

Child care, health care: Child care must be accessible and affordable for all women with children. For developing country women, especially the urban poor, health is linked to lack of sanitation, refuse disposal, nutrition, illiteracy and unemployment.

Housing design: Traditional rural family and support structures get destroyed when people are squeezed into inadequate spaces. Single-parent households need community (and private) kitchens, laundries, cooperative buying, shared toys and equipment.

• General issues covered by this group:
• Women's need for training on aspects of infrastructure and services;
• The need to recognize women as independent economic entities;
• The usefulness of an integrating approach to service provision involving women's participation in setting priorities, planning and implementation;

The need for women to participate in IYSH and for women's needs and priorities to be addressed by IYSH.

HOUSING NEEDS IN RELATION TO INCOME GENERATING ACTIVITIES OF WOMEN

Women often work in the home because they can combine such work with their subsistence production, childcare and maintenance of the home. Such informal sector activity is needed by many women because it can be easily started by an individual and does not need a lot of capital or skills training. Women are also often pushed into this type of work because of the other demands on their time, and by settlement planning and relocation strategies that ignore their work needs. At the same time, such work in the home is also ignored or frustrated by design, planning and legislation.

The group made the following recommendations:

1.   Commercial and land use bylaws preventing fairly nuisance-free income-generating activities within the house should be relaxed;

2.   In designing low-cost housing, architects and planners should provide an appropriate space for women's income-generating activities. The space

should be appropriate in terms of local climate, family health and safety, and local cultural norms;

        3.   Urban building bylaws which demand unrealistically high building standards should be changed to permit the use of local building materials and techniques;

        4.   Women should be given construction skills. This will allow them to help construct their own houses as well as giving them a marketable skill. It will also prevent cheating by contractors;

        5.   Market places and small workshops should be easily accessible, properly located and of a design affordable by the poorest women;

        6.   Urban planning bylaws should make proper provision to allow residents to keep small stock and cultivate vegetable gardens;

        7.   Women who do income-generating activities within the home often do not have adequate marketing facilities or information due to their isolation in separate households. Therefore institutions which lead to fairer marketing practices and prevent exploitation of female producers or home workers should be developed. Marketing co-ops, training and other support services for women were mentioned.

HOUSING PROBLEMS FOR RURAL WOMEN

Women have a substantial task in building and upkeep of the home. In some traditional societies women are responsible for house construction. In others there are taboos against it, but they may still be responsible for collection and preparation of building materials, plastering floors, finishes, maintenance and repairs. The availability and cost of building materials, both traditional and modern, are of concern to women. Supplies of traditional materials are rapidly disappearing because of cash-cropping and other competing land uses. Rural training programs on use of modern building construction are rarely accessible to women.

Women in some countries do not have the right to establish their own land or buildings. Widows, divorced women, and these days unmarried mothers, live in the compound or dwelling of a male relative. With increasing pressures on land, sons have greater access and more of the young women have to go to towns, some into prostitution or other illegal activities such as brewing. Other families are separated by male migration, the wife remaining on a subsistence farm, but without legal rights. Cultural traditions and family ties protect women to some extent. However, among rural as well as urban women, female-headed households are on the increase and their problems need to be faced.

FEMALE-HEADED HOUSEHOLDS AND HOUSING NEEDS

The number of female-headed households is rising rapidly in all parts of the world, both in urban and rural areas. This is a new social development which does not yet receive sufficient attention from policy makers. Migration by men in search of jobs, economic and social problems due to low incomes, age difference between husband and wife, and pregnancies of teenage girls can be considered the main causes.

Taking all households of the world together, at least 30 percent of them consist of a mother and her children without a permanent husband. This statistic was reflected in this working group, of which 30 percent of the members (two out of six) happened to be themselves female household heads.

The group stressed that many single mothers are trapped in the vicious circle of poverty. Earning a low income, they cannot afford to pay anyone to look after the children. This restricts them to a small range of jobs which pay little. Having no free time, these single mothers cannot go for further training to upgrade their skills. This again limits them to low paying jobs. In other cases the burden of child care falls on small girls, leading to accidents and lack of female education. Worse still, it leads to growing numbers of abandoned and street children. The provision of adequate, accessible and affordable childcare centres is therefore a very high priority.

Many countries have low-income housing projects, but they are insufficient in number. Single mothers suffer most as they are often given a low ranking on the waiting list. Many mothers spend almost 50 percent of their income on housing. Having so many responsibilities at the same time makes time very precious to single mothers. Accessible and reliable means of transport is therefore of the utmost importance to them.

The group pointed out that female-headed households in particular need the support of neighbours to share household chores and especially childcare. Single mothers should get together in an organization so that they can speak out with a strong voice and defend their interests. They must take part in public decision-making about housing matters, since this concerns the well being of the nation's children.

The group recommended that:

1.   The needs of female-headed households be recognized as being of great importance;

2.   The consideration of female-headed households be guaranteed in national and local habitat policies;

3.   Childcare centres be developed to enable these women to contribute their potential; this should be included in habitat policy making at all levels; such centres should be available at low cost and 24 hours a day for women on split shift;

4.   Transportation be easily accessible;

5.   Housing for female-headed households be adapted according to their needs and include time and labour saving devices such as food storage and laundry facilities.

LEGAL CONSTRAINTS AND OBSTACLES AFFECTING WOMEN AND THEIR ACCESS TO CREDIT AND MATERIALS

This group discussed legal aspects of women's access to land, housing and credit, which are very interlinked, as well as customary constraints.

In many developing countries, women's legal rights to land and property ownership are restricted, particularly by inheritance laws. This causes hardship, especially to female-headed households already affected by poverty. There is a vicious circle of lack of money to buy land and lack of title deeds as security for access to credit. Many countries have a mixture of legal and customary traditions which are difficult to sort out. Some countries are changing their laws to permit equal access for women. But even where laws are changed, behaviours restrict women's access to land, housing and credit.

Obstacles to women's participation include lack of women decision-makers, women's needs being not included in plans and budgets, rigid sectoral ministries and lack of political strength at the local level, too many other demands on women's time, legislation, customs, some governments' repressive attitudes against women's participation, lack of women's literature and women having to "reach out to a man's world."

The group discussed the need to reach the poorest, where women predominate, and pointed out that "welfare" type policies of governments which assume a trickle-down effect do not work for the poorest. Increasing absolute poverty, the growing gap between rich and poor countries, and the hidden poverty in wealthy countries were also discussed.

The following recommendations were made by the group to the United Nations:

1.   Recognition of the different needs of men and women (gender considerations) must be included in government planning, including use of foreign and bilateral aid;

2.   IYSH must focus on women's needs and priorities and include women at all levels in planning and implementation of activities.

CONTINUATION AND GLOBAL NETWORK

In summary, Anje Wiersinga of the Netherlands Council of Women said the workshop's objective was to exchange experience on women's needs in human settlements and identify strategies on how to proceed. An additional objective is to follow up the workshop by forming a global network on women and human settlements. She stressed the importance of existing NGOs and networks working together and of linking developed and developing country women.

The workshop registration forms were used to register in the new Global Network on Women and Habitat. Interested participants will form the basis of the network which, it is hoped, will link with existing networks and newsletters, including:

● Women's International Network (WIN)
● Match International, Canada
● Settlements Information Network Africa (SINA)
● Women and Environments
● Planners Network

It is hoped this network will continue to promote and disseminate the ideas and strategies for women launched at Forum 85 and summarized in this document. Those interested in participating in the network should contact:

Habitat International Council, c/o IULA, 41 Wassenaarseweg, 2596 CG The Hague, Netherlands; or Netherlands Council of Women (NVR), laan van Meerdervoort 30, The Hague, Netherlands.

Reprinted by permission from **Women and Environments**, vol. 8, no. 1, pp. 7-9. (Subscriptions: $13/yr. outside N. America: $18. From: Women and Environments, Centre for Urban and Community Studies, 455 Spadina Ave., Toronto, Ontario M5S 2G8, Canada). A longer version appeared in SINA (Settlements Information Network Africa), no. 9, 1985.

17 Women and property

FRAN HOSKEN

At the 1976 United Nations HABITAT Conference in Vancouver, Canada, the issue of women's property rights was dramatized by a divorce case that made headlines in the local papers and was widely discussed at the Conference.

A wealthy Canadian farmer divorced his wife of more than 30 years. The wife and her minor children were left penniless, dependent on welfare. The farmer kept the prosperous farm which both he and his wife had built up together over many years; however, even though the wife's contributions and work in developing this valuable property were as great as her husband's, she had no legal right to any of the property!

Women in too many countries where property rights discriminate against women on gender grounds, and where married women especially are deprived of property rights by the marriage contract, are still similarly affected. Many cases record that women discover, upon getting divorced, that they have no legal right to the family home which they thought they owned. Traditional legal real estate documents exclude a wife from home ownership, even if both husband and wife financially contributed to its purchase. The house is registered in the husband's name alone.

In some countries, men may dispose of their wives' property and real estate, including the family home, without the consent of the wife, even though the property may be registered under both their names. Women have found themselves evicted from their homes after their husbands had sold or gambled away the property, without any consultation.

In the USA, special credit and banking legislation had to be passed because it was found that -- especially where home mortgages were concerned -- banks discriminated against women solely on the basis of sex.

In socialist countries, land and real estate is public property; therefore, very different conditions of land ownership and real estate prevail. Recently, many families working on collective farms have been given access to private plots of land to grow their own food crops; female vs. male rights to such family plots and/or homes should be investigated as well as how these arrangements, including different forms of access to land, are organized and affect women.

The property rights of women differ vastly all over the world as shown in the study *Law and the Status of Women: An International Symposium,* published by the United Nations Centre for Social Development and Humanitarian Affairs in Vienna, which briefly surveys women's property rights among other legal issues.

Where Moslem (Sharia) Law is recognized, daughters inherit only half what their brothers receive, including access to land. Married women in many Moslem societies retain and control their own property in their own names and many dispose of it freely as they wish. Unmarried women or widows, however, are often compelled to give their land and property to a male member of the household to "manage" because women are deemed "incapable" of doing it.

In some Indian states, women are excluded from managing their property and must hire a male manager who is then in control.

In many countries, property rights are a local concern, dependent on ethnic or local traditions that may differ greatly within one country or state.

For instance, in the *Country Reports on Human Rights Practices for 1983,* (the Country Reports on Human Rights Practices are submitted annually to the US Committee on Foreign Affairs (House of Representatives) and the US Committee on Foreign Relations (Senate) by the US Department of State), the status of women is discussed briefly in each country report, including women's access to property.

The 1983 Report documents that in many African countries tradition still excludes women from access to land and from all land ownership in their own name.

This situation seriously diminishes food production since women are the main subsistence farmers in most of Africa. Per capita food production has been decreasing over the past 10 years, especially in sub-Saharan Africa, as women food farmers are increasingly pushed off the most productive land by male farmers who grow cash crops for export.

Cash crop growers in Africa get technical aid, modern tools, fertilizers and credit from the government, which is interested in agricultural production for export. Female subsistence farmers get no support; on the contrary, they are often obliged to work as agricultural labour for their husbands free or at a minimum wage, neglecting their food crops.

Decreased food crop production leads to widespread hunger among the women and children who remain in rural areas -- quite aside from the effects of recent devastating droughts -- while the men leave for the towns.

Access to rights to land in traditional agricultural societies affects the status, the well-being and the productiveness of each social group. But especially women and their children who, as a result of discrimination in land rights, are the largest group of the poor and the hungry in every developing country.

In many African countries, women cannot inherit or own land, and face barriers in obtaining access to land for agricultural purposes.

192

CREDIT WITHHELD

Credit also is rarely available to women farmers in their own name since without land, they have no collateral. In Burundi, Botswana, Kenya, Burkina Faso, Swaziland, Liberia, indeed, most of sub-Saharan Africa, women lack property rights as the above cited Country Reports confirm. But a systematic survey of Africa has not been made.

At the opening Conference in March 1984 of the newly-formed Women's League of Zimbabwe, Teurai Ropa Nhonga, Secretary of the Women's League, demanded that married women should have property rights which they still lack, as reported in the Zimbabwe Herald.

In Kenya, which has a sophisticated, modern urban sector, a loan application for a kindergarten project was recently rejected by Kenyan banks, though it was made by the President of the National Council of Women, also a member of Kenya's Parliament. The reason: bank credit is not available to women!

Land reform legislation, where it exists, does not seem to consider women farmers as persons. As the study by Lisa Bennett *The Legal Status of Rural Women: A Review of those Aspects of Legal Status which Limit the Economic Participation of Women in Rural Development*, published by the FAO, reports, land reform in Ethiopia -- by virtue of designating the "head" of each family as the beneficiary of land distribution -- resulted in excluding women altogether from all land holdings in their own right. If anything, the reform made their situation worse, especially in polygamous households.

Often, land reform, by using modern legal tools, also deprives women of their customary rights of access to land, for instance, in sub-Saharan Africa.

ALONE AND LANDLESS

The situation of Asian and African women farmers is worsened when men leave to seek employment in towns. Women and children do the farming alone on land the women are not entitled to own, and from which they may be evicted at any time.

The situation of rural widows is often desperate, as they lose access to land on the death of their husbands and thus the prime source of support for themselves and their children. Such is the case in many countries of Africa, for instance Kenya, and also in India.

Urbanization schemes, for instances sites and services programmes, in their allotment of plots, generally consider only "heads of families" as eligible -- that is, men. Even though a man may have several wives, each man is still eligible for only one plot -- depriving his other wives and children of access to land and housing. In her book *The Domestication of Women: Discrimination in Developing Societies*, Barbara Rogers documents this exclusion of women from such schemes.

In most of sub-Saharan Africa, a man is not legally obliged to support his wives or children and can divorce his wife unilaterally, usual in most Moslem societies, without her consent. She is then evicted from her home and house and loses all access to land.

Traditionally, land in Africa was community property. The village chief assigned land to each man according to the number of wives he had, as each wife, through her husband, was entitled to enough land to grow food for herself and her children as well as to feed her husband and any male members of his family.

At present, in modern agricultural development schemes in Africa, especially internationally financed ones, all land is assigned to the male family head -- in the assumption that he is responsible for the upkeep of women and children. In reality, it is the woman who is obligated to provide food for her husband and her family.

In addition, in many African countries, what she earns from her work belongs to the husband.

In urban areas, the systematic disenfranchisement of women from property ownership is now being recorded and registered in all legal documents. In Africa, where urbanization is greater than anywhere and cities are growing by 10 percent or more per year, the exclusion of women from land ownership will seriously affect their status in coming years.

At present, up to 90 percent of women in most African countries are living in rural areas where land is still plentiful. But, as more and more people move to urban areas, the legal inability of women to own and control land virtually excludes them from economic development, from access to credit, and thus from developing their own economic base, pushing them thus in even greater numbers into prostitution and/or poverty.

The damaging effects of discrimination against women in land and property ownership have not been sufficiently recognized or emphasized. Indeed, the overwhelming injustice of legal systems that deliberately disenfranchise women and exclude them by law from property ownership has never been discussed.

Equal access to land as the primary resource, especially in agricultural societies, is of overwhelming importance to women, and this must be the basis for a demand for legal equality for women and new legislation. In urban areas, access to land as a basis for establishing credit is the condition sine qua non for trade and business establishment.

NOTE

The author, trained as an architect at the Harvard Graduate School of Design and MIT, is a specialist on urban/international development worldwide. Writer and lecturer, she is also the editor of the WIN News, the publication of the Women's International Network (WIN). She is currently raising funds for the study on property rights and may be contacted at 187 Grant Street, Lexington, MA 02173, USA (617) 862-9431.

This article has been excerpted from **Development Forum**, Oct. 1984.

18 Women, urbanization and shelter

FRAN HOSKEN

The UN designated 1987 the International Year of Shelter for the Homeless to draw attention to the unmet shelter needs around the world. With increasing urbanization, the number of homeless people has been growing steadily worldwide. Women and children are the majority of those without shelter -- with women-headed homeless families increasing in every society. Since the 1976 UN Human Settlements Conference in Vancouver, Canada, the contributions by professionals have been mostly concerned with analyzing the many seemingly overwhelming problems of urbanization. Few solutions have been offered given the poverty of most city administrations -- especially those in developing countries which face the greatest influx of immigrants and have practically no means or money to deal with them in an organized professional and politically acceptable way.

Urbanization can be seen as a unique opportunity for people, and women especially, to change their lives to escape from oppressive traditions of the past and village life which has always excluded them from positions of control. Rural women in developing countries are socialized from childhood to perform the hardest labour, they are constantly threatened by hunger and ill health, isolated and under the rule of male family members.

Urbanization, in such a situation, is a welcome opportunity for change: urban living offers education, a variety of different lifestyles and most of all economic rewards for hard work and individual enterprise. Urban living provides contact with new ideas, technology and opportunity for training and information from around the world. In fact, it offers a whole new way of life especially to women who traditionally have had to provide the food and much of the farm labour.

PERSONAL INITIATIVE

In an urban environment, it is each person's initiative that counts and that is rewarded. Though women face many of the same problems as in rural areas, such as providing food, water, housework and childcare, they also have many opportunities to earn their own money and have access to education, self-development and learning new skills. The city also offers many services, including health care, information about family planning and women's rights, as well as how to lead an independent life based on self-support and much more -- there is upward mobility available to women as persons in their own right.

Instead of deploring "urban problems," these questions must be asked: How can urban opportunities be made more accessible to women immigrants to enable them to help themselves? What has to be done to make urban services available to women who are the real creators of urban community life? What do women need to help themselves and their families to a better life and future?

URBAN IMMIGRATION

First, it is necessary to analyze urbanization and define what it really means for those who come to the cities in ever larger numbers and especially women and their families. Urban immigration -- the move from rural areas to the cities -- is a worldwide phenomenon. It is estimated that before the end of the century the majority of the world's population will live in urban settlements of some kind, while throughout history the vast majority of all people have lived on and from the land -- that is, as peasant farmers. The 1986 "State of the World Population Report" says:

"More than 40 percent of world population currently lives in urban areas. This will increase to 50 percent shortly after the turn of the century. Developed regions have been more than 50 percent urban since the mid-20th century. Developing countries are expected to pass this mark in the first quarter of the next century."

The migration to urban areas is now peaking in Africa, where many cities and towns are growing by 10 percent or even more each year, creating enormous health, sanitation, supply and housing problems. It means that cities are doubling their inhabitants in less than 10 years.

At present, in most parts of the world, with the exception of some Latin American countries, men are leaving the rural areas first; they go to the towns and cities, leaving their families behind in the villages. Most African towns have a large surplus of men, while women are left in the villages to do all the subsistence farming to feed their families. But recently in Africa also, more and more young women are joining the move into the cities; many follow their husbands and bring their children along.

In Asia, the migration to urban areas, mostly by family groups, started several decades ago. By now cities, and especially the capitals all over Asia, have grown into huge urban agglomerations of millions of people that are surrounded by squatter settlements. Yet despite these hardships and the squalor of their living conditions, most immigrants prefer their present situation to village life.

In many Latin American countries, rural women work in the households of well-to-do urban families while their own families remain in the villages. But, increasingly, whole families are leaving the rural areas in search of a better life -- as shown by the huge squatter settlements surrounding many cities, for instance Lima, Santiago or Brasilia.

What does this migration to a town or city mean to a woman and her family, and why are more and more people leaving the rural areas and moving to a town?

Moving into an urban environment offers possibilities that do not exist in rural areas. There are handsome buildings, parks and wide streets full of people; entertainment and festivals that can be shared; urban "services," new goods, and clothes and all kinds of food that attract the newcomer; incentives to take part in this new, exciting and seemingly easy way of life abound.

Most cities in developing countries by now are surrounded by squatter settlements of rural immigrants. Many also settle on any vacant lots in the cities, under bridges, between buildings, indeed on every available piece of land, building some sort of temporary shelter. Since immigrants do not own the land on which they build, they are subject to instant eviction as their shacks can be, and often are, fire and health hazards.

Sites and services (S&S) projects are organized and funded by the public sector as a response to the urgent needs of urban immigrants who are unable to pay for any housing. S&S projects mean that public land, usually open fields surrounding the cities, is divided into rows of individual plots connected by roads that are built first and equipped with water lines and other services. A plan is made to include space for future neighbourhood shops, schools, markets, etc., usually surrounding a centre with public facilities such as administration buildings and clinics to be built later. The plots are rented (or sold on an installment plan) at very low prices to families who are required to build a permanent shelter for themselves within a given time.

S&S projects can be described as the infrastructure, that is, the physical component of planned new communities. This infrastructure -- roads, water supply, sanitation, electrical and other services -- requires public investments and continuous public support and therefore cannot be built by individual families. S&S projects provide a permanent way to settle immigrants, encouraging them to build their own houses without fear of eviction.

The housing departments of governments are in charge of planning and developing S&S projects -- often with international financing and technical assistance. For instance, the World Bank, the US Agency for International Aid (AID) and other Western governments support and finance such projects. Various kinds of new settlements have been built or are under construction, for instance, in Zambia, Kenya, Malawi, Senegal and other African countries; also Korea, India and other parts of Asia and all over Latin America, including Chile, Argentina, Brazil, Colombia and Peru.

S&S projects give women a unique opportunity to become active participants in community-building -- practically from the start -- to organize community life and services in new ways according to their and their families' needs. While most men go into town to work, women, especially those with small children, spend more time in the new community. For instance, visiting such new settlements as the Copperbelt Towns of Zambia, one can see women building houses, digging ditches and carrying on all kinds of construction work. Women also decorate their houses with different designs and are, of course, in the forefront of all marketing activities -- buying and selling everything from vegetables to old tin cans, charcoal and second-hand clothes -- quite apart from washing and haircutting to childcare.

Economic self-sufficiency of the new settlement is an immediate goal: the necessary supplies and services should be provided within the community by residents, rather than buying the goods and services from outside. Here women can play an all-important role -- using their own houses as trading centres.

COMMUNITY MANAGEMENT

S&S projects need to be supported by community management. The money earned by those who have jobs outside the new settlement should be spent on services and goods produced by community members or within the new settlement, thus providing a growing capital base for community services and improvements. A financing mechanism such as rotating loan funds and cooperatives should be organized with assistance and initial financing provided by the community management.

Women are in an excellent position to organize and provide the necessary services as well as marketing and trade until such time as the community elects its own administration.

Building a home requires a major physical as well as financial effort by the immigrants, aside from their having to live in a new way in a very different kind of environment. The essential questions that must be raised are:

- What makes S&S projects into successful communities for people? What can be done to enhance their economic and social development which supports the building of the physical environment?
- How can the potential of women for the human and social development of the new community be fully mobilized?

The criteria listed below are designed to support individual families in the great effort to build their own homes as well as assist in the economic and social development of the whole community. Managers and their international financiers must first recognize women's vital contributions in community-building and then maximize the opportunities for them to participate as full partners in every phase of the work.

Further, the role of women as community organizers, as guardians of safety and as developers of a new social base must be supported by the physical plan and given attention by the S&S administrators who run such programmes. For the difficult task of creating homes that are more than shelter, and communities that are more than streets and buildings, the full participation of women is needed.

- Land/plot ownership or rental. Women and men must be guaranteed equal access to plot ownership or leasehold (or equally shared joint ownership) providing both partners with equal rights and responsibilities, requiring the written consent of both co-owners to sell or dispose of the plot. Women as heads of families must be given the same rights and access to plot ownership as men, as well as the same access to credit and financing.

- Land use regulations. A viable land use plan should be prepared according to local regulations to protect settlers as well as safeguard health and the public interest while preventing land speculation. No plot use restrictions should be made (e.g., running a small business from one's home) unless the activities interfere with the neighbours'

198

rights or create a public nuisance (smoke or other kinds of pollution).

- **Plot sizes.** Plot should be large enough to grow some vegetables and/or keep small animals for food. Alternatively, communal garden plot areas should be designated, where plot owners can have gardens. Traditional families often include grandparents and unmarried relatives. A "family" may be two or 20 people. Plot sizes should be distributed according to family size/need.

- **Building materials and supplies.** Stores should be run by the plot/community administrator's office to sell building materials at cost. Credit must be available on an equal basis to women and men.

- **Community organization and leadership.** Community organizing -- leading to local self-government -- should be based on the neighbourhood structure, with one woman and one man elected from each neigbourhood to assure equal representation.

- **Extra room rentals.** Some plot occupants build additional rooms for rent. In many cases, this is the only way they can finance the plot and build. However, rental opportunities also are abused by speculators and absentee landlords; rules to protect the community must be spelled out.

- **Community activities and services.** Plot occupants and especially women should be assisted in starting small businesses, service enterprises and markets within the community as a means to keep income within the new settlement, rather than buying the services and products outside. A special credit facility should be created for that purpose, for instance, a rotating fund run by women for women entrepreneurs. Special plots for commercial activities ("corner stores") should be planned into each community and run as consumer cooperatives by local women.

- **Self-help cooperatives.** Cooperative self-help and training programmes should be developed by community leaders with equal participation of women. Construction cooperatives, whereby plot owners of one area work together exchanging labour, often get the job done much quicker.

- **Access to transportation.** Inexpensive transportation from the town to the site as well as within the community is essential for economic viability. Such a local transportation system offers new employment opportunities, especially to women (as drivers, etc.). Credit to organize a local transport service should be offered to women on an equal basis with men.

For women, home ownership is an important goal and incentive to demonstrate achievement and leadership in quite a tangible form: it can serve as a status symbol and resource for all women in the community. For instance, a house jointly owned by women in each new community can serve as an education/meeting/organizing/recreation centre for women, including childcare. It also can provide shelter for women who need protection from abusive husbands and can serve many other functions -- as needed by women -- to provide a base and support.

The development criteria outlined above are designed to encourage new settlers not only to build new houses and a new physical environment, but to develop a different and more productive way of life based on mutual support and sharing of rights and responsibilities among all people. The building of a new community is a learning experience that offers a real opportunity for urban immigrants to work for a better future and more productive life that leaves behind the notions of superiority and inferiority attached to gender and race, and all its damaging stereotypes.

Reprinted with permission from **Development Forum**, May 1987.

19 Monica's life: A continuous fight for shelter

UN CENTRE FOR HUMAN SETTLEMENTS

Monica Wanjiru is a Kenyan grandmother of some 53 years of age. She was born and raised in a farming area of the Rift Valley in Kenya. Her deceased parents were farmers with a small plot in the valley and Monica still has a brother on the family farm and three married sisters nearby.

Monica completed Grade 3 of primary school in the late 1930's before dropping out and taking up other household responsibilities of a growing girl. Today she can still sign her name and count enough numbers so as not to be cheated in simple business transactions.

By the time she was 16, Monica had married a farmer. During the independence struggle he died, and as a widow of the freedom struggles, Monica was able to move into Nairobi. She and her four children took up residence in a single room the city council allocated to her in the Bahati African Housing Estate. Later she had four more children in the city.

The Bahati estate is only about a mile from where Monica now lives in a rural type (but semi-permanent) mud and wattle home of her own construction. In 1958 the Bahati Community Centre was paying 89/-shs.k. a month on Monica's behalf for the rent of her one room with an outside kitchen and a common toilet shared by several households. She herself was earning a living at the community centre by weaving traditional banana fiber baskets for sale to tourists and by selling vegetables among her near neighbors. By 1969, however, the community centre stopped paying rents in Bahati. As several of her eight children had to pay school fees, Monica could no longer afford the monthly rent of that single room in permanent materials.

In 1969 she and her large household joined other squatters on waste land at the bottom of Bahati hill, right on the banks of the ever more polluted Nairobi River.

201

Fig. 1 Housing conditions common for many women in the Third World. Source: Mark Edwards/UNCHS (Habitat)

Monica, with the help of her sons and daughters quickly erected a single room shanty made out of packing cases and cardboard as well as mud and wattle. She lived in that shanty from 1969 until 1984 when the Undugu (Brotherhood) Society of Kenya and the local chief allocated her a small plot of land on the other side of the river and the Netherlands Embassy supplied her (and 200 of her near neighbors) with sturdy poles, cross ribbing, a strong door and galvanized metal roofing for the self-help construction of a semi-permanent home in traditional rural design. This may explain in part why Monica appears to be a happy and optimistic homeowner, one for whom the words "care free" had finally taken on some real meaning.

Between the year 1969 and 1984, when she was living in her crate and cardboard shanty, Monica's home was repeatedly burned down. Several times by the staff of the city council who engaged in extensive squatter clearance operations between the years 1970 and 1975. At other times, her shanty, which was built wall to wall with her neighbors, burned when cooking or beer brewing fires broke out on the block and quickly spread from one house to another. In one of these fires Monica and her children lost everything they owned: beds, bedding, chairs, clothes, school books, etc. During those years, there were many nights when the whole family slept out in the wind and the rain. However, as soon as the local furor and press exposure subsided, perhaps only two or three weekends later, she and her neighbors were back building new shanties out of used crates, plastic and cardboard purchased from hawkers working out of the city dump. She, in fact, can rebuild the whole shanty or "igloo house" in one working day.

Monica's uncle had taken two of her children back home to raise them in the Rift Valley. She does, however, remember many times when the other six went to be hungry and crying. There were other occasions when they were sent home from city schools for a week, month or a term because their fees were late or their uniforms incomplete or worn out. Shoes and sweaters were the most costly items. On those occasions Monica worked harder during the day and went to bed at night hungrier than they. She reminisces about a very bad time when two of her children caught serious chicken pox and she had to sleep with them for more than a week in the city hospital.

Monica's present optimism seems to date from a time in 1984 when social workers from the Undugu (Brotherhood) Society of Kenya set up an office and began surveying as well as organizing their Kanuku "village" community. These social workers had the chief's permission to resettle the squatters on the other side of the Nairobi River, since the city sanitation works were taking over their traditional site.

Since Monica was by now a grandmother seven times over and had two of her sons' households living with her in extensions to the shanty, she and her sons were allocated three very small plots around a miniature open courtyard where they could each build a two-room hut in the "New Kanuku" village. When she was shown the plots and allocated the construction materials (trees, a door and metal roofing), Monica and her two sons set to work constructing their eighth and, hopefully, final home in Nairobi. They had to buy tools, nails and windows for themselves aside from contributing all the labor. Soon they also hope to receive (from the Netherlands Embassy) a few bags of cement with which to permanently plaster the outside of their new homes. Each of the three houses was completed in three weeks. The entire job took just under three months.

Monica attributes her current optimism (1986) to the fact that she finally has a bit of peace and quiet in her life. She resides in her own safe, secure and water proof home. She has been resettled in the midst of her old Kanuku neighbors. She can still sell potatoes and charcoal from a roadside stand and for the past two years her neighbors have elected her chairwoman of the local Women's Society for Progress. She is a respected elder who has seen much of life and whose opinion is valued. One of her sons works as a sweeper in a hospital while the other works in the informal sector of Nairobi economy, cutting used inner tubes into the long rubber bands which local residents use for tying all kinds of packages and selling recycled cardboard to other squatters. There are many times during the month when the whole family eats well, although there are still occasions when hunger visits their door. Monica feels she will be allowed to live out her days in peace here. She has no other property in Kenya. This is her house and she hopes to go on improving it.

Reprinted with permission from the **Bulletin of the International Year of Shelter for the Homeless**, no. 6, published in August 1986 by the United Nations Center for Human Settlements.

204